THE ADLARD COLES BOOK OF

DIESEL ENGINES

FOURTH EDITION

TIM BARTLETT

Published by Adlard Coles Nautical
an imprint of A&C Black Publishers Ltd
36 Soho Square, London W1D 3QY
www.adlardcoles.com

First published as The RYA Book of Diesel Engines 1998
Reprinted 2000, 2002
Second edition 2002
Third edition 2005
Fourth edition 2011

ISBN 978-1-4081-3116-9

A&C Black uses paper produced with elemental chlorine-free pulp, harvested
from managed sustainable forests.

A CIP catalogue record for this book is available from the British Library.

Typeset in 10/11 Concorde Regular by Margaret Brain.
Printed and bound in Spain by GraphyCems.

Note: While all reasonable care has been taken in the publication of this book,
the publisher takes no responsibility for the use of the methods or products
described in the book.

The photographs in this book were provided PPL Media Ltd, Arundel, West
Sussex with the assistance of Arun Craft Ltd, Littlehampton, West Sussex and
Motortech Marine Engineering, Birdham, Chichester, West Sussex.

There is also a DVD available to complement
this book available from the RYA or, if in
difficulty, direct from Amberley Marine on
Tel: 01628 826104, *Fax:* 01628 828322 or
e-mail amberley.marine@btinternet.com

Contents

Foreword to the First Edition

Every year the rescue statistics published by the RNLI show that the most common cause of Lifeboat launches to pleasure craft is machinery failure. In the case of motor cruisers this does not come as any great surprise; one might expect loss of motive power to figure high in the list of problems. The fact that engine failure is also the most common cause of sailing cruiser rescues is less predictable and serves to confirm just how important it is to keep the engine in good running order.

In response to these statistics, the RYA introduced a one-day course on diesel engine operation. The syllabus is, very broadly, the material covered in this book, although the depth into which it is possible to go in such a short course is inevitably rather limited. The aim of both the course and of this book is not to create instant diesel mechanics, but to provide boat owners with a better understanding of how their engines work and what they must do to keep them working.

While it would be great if everyone could carry out all the servicing and repairs on their own engines, this is not a realistic proposition; few boat owners have the time to become skilled mechanics and not many boats carry the tools, spares and equipment to provide the full workshop support needed for complex repairs.

What is achievable by every owner is an understanding of the importance of routine engine management, how to rectify the most common and relatively simple problems which occur and how to recognise the warning signs that an engine needs expert attention.

Fortunately, most diesel engines are reliable and relatively trouble free in operation, so boat owners do not spend a high proportion of their time confronted by smoky exhausts, screeching temperature warning alarms or engines that obstinately refuse to start. Hence much of the knowledge acquired on a diesel engine course is seldom put into practice. This reinforces the need for a clear comprehensive reference book, both to back up the knowledge gained on a course and to provide a guide for those who prefer to teach themselves.

Bill Anderson
Former RYA Training Manager

Foreword to the Fourth Edition

Whilst the last six years have seen minimal changes in the 'nuts and bolts' of diesel engine maintenance, mechanical failure continues to be the main cause of rescue call-outs to cruisers. The need for sailors to learn about engine structure and the processes involved with fuel, air, cooling, oil, electrical and control systems, is clearly as important as ever.

This new edition remains a highly valuable guide, and can be read in conjunction with the RYA's Diesel Engine course. It has now been updated throughout with colour photos and diagrams, all to further aid the understanding process.

1 Why Choose a Diesel?

I still remember the time when, as a boy, I was given my first ballpoint pen. It was one of those with a knob on top that, when pressed, made the nib emerge and when pressed again made it retract. Like most small boys, I amused myself by clicking it in and out for a while. The clicking, I recall, seemed much more fun than writing.

It wasn't long, though, before that novelty wore off – and not much longer before my new pen had 'come to bits' as I tried to find out how it worked. I suppose most of us have done much the same thing, and I'm quite convinced that the outcome of that experience determines our future attitude to all things mechanical.

If you are one of those for whom the pen never clicked again, take heart. Remember that for all their apparent complexity, engines depend on a sequence of simple processes. They don't have souls, or wills of their own, so if you can make sure that those processes go on happening in the right order, your engine just has to keep on running. The flip side of the coin is that if you don't, your engine can't keep going out of any sense of affection, loyalty, or self-preservation!

That much, at least, applies to all engines, whether you're talking about the electric motor of a vacuum cleaner or the jet engines of an airliner. Every type of engine, however, has its own strengths and weaknesses that make it more suitable for some purposes than others. That's why you don't find jet-powered vacuum cleaners or electrically powered aircraft, and why you're more likely to have a diesel engine powering your boat than your lawnmower.

Compared with a petrol engine, for instance, a diesel engine is likely to be expensive, heavy and slow to respond. On most boats, though, these drawbacks are worth putting up with in order to take advantage of a diesel's main attributes:

- Reliability
- Long life expectancy
- Low running costs
- Non-explosive fuel

Even a diesel engine, however, will deteriorate if it is neglected, and could ultimately corrode away to become a useless lump of rusty metal. To take advantage of its reliability and long life expectancy it needs to be looked after. Of course you can pay someone else to do the work for you, but that eats away at the advantage of low running costs.

The aim of this book is to help you get the most out of the capital invested in your engine, by making the most of the advantages you've already paid for – reliability, longevity and economy.

A fringe benefit of doing your own maintenance will be familiarity with your engine and the tools you use to work on it. Then, if things *do* go wrong, you have a sporting chance of either being able to solve the problem yourself, or of giving a professional mechanic something more to go on than 'it just sort of stopped'.

2 | The Basic Engine

As I pointed out in Chapter 1, diesel engines don't have souls or wills of their own, but depend on a sequence of simple processes.

The most fundamental of all those processes takes place deep inside the engine. It's the one that gives internal combustion engines their name, because it involves burning air and fuel inside a confined space.

The basic process

The confined space is the *cylinder* – a vertical tube, machined into the heavy metal *block* that accounts for most of the engine's weight and bulk. The top of the cylinder is closed by another heavy casting called the *cylinder head*. Tunnels in the cylinder head allow air and exhaust gas to flow in or out of the cylinder, controlled by *valves*.

The bottom of the cylinder is formed by the *piston*, another machined metal casting that is designed to slide up and down inside the cylinder, with springy metal *piston rings* forming an almost gas-tight seal between the piston and the cylinder walls.

Don't bother, for the moment, about how we get a mixture of fuel and air to burn inside the cylinder: just accept that as it burns it produces a mixture of water vapour, carbon dioxide and small quantities of some more unpleasant gases such as sulphur dioxide and oxides of nitrogen. It also gets very hot.

Fig 1 *The four-stroke cycle.*

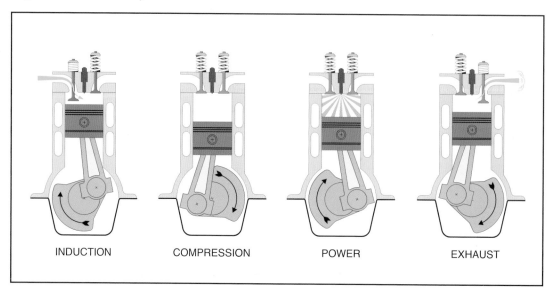

INDUCTION   COMPRESSION   POWER   EXHAUST

The rise in temperature makes this gaseous cocktail expand – increasing the pressure within the cylinder, and driving the piston downwards. The piston is attached to a connecting rod, or 'con rod', whose other end is coupled to the *crankshaft*. Just as the cranks of a bicycle convert vertical movements of the rider's legs to a rotary movement of the wheels, the crankshaft converts the downward thrust of the piston into a rotary movement of the shaft.

One end of the crankshaft carries a heavy metal *flywheel*. Once the flywheel has started turning, its momentum keeps it going, so the crankshaft keeps turning with it – pushing the piston back up the cylinder. As it does so, one of the valves in the cylinder head opens, allowing the hot gases to escape.

As soon as the piston reaches the top of its travel, the still-spinning flywheel and crankshaft drag it back down again. At this point, the exhaust valve shuts and the inlet valve opens, allowing fresh air to flood into the expanding space inside the cylinder.

This time, as the piston reaches the bottom of its stroke, the inlet valve closes. With both valves shut, and the momentum of the flywheel driving the piston back up again, the air inside the cylinder is compressed.

If you compress any gas, it gets hot. You can feel the effect for yourself by putting your finger over the outlet hole of a bicycle pump and pumping the handle. Even after several hard strokes, a bicycle pump is unlikely to develop more than about 100 psi, but the pressure inside a diesel engine's cylinder rises to over 500 psi in less than $1/100$ second. Its temperature rises, as a result, to something in the order of 800°C.

Diesel fuel doesn't burn easily under normal conditions, but if you spray a fine mist of it into hot pressurised air, it will ignite spontaneously. The engine's fuel system is designed to do exactly that – producing, in the cylinder, the burning mixture of air and fuel required to start the cycle all over again.

So there you have it: the basic operating cycle of a diesel engine, made up of four distinct strokes of the piston. You can think of them, if you like, as 'suck, squeeze, bang, blow', though in more conventional terminology they're called Induction, Compression, Power and Exhaust.

Valves

The work of the valves is vital to the whole sequence: they have to open and close at precisely the right moments, allowing an unrestricted flow of air or exhaust gas when they're open, yet forming a perfectly gas-tight seal when they're shut.

Each valve is roughly mushroom-shaped, with a long straight stem and a flat circular head, whose edge is bevelled and precision-ground to match the slope of the hardened *valve seat* that surrounds the mouth of the tunnel in the cylinder head. For most of each cycle, each valve remains shut, pulled firmly against its seat by one or two very strong *valve springs*. It's opened, when necessary, by a component called a *rocker*, like a miniature seesaw that pivots on another shaft running across the cylinder head.

Meanwhile, a component called the *camshaft* is being driven by the crankshaft, but at half the crankshaft's speed. On it are carefully machined bulges, called *cams*, that are shaped and positioned so that each in turn pushes upwards against a rocker at the right moment in each cycle. As one end of a rocker is pushed upwards, the other end moves downwards to push the valve open.

Although the principle is standard, there are plenty of variations on the theme. The

Fig 2 *Valve gear.*

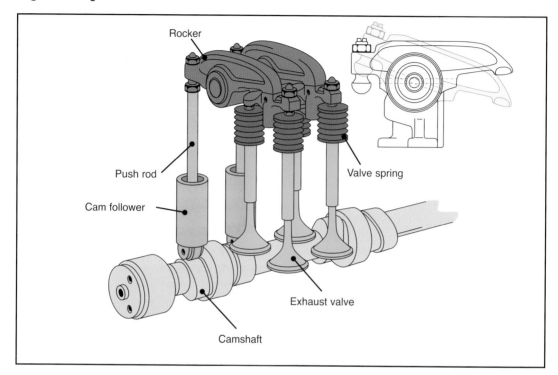

camshaft, for instance, may be driven by gears, or by a chain and sprocket system, or by a toothed rubber belt, and it may be mounted high on the engine with the cams pushing directly on the rockers; or lower down and relying on *push rods* to transmit the movement of the cams to the rockers. In this case, the ends of the push rods don't rest directly on the cams but sit in small bucket-shaped components called *tappets* or *cam followers*. In some engines, the cam followers are fitted with rollers to reduce wear: in others, they are designed to rotate so as to spread the wear more evenly, while some engines have hydraulic tappets which adjust themselves to correct for wear as it happens.

Whichever of these applies to your particular engine, do bear in mind that the whole system will have been set up so that each valve opens and closes at precisely the right moment in the cycle. Small

amounts of wear and tear can be corrected by means of a simple adjustment, but it's asking for trouble to tinker with the gears, belt or chain unless you know exactly what you're doing.

The two-stroke cycle

It seems rather wasteful to have the piston going up and down like a yo-yo, but only producing power on one of its four strokes. There is an alternative, called the *two-stroke* cycle. Apart from the fact that it produces power on every second stroke of the piston, the diesel two-stroke has very little in common with its petrol-oil counterparts on lawn mowers and outboards, and its use is mainly confined to the very large engines that drive ships. The one exception is the Detroit Diesel range, which includes two-strokes down to 270 hp.

Fig 3 *The two-stroke cycle.*

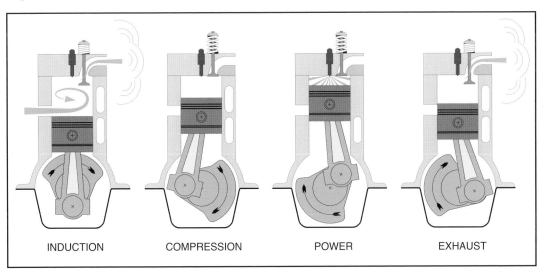

| INDUCTION | COMPRESSION | POWER | EXHAUST |

They are physically different from conventional four-stroke diesels in that they have no inlet valves. Instead, air is pumped into the cylinder by a mechanical blower – a *supercharger* – through *ports* half-way up the cylinder walls. (See Fig 3.)

When the piston is at the bottom of its travel, these ports are above the level of the piston, so, with the exhaust valve open, clean air flows into the cylinder and blows the previous stroke's exhaust gas out of the top.

As the piston rises, the exhaust valve shuts, and the piston itself closes the inlet ports, trapping the air inside the cylinder. The compression stroke continues, just as in a four-stroke engine, and is followed by the power stroke driving the piston downwards.

Just before the piston reaches the level of the inlet ports, however, the exhaust valve opens, allowing the exhaust gas to start escaping. As the piston descends still further, it uncovers the inlet port, allowing fresh air into the cylinder, to start the sequence all over again.

The advantages and disadvantages of two- and four-stroke engines are pretty evenly balanced: power for power, two-strokes are smaller and lighter, but are slightly less fuel-efficient, and because they are produced in very much smaller numbers they tend to be relatively expensive. Most of their repair and maintenance procedures are similar, though, so we'll concentrate on the more common four-stroke engine throughout this book.

Variations on a theme

One apparently subtle variation is the distinction between *direct* and *indirect* injection.

Fig 1 illustrating the four-stroke cycle shows a direct injection engine: the fuel is sprayed directly into the cylinder. In practice, the top of the piston is usually carved away to form a hollow, called the *combustion chamber*, shaped to ensure that the fuel and air mix as thoroughly as possible.

In an indirect injection engine, the piston crown is usually flat, and the combustion chamber is deeply recessed into the cylinder head, with only a narrow opening between it and the cylinder. The idea is that the turbulence created when air from the cylinder is forced into the

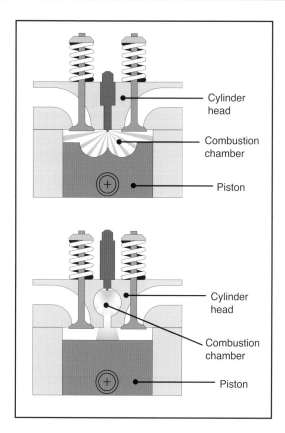

Fig 4 *Direct injection (above) and indirect injection.*

combustion chamber ensures more thorough mixing of the air and fuel, and a more progressive increase in cylinder pressure during the power stroke.

Historically, at least, indirect injection engines have been regarded as quieter and cleaner but harder to start, because the cylinder head absorbs a lot of the heat created during compression. Unfortunately, the heat lost to the cylinder head and the effort required to force air and burning gas in and out of the combustion chamber make them rather less fuel-efficient overall.

Developments in piston design are now allowing modern direct injection engines to catch up with the indirect engine's advantages without the drawbacks, so indirect injection seems destined to fade away.

...Things to do

Checking valve/rocker clearances – once per season

There isn't much an amateur mechanic with a limited tool kit can (or should) do to the major components inside the engine apart from making sure that it has a good supply of fuel and air and clean lubricating oil.

You can, however, check and adjust the gap between the rocker and the valve. There has to be a gap – usually about the thickness of a fingernail – to allow for the different rates at which the various components expand and contract as they warm up. Without it, there's a very real risk that the valves won't shut completely: they may even come into catastrophic contact with the pistons. If the gap is too large, the valves may not open as far as they should, and the engine will certainly be noisier than it should be.

1 Read the engine manual to find out what the valve/rocker clearances should be, and whether they should be adjusted with the engine cold or at normal running temperature. Note that the clearances for inlet valves may be different for those for exhaust valves, because exhaust valves get hotter.

2 Remove the rocker cover (A) – a relatively thin metal box on top of the engine, usually with the oil filler cap in the middle. Some engines have a separate rocker cover for each cylinder, or for each of two or three groups of cylinders.

3 Check the gap on each valve in turn, when the valve is completely closed and the gap is at

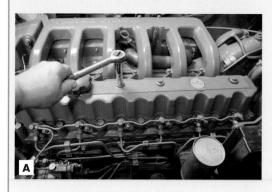

its widest. There are two ways of finding out when this happens. On a multi-cylinder engine, the best way is to find the 'magic number' for your engine by adding one to the number of cylinders. For a four-cylinder engine, for instance, the magic number is five.

4 Turn the engine slowly by hand, if necessary using a spanner on the crankshaft (big nut on the lowest of the pulleys at the front of the engine). Watch the rockers moving as you do so, until the two rockers for one cylinder are 'on the rock' – that is, when one is rising and the other falling – signifying that this particular cylinder is at the end of its exhaust stroke and just beginning its induction stroke. Subtract the number of this cylinder from the 'magic number' to find the number of the cylinder that is ready to have its valve clearances checked. If, for instance, you have a four-cylinder engine and number 2 cylinder's valves are on the rock, number 3 cylinder is ready, because 5 – 2 = 3.

5 On a single-cylinder engine, the clearance for one valve should be checked when the other valve is fully depressed. You can use this approach for a multi-cylinder engine, but it will take longer! (B)

6 Slacken the lock-nut on the rocker whose clearance you are about to adjust, and then unscrew the threaded adjuster about one or two turns.

7 Set a feeler gauge to the clearance specified in the engine manual, and slip it between the valve stem and the rocker (C). Gently wiggle the feeler gauge whilst tightening the adjusting screw, until you can feel the feeler gauge being nipped between the valve stem and the rocker.

8 Leave the feeler gauge in place, and hold the adjusting screw with a screwdriver while you tighten the lock-nut. When it's tight, wiggle the feeler gauge again to check that you haven't upset the adjustment: you should feel a slight resistance, but it shouldn't be jammed tight.

9 Repeat the process for each valve in turn, then replace the rocker cover, making sure that the cork or rubber sealing gasket is smooth, undamaged and properly seated.

B

C

3 | Fuel System

Otto Diesel's original patent application for what we now know as a diesel engine was pretty vague about the kind of fuel it might use: he even suggested coal dust as a possibility. Some boatowners seem almost equally vague: every year lifeboats have to tow in boats that have simply run out of fuel!

There's more to getting fuel into an engine, though, than simply pouring the stuff into the tank.

Diesel fuel doesn't burn very easily, and in order to burn quickly, cleanly and reliably it has to be in the form of fine droplets, like an aerosol spray. You'll remember from the previous chapter that the air in a diesel's cylinders is made hot by being compressed to 20 or 30 times its normal atmospheric pressure, so producing an aerosol spray inside the cylinders means that the fuel has to be at an even higher pressure – in the order of 2,500 psi.

It's also essential for the proportions of fuel and air to be exactly right, so each squirt of fuel has to be very accurately measured. If you think of a typical four-cylinder diesel developing 80 hp when it's running flat out at 4,000 rpm, it will be burning about 4 gallons of fuel an hour. Each cylinder will be receiving 2,000 squirts of fuel every minute – making 8,000 squirts per minute, or 480,000 squirts per hour. Each squirt, then, must be less than 10 millionths of a gallon, 0.04 ml, or less than a hundredth of a teaspoon. At low loads the amount of fuel sent to the cylinders has to be even less.

It's hardly surprising, then, that the fuel system includes some of the most sophisticated and expensive parts of the engine, responsible for achieving pressures of almost 200 atmospheres, measuring doses of fuel accurate to less than a thousandth of a millilitre, and repeating the process perhaps half a million times an hour!

The basic system

The fuel system starts, however, with the crudest component of all: the tank. It's worth bearing in mind, though, that a full tank can be very heavy, so it needs to be well supported and secured against the boat's motion. A big tank – anything over about 5–10 gallons – should include internal baffles to stop the fuel sloshing about, and any tank needs a vent, or 'breather', to let air in as the fuel is used up.

Unfortunately, the fuel received from the hose may not be perfectly clean, and the air that comes in through the breather will almost certainly be moist enough to allow condensation to form inside the tank. The end result is that the tank will include some dirt and water.

To prevent this reaching the engine, the engine installation should include a component known as a *primary filter, pre-filter, separator, sedimenter* or *filter-agglomerator*, usually mounted on a bulkhead in the engine compartment rather than on the engine itself.

The *lift pump* is responsible for pulling the fuel out of the tank, through the primary filter, and passing it on to the rest of the system. In most cases, it's a simple

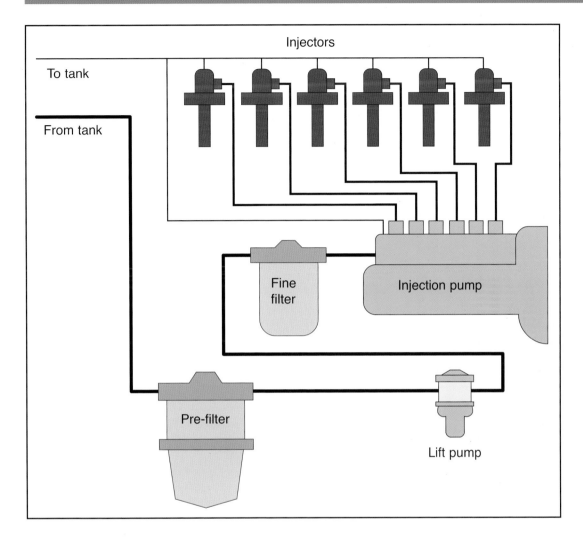

Fig 5 *General layout of fuel system.*

diaphragm pump, very much like a miniature version of a manual bilge pump. It's driven by the engine, but usually has a hand-operated *priming lever* so that you can pump fuel through the system without running the engine.

The fuel then passes through another filter, sometimes known as the *main filter* or *secondary filter* or *fine filter*, whose job is to remove particles of dirt that – at less than a thousandth of a millimetre in diameter – may be too small to see, but that are still capable of wearing the very finely

engineered surfaces of the rest of the system.

If a diesel engine has a 'heart', it has to be the *injection pump*, because this is where the fuel is measured and pressurised.

Injector pipes, with very thick walls to withstand the pressure, carry the highly pressurised fuel from the injection pumps to the *injectors* that spray it into the cylinders.

Some of the fuel that is pumped to the injectors, however, never actually reaches the cylinder but is returned to the tank through a *leak-off pipe*, or *return line*.

The single-element injection pump

There are three main types of injection pump, of which the simplest is the kind found on single-cylinder engines. Even if you have a multi-cylinder engine, it's worth knowing a bit about the *single-element* 'jerk' pump, because many multi-cylinder engines use derivatives of it.

The principle is much like that of a bicycle pump or an old-fashioned bilge pump, with a piston (usually called the *plunger*) moving up and down inside a cylinder. A hole called the *spill port* in the side of the cylinder allows fuel to flow into the cylinder when the plunger is at the bottom of its travel. As the plunger rises, however, it covers the port to shut off the flow and trap some fuel in the cylinder. As it continues to rise, the trapped fuel has to go somewhere, so it escapes by lifting the delivery valve off its seat, and flowing out into the injector pipe.

Principle of the jerk pump

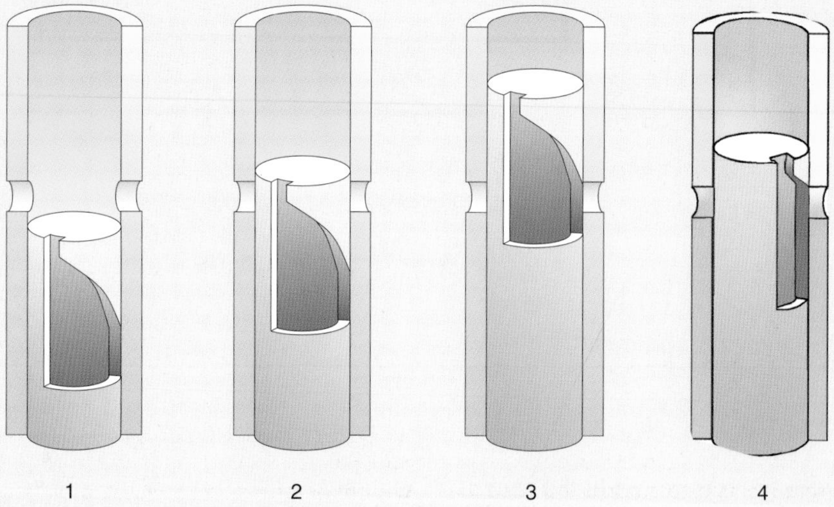

1   2   3   4

Fig 6 *Jerk pump.*

1 When the plunger is at the bottom of its travel, fuel flows into the pump cylinder through one of the ports.

2 As the plunger rises, it blocks off the ports and pressurises the fuel, driving it out of the top of the pump cylinder.

3 As the piston rises further, the helical cut-out reaches the spill port: fuel can flow down the groove and out through the spill port. The pressure is released so no more fuel reaches the injector.

4 Rotating the plunger means that the cut-out reaches the spill port at an earlier stage in the plunger's travel. The effective stroke of the plunger is shortened, so less fuel is delivered.

In-line injection pump

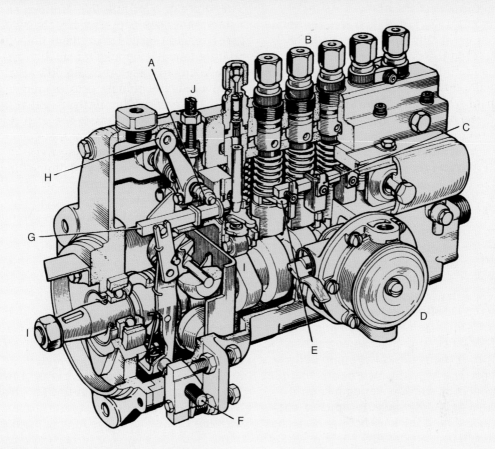

Fig 7 *An in-line fuel injection pump.*

Key

A Excess fuel button for cold starting.
B High pressure fuel line connectors that feed the injectors. Six in this case for a 6-cylinder engine.
C Control fork that moves levers on the plunger arm on each pump to control the quantity of fuel injected.
D This model has the low pressure fuel pump built on to the side of the injection pump. This is a diaphragm type driven from the injection pump's camshaft rather than from the main engine camshaft.
E The actuating arm that along with C moves the pump element to control the amount needed for injection at various engine speeds.

F Control lever connected by cable to the helm position.
G Control rod assembly which is moved by F and a combination of the excess fuel device, the engine governor and the stop control to provide exactly the right control of the pumping elements to suit the particular running or stopping conditions.
H Stop lever.
I Cam and roller cam follower which drive the pumping elements. This is a pump which requires the gallery to be topped up with engine oil for the internal lubrication of the moving parts.
J Maximum fuel stop screw, usually has a seal placed through it to prevent tampering.

The measuring part of the fuel pump's job is taken care of by a spiral-shaped cut-out in the side of the plunger. As the piston nears the top of its travel, the spiral cut-out eventually comes level with the spill port in the side of the cylinder, allowing fuel to flow round the spiral and out of the spill port.

Pushing or pulling on a toothed rod called the *rack* makes the plunger rotate, so the spiral can be made to uncover the spill port at any stage in the plunger's stroke, varying the amount of fuel that is delivered without having to change the distance the plunger actually moves.

This is significant, because the up and down movement of the plunger is achieved by the action of a cam, very similar to the cams that operate the valves in the engine's cylinder head.

It's worth noting that thin metal packing pieces called *shims* are usually fitted between the base of the pump and the cylinder block or crankcase. Increasing the number of shims raises the pump body, so the ports are higher, which means that the pump doesn't start delivering fuel until slightly later in the cycle. In other words, the number and thickness of the shims has a critical effect on *timing* – the moment at which fuel is sprayed into the cylinder – so if you remove the fuel pump for any reason, it's essential to make sure that you retain all the shims and put them back when the pump is re-installed.

The in-line injection pump

A few multi-cylinder engines use a separate single-element fuel pump for each cylinder, but it's more common to find all the separate elements combined into a single component that looks rather like a miniature engine. It's called an *in-line pump* because it consists of several jerk pumps in line, driven by a camshaft in the pump body instead of in the engine block.

The rotary injection pump

The *rotary* or *DPA injection pump* is lighter, more compact, and can cope with higher engine speeds than the in-line type, so it's eminently suitable for small, high-revving engines. Unfortunately, it's also more vulnerable to dirty or contaminated fuel and – unlike an in-line pump that may fail on one or two cylinders but keep going on the others – a DPA pump that goes wrong will often pack up altogether.

The reason for this 'all-or-nothing' operation is that a DPA pump consists of a single *high pressure pump*, distributing fuel to each injector in turn through a spinning rotor.

The lift pump supplies fuel to the injection pump at one end, where a vane-type *transfer pump* – similar in principle to the engine's raw water pump – increases its pressure. The fuel then flows to the high pressure pump through the *metering valve*, which controls the amount of fuel that will be delivered to the engine's cylinders.

The high pressure pump consists of two small plungers built into a rotor. Fuel from the metering valve flows into the space between the two plungers forcing them to move apart. As the rotor turns, however, bulges on the *cam ring* that surrounds it force the plungers back inwards.

Fuel, now at very high pressure, is driven out of the space between the plungers and through a drilling in the rotor, which directs it to each injector pipe in turn.

Injectors

The injectors convert the tiny squirts of high pressure fuel into an atomised spray in the cylinders. They are usually cylindrical in shape, about 6 in (15 cm) long and 1 in (25mm) in diameter, but are clamped into the cylinder head so that only a couple of inches of the injector body and a couple of pipe connections are visible.

Rotary injection pump

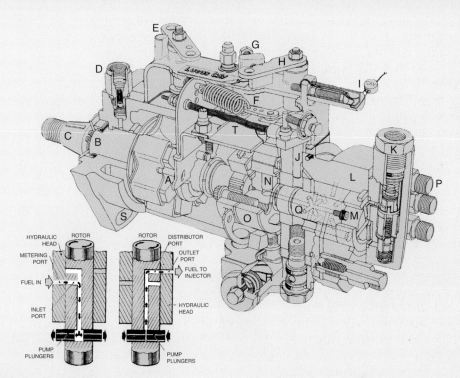

Fig 8 *Rotary injection pump.*

Key

A Centrifugal governor weights provide sensitive speed control.
B Front bearing oil seal and retaining circlip.
C Tapered drive shaft.
D Back leak connection feeds excess fuel which has also helped lubrication of the pump back to the fuel filter.
E Shut off lever, hand operated by cable control.
F Return spring to hold speed control lever against idle stop.
G Idling speed control stop.
H Speed control lever usually connected to helm position by cable control system.
I Maximum speed stop and adjusting screw sealed to prevent tampering.
J Fuel metering valve, governor controlled.
K Low pressure fuel inlet with nylon filter below it.
L The stationary hydraulic head which houses the transfer pump (M) and the distributor rotor (Q).
M The transfer pump which transfers low pressure fuel from inlet (M) to high pressure plungers

(N) via metering valve (J).
N High pressure pump plungers are driven outwards by fuel pressure from (N) and pushed inward by the lobes on the cam ring (O).
O Cam ring.
P High pressure outlet pipe connections to injectors.
Q The distributing part of the rotor contains a central axial passage (dotted) and two radially drilled ports. The distributing port aligns successively with each high pressure outlet port to P, there being one for each cylinder of the engine. A similar number of inlet ports in the rotor align successively with a single port in the head, called the metering port, and admits the fuel from (M) under the control of the governor. See inset.
R Fully automatic advance device.
S Pump fixing and locating bolt slot that allows rotation of pump about axis for timing. Score marks across engine and pump flange can help re-install pump to same timing position.
T Governor spring.

The principle of a mechanical governor

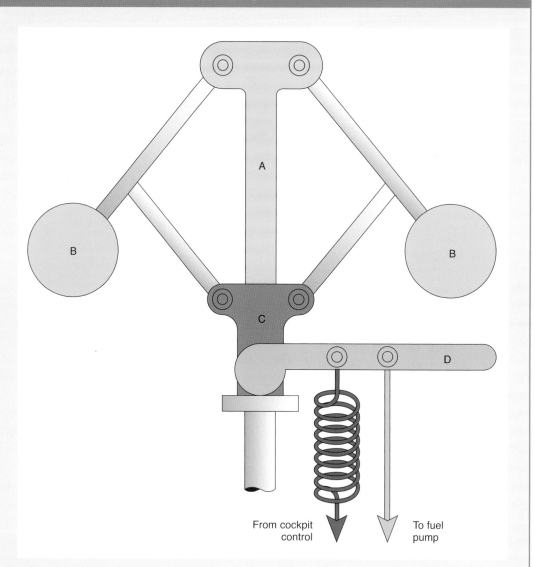

From cockpit
control

To fuel
pump

Fig 8a *The principle of the mechanical governor.*

The shaft (A) is driven by the engine, so as the engine speed increases, the weights (B) try to fly outward. The linkage (C and D) is arranged so that this movement tells the fuel pump to slow the engine down.

The cockpit control is connected to the spring. When the control is pushed forwards, for higher engine speeds, the increasing tension in the spring makes it more difficult for the flywheel weights to slow the engine down, so the engine speed increases.

The balance between the governor weights and the spring tension keeps the engine running at a constant speed, set by the cockpit control, even if the load varies.

The mechancial governor inside a diesel injection pump is more sophisticated than this, but the principle is identical.

The injector body is basically a tube, almost completely filled by a *needle valve*, *push rod*, and a strong *spring*. Fuel from the injection pump enters the side of the injector from the injector pipe, and then flows down a narrow passage to the *pressure chamber*, just above the nozzle.

The *nozzle* is sealed off by the needle valve, which is held in place by the push rod and spring. When the injector pump

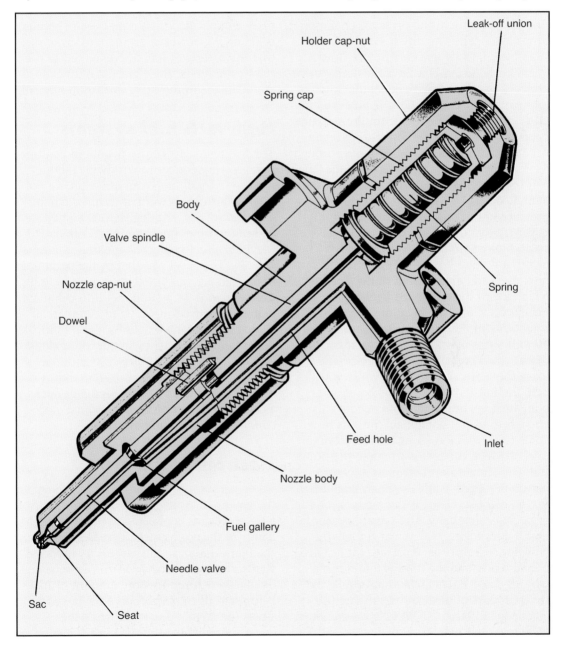

Fig 9 *Injector.*

delivers one of its pulses of fuel, the pressure within the pressure chamber rises sufficiently to lift the needle valve off its seat. Fuel then rushes out of the nozzle so quickly that it breaks up into a spray. Of course, this sudden escape of fuel means that the pressure in the pressure chamber drops again, allowing the needle valve to snap back into its seat to stop the flow.

Although the movements of the needle valve are very small, they happen so quickly that lubrication is essential. This is achieved by allowing some of the fuel from the pressure chamber to flow up the injector, past the needle valve and push rod, and out through the leak-off pipe at the top to return to the tank.

If too much fuel took this route, it would entirely defeat the object of the exercise: the pressure in the pressure chamber would never rise enough to lift the needle valve, so no fuel would get into the cylinder. The fact that it doesn't is entirely due to the very high precision engineering of the injector, which keeps the clearance between the needle valve and the injector body down to something in the order of 0.001 mm (about 40 millionths of an inch). That's so small that if you were to strip an injector and leave the body on the bench while you held the needle valve in your hand, your body heat would expand the needle valve enough to stop it going back into its hole!

There are three reasons for mentioning this, of which the first is to make the point that you should never strip an injector: it may look rugged, but it's so finely engineered that injector servicing is definitely a job for a specialist company. The second reason is that it goes a long way towards explaining why new injectors can cost several hundred pounds each, and the third is that it explains why all those filters are so important: the tiniest specks of dirt can be sufficient to abrade the surface of the needle valve enough to increase the leak-off to such an extent that the injector doesn't open properly, or to wedge the valve open and allow fuel to drip out of the nozzle instead of forming a fine spray.

The same applies to injection pumps, because there is nothing an amateur mechanic can achieve by tinkering with them, other than a lot of damage. Even the apparently simple job of removing an injection pump is more complicated than it may seem, because re-fitting it involves adjusting it to make sure that the squirts of fuel are delivered to the right cylinders at the right time: it needs confidence and the right workshop manual.

High-tech fuel systems

The last few years of the twentieth century saw growing concern, worldwide, about the use of fossil fuels and atmospheric pollution. Customers wanted cleaner, quieter cars and lorries, and legislators wanted to be seen to be doing something. Almost inevitably, fuel systems came under close scrutiny. The effect was that by the beginning of this century we started to see new, radically different ways of getting fuel into cylinders being introduced in cars and commercial vehicles. It's taking longer for these to trickle down to marine engines, and it will undoubtedly be many years before conventional fuel systems disappear altogether, but it is worth being aware of developments such as *electronic control*, *unit injectors*, and *common rail injection systems*.

Electronic control

A key part of any conventional fuel pump is the governor. At its simplest, this consists of a set of weights connected to the shaft of the pump. As the engine speed increases, the pump shaft turns faster, so the weights try to fly outwards. As they do so, they operate a mechanical linkage which reduces the amount of fuel being sent to the injectors. This, of course, slows the engine down, allowing the governor weights to move inward again.

The engine control, in the cockpit or wheelhouse, is connected to the governor by a spring. By adjusting the engine controls the helmsman adjusts the spring tension so as to increase or decrease the speed at which the shaft has to turn before the weights move outwards far enough to slow the engine down.

The aim of all this is partly to stop the engine over-revving, but it also means that when you – the user – set the throttle for a particular engine speed, the governor will keep the engine running at that speed even if the loading varies.

Simple mechanical governors like this have been used to control machinery for centuries: you can see rudimentary versions in water-mills, windmills, and on steam engines, but now their place is increasingly being taken by electronic versions which monitor other factors such as air temperature and inlet manifold pressure as well as shaft speed.

Unit injectors

Unit injectors, in principle, are almost a retrograde step: they take us back to the days when each injector had its own high pressure pump. As the name suggests, however, the modern unit injector combines the pump and injector in a single unit, mounted in the cylinder head in much the same way as a conventional injector.

In some cases the pump is mechanically driven. Each cylinder has three rockers instead of the usual two. Two of the three rockers open the valves, exactly as they do in a conventional engine, while the third one operates the plunger of a small piston-type pump in the head of the injector.

An alternative is to dispense with mechanical operation, and use hydraulics instead, with an electric solenoid (see page 46) controlling the pump plunger.

Common rail injection

Perhaps the most exciting development is known as 'common rail' or 'reservoir' fuel injection. The key feature of this is that metering and control functions have been taken away from the injector pump altogether: its sole job is to produce a constant supply of fuel at enormously high pressure – up to about 30,000psi (2,000bar).

From the pump, the pressurised fuel passes to a thick-walled tube (the 'common rail') or to an equally rugged reservoir, from which injector pipes carry it to electronically controlled injectors.

The advantages of the system are that the higher pressure means that the fuel spray from each injector is much finer, while the electronic control means that the amount of fuel, the timing and duration of each squirt, and even the number of squirts per cycle can be varied by the electronic processor to give increased fuel efficiency, less toxic exhaust gas, and lower noise levels.

The down-side of the system (apart from price!) is that it has done away with the rugged simplicity which used to be one of the advantages of a diesel engine, and has made a diesel just as dependent on electricity as a petrol engine.

• • • Things to do

There is absolutely nothing an amateur mechanic can or should do to the internal working parts of a unit injector, to electronic controls or to a common rail fuel system, without specialist expertise and equipment. But bear the following in mind:

• Regular checking and changing of fuel filters and water traps is more important than ever.
• Visually inspect electrical connections, and clean/tighten if necessary.
• On rocker driven unit injectors, check and adjust the rocker clearances in accordance with the manufacturers instructions and the procedure outlined on pages 6–7.

• • • *Things to do*

Safety first

Diesel fuel can cause skin problems, especially in people who have become sensitised by repeated contact. Avoid the risk by using protective gloves and by keeping your hands clean.

The fuel leaving the injection pump is at such high pressure that it can penetrate skin. This is particularly true of the very fine droplets that leave an injector at high speed. Never expose yourself to high pressure diesel.

1 Draining the pre-filter

The pre-filter is the part most likely to be affected by water or dirt from the fuel tank, so it should be checked frequently. The optimum interval will vary widely, depending on how clean your fuel is to start with, and how quickly you're using it, as well as on the filter itself, but after every ten hours' running is usually about right.

Many pre-filters have a transparent bowl at the bottom, so you can see any dirt or water at a glance. If yours doesn't have this, or if you can see a layer of dirt or water collecting at the bottom, you will need to drain it.

a Slacken the drain screw at the bottom and allow the contents of the filter to run off into a

suitable container such as a jam jar until clean fuel emerges.

b Shut the drain screw, being careful to avoid using excessive force (it's hollow, and can snap easily), and then dispose of the contaminated fuel carefully.

c Some pre-filters have a replaceable element similar to that in a cartridge-type fine filter, and which should be replaced in much the same way.

2 Replacing the fine filter

The fuel filter should be changed at least once a season, or after about 200 hours' use. Start by cleaning the area around the filter, and placing a bowl or rags underneath to catch any spills. If your filter is below the level of the fuel in the tank, shut the fuel cock on the tank, but remember to open it again before attempting to start the engine. In any case, you will have to *bleed* the system before starting the engine.

Spin-on filters

a Use a strap or chain wrench to unscrew the filter canister. If this isn't available or doesn't work, try a large pair of gas pliers or a set of stillsons (pipe wrench).

1

2

b Smear the sealing ring with a thin film of fresh oil, then spin the filter on until the sealing ring just touches the filter head.

c Tighten the filter another half turn by hand. Do not over-tighten it by using any kind of tool.

Cartridge filters

a Unscrew the central bolt to release the filter body (see photos above).

b Remove the cartridge, and replace it, making sure that the various springs and washers are replaced in the correct order, and that the filter is the right way up. Make sure the old rubber sealing ring isn't stuck to the filter head, and replace it with the new one supplied with the filter.

c Replace the complete assembly, making sure the filter body is correctly seated, and tighten the retaining bolt.

Water trap filters

Some filters have a bowl designed to trap water underneath the filter cartridge.

The sequence of photos above shows the fitting of a new cartridge:

a Slacken the drain tap in the bowl and drain off the contents of the filter.Then unscrew the bolt that protrudes from the centre of the bowl.

b Reassemble the filter with a new cartridge and the new seals that are supplied with it – noticing that the upper and lower seals are different.

c Tighten the central bolt gently, applying no more than about 10 lb to the end of a typical spanner.

3 Bleeding the fuel system

Even a very small amount of air in the fuel system can be enough to stop a diesel, because if air bubbles reach the injector pipes they can act

Fitting a new cartridge

as shock absorbers which prevent the pressure from rising sufficiently to open the injector's needle valve. If the engine suddenly stops or misfires, or if you have let air into the system by running low on fuel or changing a filter, you will have to remove the air by 'bleeding' the system. Special hollow bolts called *bleed screws* are provided for the purpose. In principle, the process involves working from the tank towards the engine, slackening each bleed screw in turn until clear diesel comes out, then tightening that screw, and moving on to the next. If you can't find a bleed screw, it is usually enough to slacken one of the pipe unions instead.

• • • *Things to do*

a Open the fuel cock to allow fuel to flow from the tank into the system, and slacken the bleed screw on top of the pre-filter until clear diesel – free of bubbles – comes out.

To bleed the system downstream of the lift pump, you'll have to operate the lift pump by hand, using the hand priming lever. If the hand priming lever doesn't move, it may well be that the engine has stopped with the pump lever at or near the end of its travel: try turning the crankshaft (with the starter or by hand) so that the pump is at a different part of its stroke.

3b

b Slacken the bleed screw on top of the engine's fine filter, making sure that it's the bleed screw you are undoing, not the one that holds the whole thing together! The bleed screw is higher, and usually just off centre. Operate the lift pump by hand until clear diesel emerges from the bleed screw, then tighten the screw and move on to the injection pump.

c There may be one or two bleed points on the injection pump, depending on the make and model, but they are usually smaller than any spanner in an off-the-shelf tool kit. Check with the engine manual, mark them with a dab of paint, and make sure you have a suitable spanner on board.

3c

d Changing filters is unlikely to let air into the high pressure side of the system, but if the engine has stopped of its own accord or fails to start, bleed the injector pipes by slackening the pipe unions that join them to the sides of the injectors. With the engine controls set up for a fast idle, use the starter motor to turn the engine as though you were trying to start it, while watching the fuel escaping from the unions. When no bubbles appear from one union, tighten it, then continue the process until you've re-tightened them all. Don't worry if the engine starts and runs on one or two cylinders while some unions are still slack: this is perfectly normal, and simply saves you the trouble of operating the starter.

3d

4 | Air System

Fuel, by itself, is of no use whatsoever: it needs oxygen from the air outside in order to burn. At the most basic level, this happens of its own accord: as the piston falls during the induction stroke, air rushes in past the open inlet valve to fill the expanding space. Then, when the compression and power strokes are complete, the exhaust valve opens and the rising piston pushes the exhaust gas out ready for a fresh charge of clean air.

In practice, though, the engine needs an *air filter* to stop dirt, moisture and bits of rubbish being sucked into its cylinders, and it needs an *exhaust system* to dispose of the hot exhaust gases safely and quietly. To save having a separate filter and exhaust pipe for each cylinder of a multi-cylinder engine, the incoming air is fed to the cylinders through a tubular structure called the *inlet manifold*, and the exhaust gases are carried away through a similar structure called the *exhaust manifold*.

Air filters

Unlike their cousins that power tractors and earth-moving machinery, marine diesels usually operate in a relatively clean environment: there's little danger of them having to contend with straw, dust or roadside litter. This means that their air filters can be relatively simple, so some engines operate perfectly well for years with little more than a metal box with a few baffles in it.

Most, however, have something a little more sophisticated, involving either wire gauze or porous paper.

Paper tends to restrict the air flow, so to make up for this its area has to be increased by being folded into a concertina shape. It's also difficult to clean, so once a paper filter becomes clogged it has to be replaced with a new one.

Wire gauze doesn't restrict the air flow as much, but it is less effective because the gaps between the strands of wire are bigger than those between the fibres of paper. To counter this problem – and to minimise corrosion – wire gauze filters need to be dipped in oil from time to time, so that dust sticks to them instead of passing straight through.

Exhaust systems

When it comes to exhaust systems, the boot is on the other foot: road vehicles and agricultural machinery have an easy time of it. Their engines are in compartments that are open to the atmosphere but sealed away from their drivers and passengers, so all that's required is a pipe connected to the exhaust manifold, with a few baffles to reduce the noise. A few marine installations adopt a similar *'dry'* exhaust system, usually in the form of an exhaust pipe sticking straight up from the engine compartment, with a weighted flap to stop rain or spray running down inside and heat resistant lagging to minimise the risk of fire or burns.

For pleasure craft, though, *'wet'* exhausts are pretty well standard, with water from the engine's cooling system used to cool the exhaust gas. The water is mixed with the exhaust gas in the *injection bend*, where it almost immediately turns into steam but in doing so reduces the

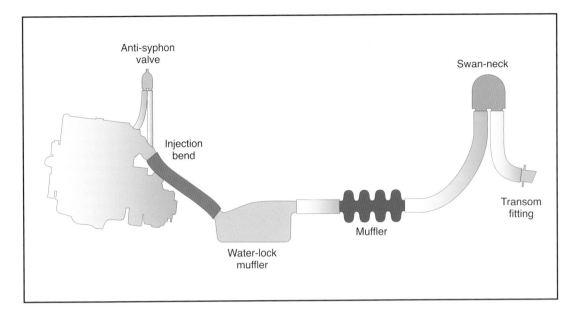

Fig 10 *The exhaust system.*

temperature of the exhaust gases from almost 500° C to about 70° C – cool enough to allow flexible tubing and GRP to be used for the rest of the exhaust system.

At that reduced temperature, the steam condenses back into water. That is why the mixing takes place in a bend: it protects the engine against the possibility of the cooling water running back through the system and into the cylinders.

If the engine is below the waterline, or very close to it, however, the injection bend alone is not enough: there's a danger that water already in the exhaust might set up a siphon effect that would allow sea water from outside to make its way back through the exhaust system and into the engine. To stop this, many boats have an extra loop in the exhaust system, known as a *swan-neck*. To guard against the possibility of waves pushing water up the exhaust pipe, some boats have a one-way flap covering the end of the pipe where it emerges from the hull; on some sailing yachts you may even find a hand-operated *gate valve* that seals the exhaust pipe com-

pletely when the engine is not being used.

The vital thing about any exhaust system is that it must not restrict the flow of exhaust gases beyond a certain limit, because if the exhaust can't get out of the cylinders, there will be no room for fresh air to get in. The effect is exactly the same as if the air filter were clogged: starved of oxygen, the engine will not be able to burn its fuel, so it will lose power and produce black smoke.

More power

Any engine is simply a device for converting the energy released from burning fuel into mechanical power. None of them are very good at it: well over 60 per cent of the energy released from the fuel is expended as heat and vibration, rather than as useful mechanical work. Engine designers are continually working to improve efficiency, but the fact remains that the power an engine can produce will always be limited by the rate at which it can burn fuel.

At the present state of development, a good rule of thumb is that every gallon of

Turbocharger

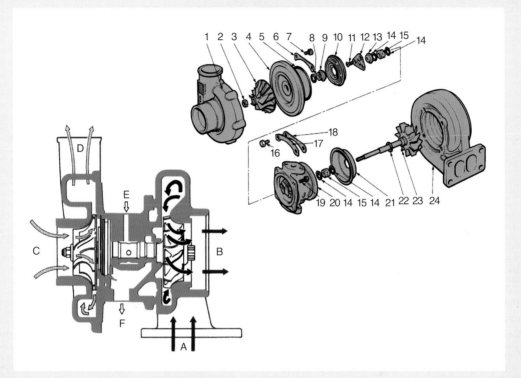

Fig 11 *Working principle and parts of the turbocharger.*

Key
Lower drawing
A Hot exhaust gases from the manifold drive the turbine.
B The exhaust gases then pass through the exhaust pipe/silencer to be cooled by a raw water injection bend fitted after the outlet.
C Air from the air cleaner is fed into the compressor.
D The compressed air is fed through the air inlet manifold to the cylinders where it can burn an increased amount of fuel compared to a normally aspirated engine.
E Lubricating oil inlet from engine's pressurised oil supply.
F Lubricating oil returns to engine sump.

Top drawing
1 Compressor-housing.
2 Lock-nut.
3 Compressor impeller.

4 Compressor diffuser.
5 'SQ' ring seal.
6 Clamping plate.
7 Hex head screw and washer.
8 Seal (split ring).
9 Oil slinger.
10 Oil baffle.
11 Flat head cap screw.
12 Thrust bearing.
13 Thrust collar.
14 Circlip.
15 Bearing.
16 Hex head screw.
17 Lockplate.
18 Clamping plate.
19 Hex head set screw and washer.
20 Bearing housing.
21 Heat shield.
22 Seal (split ring).
23 Shaft and turbine wheel.
24 Turbine housing.

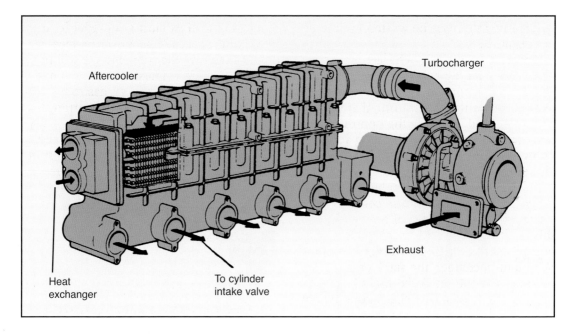

Fig 12 *Charge air cooler.*

diesel fuel will produce about 20 hp for one hour – or 10 hp for two hours, or 100 hp for twelve minutes, and so on. So if you want an engine to develop 40 hp, for instance, it needs to burn about 2 gallons per hour.

It's relatively easy to squirt more fuel into the cylinder, but that alone won't produce more power, because every gram of fuel needs about 25 g of air in order to burn. So to burn more fuel, you have to get more air into the engine.

This can be achieved in various ways:

- *Bigger cylinders* This has the advantage of simplicity and relatively low cost.
- *More cylinders* Involves more complex castings, more valves, and a more complicated fuel system, but tends to be smoother-running, and more responsive.
- *Run the engine faster* This pumps more air through the engine, without increasing its size or weight. Almost all modern diesels run faster than their counterparts of 20 years ago.
- *Force air into the cylinders* Done by pressurising it, to squeeze the equivalent of about 1¼ litres of air into each 1 litre of cylinder capacity.

The latter option has become very much more popular over the past 20 years or so, and is usually achieved by means of a blower called a *turbocharger* driven by a turbine built into the engine's exhaust system.

Unfortunately, turbochargers have to operate at high temperatures and at speeds in the order of 100,000 rpm – which give conservative marine engineers the heebie-jeebies, and produce a high-pitched whine that some people find offensive. Nevertheless, turbochargers are usually very reliable, and coax about 25 per cent more power out of an engine very efficiently, by winning back some of the energy that would otherwise be wasted in flow of hot exhaust gas.

One snag with a turbocharger is that pressurising air, especially by pumping it through a hot component like a turbo-charger, raises its temperature; therefore it tries to expand – exactly the opposite of what the turbocharger is trying to achieve! To overcome this, many engines draw their air supply through a duct lined with pipes containing cool sea water called a *charge air cooler*, *intercooler* or *aftercooler*.

You can get some idea of how effective this is by looking at the specifications of an engine such as the 90 hp Mermaid Melody. With a turbocharger, the same engine becomes the 160 hp Turbo Melody; and with an intercooler as well, it's up to 200 hp – a 122 per cent increase in power for a 3 per cent increase in weight and 40 per cent increase in price.

Variations on turbocharging

One application for which a turbocharged engine is not suitable is in a boat that spends most of its life operating at low speeds with only occasional, widely spaced bursts of high power. This is because at low power the exhaust flow won't be enough to operate the turbocharger. Exhaust gas flowing past the stationary tur-bocharger blades produces a build-up of soot, so when high power is called for, the clogged-up turbocharger can't work prop-erly. As a result, the engine won't receive enough air to burn its fuel properly, so it will produce more oily soot that makes matters even worse.

There are various ways in which design-ers have brought the benefits of turbocharging to engines that have to operate at a wide range of speeds.

One method is to fit a smaller turbo-charger, capable of operating even with the

reduced flow of exhaust gas produced at low engine speeds. This, however, means that at high revs the turbocharger will be faced with more exhaust than it can cope with, so some of the exhaust has to be diverted away through a by-pass arrange-ment called a *waste-gate*.

An alternative is to use a mechanically driven compressor called a *supercharger* at medium revs, allowing the turbocharger to take over as the engine speed increases.

• • • *Things to do*

1 Black smoke

Black smoke is almost certainly a symptom of problems in the air system.

a Check to make sure that the engine room ventilation is adequate – that the engine com-partment ventilation louvres aren't blocked by leaves or by the contents of lockers, for instance – and that the engine's air filter isn't clogged.

b On turbocharged engines, look for loose hoses or leaks between the turbocharger and the engine itself.

c Make sure the exhaust hose isn't blocked, squashed or damaged: bear in mind that flexi-ble exhaust pipes can deteriorate in time, allowing their inner layers to collapse while the outside looks perfectly sound.

2 Air filter

a Clean or replace the air filter at least once a season. Unclip or unscrew the cover, and lift out the filter element. Paper elements should be replaced if they are dirty or damaged.

b Wire gauze filters should be washed in paraffin or a solution of washing up liquid in water, and allowed to dry. Inspect the filter for rust or loose strands, and replace it if neces-sary. Otherwise, dip it in clean engine oil and drain off the excess.

c Replace the element, making sure that it's correctly seated, and replace the filter cover.

5 | Cooling System

The previous chapter mentioned that over 60 per cent of the energy produced by burning fuel in a diesel engine is wasted in the form of heat. That's almost inevitable: heat is needed to ignite each charge of fuel and air in the first place, and it's heat that expands the contents of the cylinder to drive the piston downwards. The piston sliding up and down inside the cylinder produces yet more heat by friction, as does the movement of the con rod on the crankshaft and the rotation of the crankshaft in the main bearings – anywhere, in fact, where metal moves against metal.

If all this heat were retained by the engine, it would get hotter and hotter, until it either set fire to the boat or welded some of its own parts together to become a useless lump of dead metal.

Very small engines have a large surface area compared to their volume and the heat they produce, so a lot of heat can be lost to the atmosphere by radiation – so lawn mowers, small motorbikes and light aircraft need no cooling system as such, other than fins to increase their surface area. It is very different for boats: their engines are normally larger, and are invariably tucked away in snug engine compartments. They are, however, blessed with a plentiful supply of water.

The basic system – raw-water cooling

Some of the simplest water cooling systems are found in small outboards such as the old British Seagull. Its cylinder is cylindrical, but it's inside a cube-shaped cylinder block which leaves large open spaces between the walls of the cylinder and the outer walls of the block that are filled by sea water pumped up from the bottom of the drive leg. The water absorbs heat from the cylinder, and then escapes back to the sea through a hole in the casting, pushed out by more water coming up from the pump.

Components such as the piston and crankshaft don't have the advantage of being in direct contact with the cool sea water, so they get much hotter, but are kept down to a reasonable working temperature by being able to conduct heat away to the relatively cool block.

This kind of system is called *direct cooling*, or *raw-water cooling*, and is so simple, cheap and effective that it would be surprising if it wasn't also used in small diesels.

The main difference between a diesel's direct cooling system and that of an outboard is that the diesel's cooling water has to be pumped into the boat and back out again.

The way in is through a hole in the boat and a flexible hose. The hole has to be below the waterline, so any leaks from any part of the cooling system are potentially capable of sinking the boat. This makes a *seacock* essential, so as to be able to isolate the entire system from the sea.

If the system gets blocked accidentally, by weed or rubbish, the consequences are less dramatic, but are still potentially serious. To guard against this, the system should have a *raw-water filter*.

Once the water has done its job of cooling the engine, it can be discharged overboard

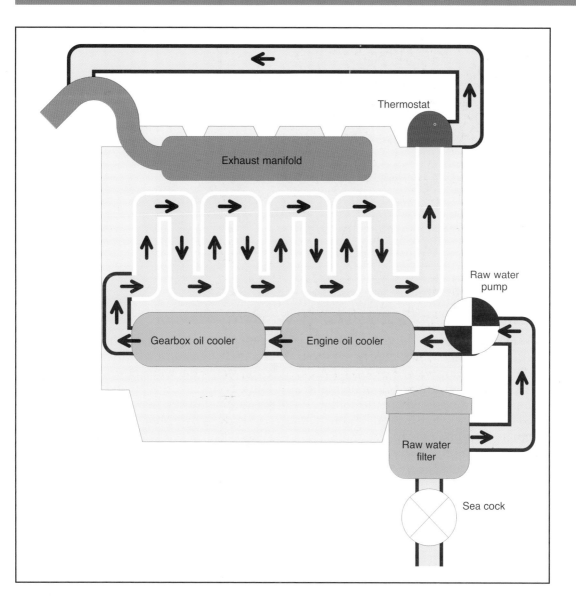

Fig 13 *Raw-water circuit.*

through a hole in the topsides. Nowadays, though, it's much more common for it to be mixed with the engine's exhaust gas in the *injection bend*, where it cools and quietens the exhaust system. To reduce the risk of water from the cooling system flooding the exhaust manifold when the engine is not running, an anti-siphon valve is usually built in just before the injection bend.

The thermostat

One drawback of raw-water cooling is that it can be too effective, especially when the engine is being started, or when it is running at low load. The engine needs some heat to ignite its fuel, so removing heat through the cooling system can be counterproductive.

To overcome this, and allow the engine to start and run at its most efficient temperature,

Removing a thermostat.

most diesels are fitted with an automatic valve called a *thermostat*, which regulates the flow of cooling water.

The thermostat is usually mounted under a dome-shaped cover where the cooling water leaves the cylinder head. It's a simple component, whose only moving part is a circular trap door of thin metal, held shut by a spring. Under the trap door is a sealed capsule of wax or alcohol which expands as the temperature of the surrounding water rises until it overcomes the resistance of the spring and pushes the trap door open.

If the thermostat were 100 per cent effective at shutting off the water flow, there would be quite a build-up of pressure between the pump and the thermostat, so the thermostat has a small by-pass hole to allow some water to flow when the thermostat is shut. Even if there's a separate by-pass hose, the hole has an important role. Without it, an air lock could keep the cooling water away from the thermostat – thereby stopping it from opening until the temperature of the engine had already risen dangerously high.

It's worth bearing in mind that there is bound to be a slight difference between the temperature at which the thermostat opens and the temperature at which it closes, so if you watch the temperature gauge closely you may well see a slow and fairly regular rise and fall in engine temperature. This is nothing to worry about: just get used to the normal range of operating temperatures for your engine.

Thermostats can occasionally jam open or closed. If yours jams open, the immediate effect will be that the fluctuation of temperature stops, and the engine runs cooler than usual, burning more fuel but producing less power and more smoke.

A more serious problem arises if the thermostat jams shut: the by-pass flow alone won't be enough to cool the engine, so it will overheat.

It's easy to test a thermostat by taking it out and putting it in a saucepan of water on the stove. As the water temperature rises, you should see the thermostat open. This should happen when the water is too hot to bear putting your hand in it, but well before it reaches boiling point.

If the thermostat has failed, a get-you-home solution is to break the wax capsule and spring away to allow the trap door to stay open.

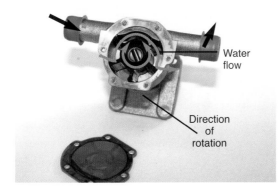

Water
flow

Direction
of
rotation

Raw-water pump: note that the vanes rotate clockwise, and that the water flow is in the same direction (ie the 'long way round').

Raw-water pump

There are many different ways of pumping water for raw-water systems, but the most common by far is the 'flexible impeller' type of pump – often known by the trade name *Jabsco*.

The flexible impeller looks like a paddle wheel, with several flat blades or vanes sticking out from a central hub. It's a tight fit inside a cylindrical casing, and is made even tighter by a bulge in the wall of the casing, between the inlet and outlet pipes.

As the impeller turns, each vane in turn

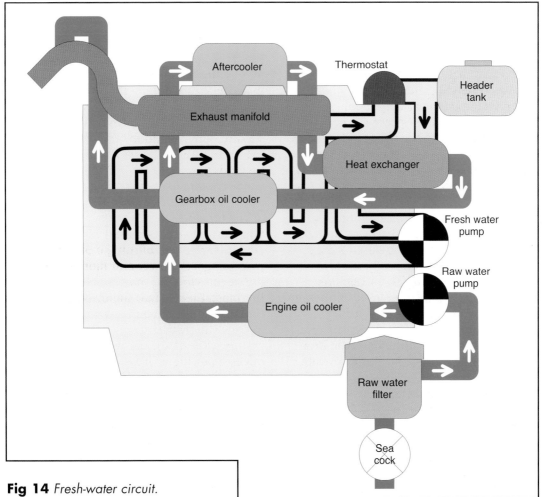

Fig 14 *Fresh-water circuit.*

has to bend to get past the bulge. This reduces the space between the bent vane and the one in front. As the vane clears the bulge, it straightens out again, increasing the space between the two vanes and pulling water in from the inlet pipe. As the impeller continues to rotate, the water trapped between the two vanes is carried around with it, until it reaches the outlet pipe. At this point, the leading vane encounters the bulge in the casing and has to bend again to get past it. This reduces the space between the two vanes, and forces the trapped water into the outlet pipe.

Anodes

Warm sea water is ferociously corrosive, so an engine with raw-water cooling needs something to reduce the effect. Just as most boats have sacrificial zinc anodes below the waterline to protect exposed metal parts, so do most raw-water-cooled engines. Engine anodes come in many shapes and sizes, though they are often in the form of rods, about the shape and size of a man's finger, which screw into holes in the engine block.

Sacrificial anodes are very effective, but are inconspicuous and easily forgotten, so do check the engine instruction manual to find out where they are and when they should be replaced.

Indirect cooling

An alternative solution to the problem of corrosion is to keep sea water away from the engine altogether, and use fresh water – usually mixed with antifreeze as further protection against corrosion.

This is exactly the same as the way car truck and tractor engines are cooled, so it is particularly common in engines over about 50 hp (which are almost invariably based on designs intended for use in vehicles).

Fresh-water cooling has other advan-

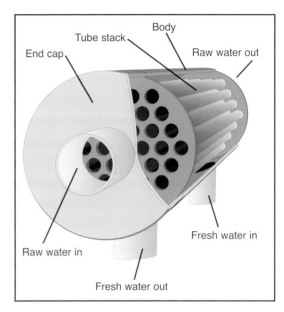

Fig 15 *Heat exchanger.*

tages besides reducing the risk of corrosion: it offers closer control of the engine's operating temperature, and allows it to run slightly hotter without salt deposits building up in the pipe-work. Both of these make the engine more efficient, so fresh-water cooling is gradually becoming more common even on engines as small as 10 hp.

The big difference between a boat engine and its stable-mate in a car or truck is that a boat engine doesn't use an air-cooled radiator to cool the water that has cooled the engine. Instead, it uses a *heat exchanger*, made up of a bundle of small-bore tubes or thin hollow plates inside an outer casing. The fresh water flows through the casing, while raw (sea) water flows through the tubes or plates.

Fresh-water cooling, then, involves two sub-systems: a fresh-water system that cools the engine, and a raw-water system that cools the fresh water. For this reason, it's often known as *indirect cooling*.

Apart from the heat exchanger, the components involved in an indirect system are much the same as those that make up a raw-water system, because the raw-water side still has to have a seacock, filter, pump and injection bend. Only the thermostat is missing, because it is now part of the fresh-water system.

Two extra components are involved in the fresh-water side: a *header tank* to provide a reserve of cooling water and give room for the water to expand and contract as its temperature changes; and a *circulating pump* to drive water through the system.

The header tank is often combined with the heat exchanger, to form a substantial box-like component mounted high on the front of the engine. It's topped by something very much like a car's radiator cap and serving almost exactly the same purpose – keeping coolant inside the system even when it tries to escape as steam, but acting as a safety valve if the pressure rises too high.

Like a radiator cap, the header tank cap can eventually fail, when the sealing ring is damaged or when the spring loses its resilience. Either of these will lead to a steady loss of water, which could eventually lead to the engine overheating.

Doom and gloom merchants will tell you (quite correctly) that loss of water and overheating are among the symptoms of a blown cylinder head gasket. It could save you a lot of money if you try replacing the header tank cap before leaping to the assumption that the pessimists are right!

Circulating pump

Compared with the raw water pump, which may have to lift water from the sea, the fresh water pump has the relatively simple task of creating a flow of water through an enclosed system. This means the pump itself can be the simpler *centrifugal* type, which is less prone to wear and tear.

The outer casing is dome-shaped, with the inlet pipe at its centre and the outlet pipe emerging from the edge. Inside, the impeller is virtually flat, but has curved

Fresh water circulating pump.

vanes sticking up from its surface like the fan of a hover mower. As the impeller spins, the vanes set up a swirling movement of the water inside the casing. Centrifugal force, helped by the curvature of the blades, drives the water out into the outlet pipe, while more water rushes in through the inlet pipe to fill the space that would otherwise be left in the centre.

There is little to go wrong with a centrifugal pump until – after several thousand hours' running – the bearings that support its shaft start to wear, producing a high pitched and almost continuous squeak. When this happens, it's a fairly simple job to rebuild the pump with new components and even easier to replace the whole thing.

Skin cooling

A variation on indirect cooling, popular in steel canal boats and some small commercial vessels, is known as skin cooling or by the somewhat misleading name of 'keel cooling'.

Essentially it replaces the heat exchanger by tubes or by a tank that is in direct contact with the side or bottom of the vessel. Coolant passing through the tank or tubes discharges its heat through the metal skin of the vessel, into the surrounding water.

Skin cooling systems require very little in

••• *Things to do*

Safety first

Remember that when the engine is warm, the fresh-water system may be full of very hot water or steam, and under pressure.

The raw-water system is directly connected to the sea. Any leak is potentially capable of sinking the boat.

1 Clearing the raw water filter

The raw water filter should be checked, and cleared if necessary, each day that the engine is to be used, and whenever there is an unusual rise in engine temperature.

If your filter has a transparent cover, putting a table-tennis ball inside can save time and trouble because movement of the table-tennis ball is a clear sign that water is flowing through the filter. Otherwise, when you start the engine, get into the habit of checking that water is coming out of the exhaust pipe.

Raw water filters differ in design and construction. In general, though, the procedure is:

a Shut the raw water seacock.

b Remove the cover: this may involve undoing several nuts, unscrewing the cap as though you were opening a jam jar, or releasing a clamp.

c Remove the filter element – usually a cylinder of perforated sheet metal, wire gauze, or a net of nylon mesh covering a metal frame – and clear out any weed or debris.

d Put the filter back, making sure that any locating studs fit into their notches, and that the top of the filter is at the same level as it was before.

e Replace the filter cover, making sure that it is screwed down handtight.

f Open the seacock and inspect for leaks around the cover. *Don't be tempted to leave this while you do your other daily checks – it's too easy to start the engine with the seacock closed!*

2 Checking the header tank

If your engine has an indirect cooling system, the level of water in the header tank should be checked whenever you check the raw water filter.

2a

2b

a Unscrew the header tank cap. If the engine is warm, protect yourself by covering it with several layers of cloth (such as an old towel), and unscrew it very slowly to allow any pressure to be released gradually. Some types have a 'bayonet' fitting: these have to be pressed down against the spring pressure before they can be unscrewed, but take only a quarter turn to release: some have a two-stage unscrewing action that allows them to be partly unscrewed to release any pressure, then require a second push and twist action to release them completely.

b Most manufacturers recommend that the water level should be between 1 and 3 in (25 and 76 mm) below the top of the tank: in general, if you can touch the water with your finger, it's full enough. If not, top it up with clean fresh water mixed with antifreeze. Replace the cap.

3 Replacing the raw water pump impeller

Although 'Jabsco'-type pumps are virtually standard there are many different models, so it's a good idea to carry at least one spare on board,

3a

3c

3b

3d

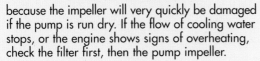

because the impeller will very quickly be damaged if the pump is run dry. If the flow of cooling water stops, or the engine shows signs of overheating, check the filter first, then the pump impeller.

a Undo the screws holding the pump's front cover in place, and remove it. Peel away the remains of the paper gasket that may be stuck to the cover, or the body, or a bit of both.

b Pull out the impeller with a pair of pliers. If it won't come out, or if you have no suitable pliers available, it can be prised out using two screwdrivers, but be very careful not to damage the softer metal of the pump body.

c If the impeller has disintegrated, try to piece it together so as to be certain there are no missing pieces wandering around the cooling system where they could cause blockages later. If there are any missing pieces, try to find them if you can: dismantle the pipe-work between the pump and the heat exchanger to see if they are stuck at a bend, or look in the heat exchanger itself.

d Smear the new impeller with washing up liquid, and slide it on to its shaft, making sure that

3e

the vanes are bent the right way and that it is properly located on the drive key or pin that protrudes from the shaft. Notice (see photo on page 29) that the water always takes the 'long way round' in its trip from the inlet pipe to the outlet and that the vanes trail backwards like the sparks from a Catherine wheel.

e Use a little water or washing up liquid to temporarily stick the new gasket that is supplied with the impeller in place on the pump body, and then replace the cover plate.

••• Things to do

4 Replacing internal anodes

Check with your engine instruction manual to see how and when to replace internal anodes.

the way of maintenance, but it is important to check the coolant level regularly, and to make sure any hoses are in good condition. Every couple of seasons or so, replace the coolant with a fresh mixture of antifreeze and water.

Oil cooling

One tends to assume that an engine needs oil for much the same reason as a bicycle or a door hinge – to reduce friction so that things move or slide over each other more easily. That, however, is only one of its jobs: it also plays an important part in carrying heat away from the engine's most intimate working parts. Some engines, for instance, even have a system that squirts a jet of oil against the underside of each piston.

In a car, the heat that the oil has collected as it travels around the engine is dissipated from the sump, hanging down below the engine in the rush of air passing under the vehicle.

For obvious reasons this doesn't apply to marine engines, so many – particularly those over about 50 hp – have an *oil cooler*.

An oil cooler is another heat exchanger, similar to the main heat exchanger but smaller, that uses the engine's raw-water system in order to cool the oil. A second oil cooler is often used to cool the gearbox oil.

6 | Oil System

One of the quickest and most sure-fire ways to wreck an engine is to run it without oil, because even a smooth or polished surface has minute imperfections called asperites. These jagged spikes and ridges may only be a millionth of an inch high, but as metal moves against metal, the asperites on one surface collide and interlock with those on the other, and then have to bend or break to allow the movement to continue.

The cumulative effect of repeatedly bending or breaking thousands of asperites soon produces visible damage to the surface, known as wear. The effort expended in doing so is friction.

Each collision also generates heat, with local temperatures sometimes rising to as much as 1,600° C – enough, in severe cases, to weld the surfaces together.

Oil solves the problem by separating the two metal surfaces with a thin layer of fluid, and filling the tiny valleys between the asperites: reducing wear, allowing moving parts to move more freely, and stopping them welding themselves together.

Cleans, cools and protects

Lubrication is undoubtedly the oil's main job, but it has a number of subsidiary functions. These were neatly summed up by one of the oil companies whose advertising slogan, at one time, was 'cleans, cools and protects'.

- It cleans the engine by flushing away tiny particles of carbon or metal, and neutralising the acids produced from burning fuel.
- It cools the engine by carrying heat away from hot spots that can't be reached by the engine's water cooling system, such as the pistons and main bearings.
- It protects the engine by covering the metal parts to exclude air and moisture that would otherwise cause corrosion.

One significant job that the advertising agency forgot is that oil also helps to create a gas-tight seal between – for instance – the piston rings and the cylinder walls.

Pressurised oil systems

A few very simple engines have no oil system at all. Two-stroke petrol engines, for instance, run on a mixture of oil and petrol, and rely on the engine's demand for air to pull the petrol-oil mixture through the areas where oil is needed. Some small four-stroke engines rely exclusively on 'splash-feed' lubrication, in which a spike or paddle, protruding from the bottom of the con rod, flings oil around the inside of the crankcase, the bottom of the cylinder, and the underside of the piston.

You don't have to move far up the scale, though, to reach engines in which pressurised oil systems are standard. They use an oil pump to lift oil out of the *sump* and through a filter, before pushing it through a maze of *oilways* to the crankshaft, camshaft and rocker bearings; to the con rods and pistons; and out to ancillaries such as the turbocharger and fuel pump.

Gravity then returns the 'used' oil to the sump.

Most of the lubrication system – like the pistons and main bearings that it serves – are deep inside the engine, and out of reach of a limited onboard tool kit. User maintenance is confined to making sure that the engine has a good supply of clean oil by topping up and changing the oil at regular intervals, and changing the filter.

In the longer term, it is a good idea to keep an eye on the oil pressure gauge. Some internal wear is inevitable, so as time goes by, the gaps between some of the moving parts will increase, making it easier for oil to seep away. This doesn't just mean that the lubrication around the affected part will be less effective: it also means that less oil will reach other components, leaving you with an escalating trail of damage throughout the engine.

Good operating practices delay the onset

Oil system

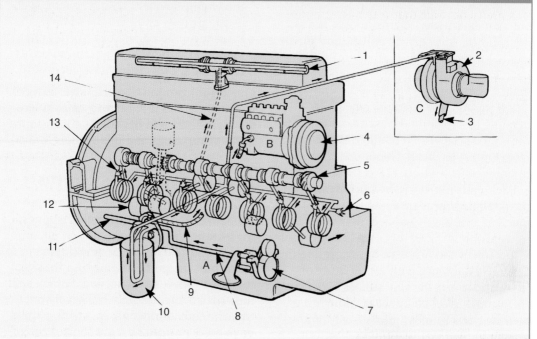

Fig 16 *The engine lubricating oil circuit.*

Key
A The sump and coarse filter.
1 Rocker shaft.
2 Turbocharger (some petrol and diesel engines only (C)).
3 Oil drain to oil pan from turbocharger.
4 Lubrication for fuel injection pump (some 'in-line' diesel pumps only (B)).
5 Camshaft bearings.
6 Spray to timing gear.

7 Oil pump.
8 Feed pipe to filter and thence to main oil gallery.
9 Feed to diesel fuel in-line injection pump (see 4 above).
10 Oil filter.
11 Main oil gallery.
12 Big end bearings.
13 Main bearings and piston cooling nozzles.
14 Metered oil feed to rockers and rocker shaft.

of wear: in particular it pays to remember that until the engine has been running for a few moments, it will be dependent on the oil which has been left clinging to its bearing surfaces. If the engine has been idle for very long, those surfaces may be almost completely dry, so if it is started with full 'throttle' and roars into life as soon as the key is turned, a lot of wear will take place before any new oil has had a chance to reach the parts it is supposed to protect.

Oil grades and classes

It is pretty obvious that if the oil is to do its job of separating two moving parts, there has to be a gap between them that the oil can fill. This, however, means that if the oil were perfectly fluid it would simply escape through the gap, so to be effective an oil needs a certain *viscosity*, or 'thickness'.

This seems to imply that a 'thick', viscous oil is better than a 'thin' one, but that is certainly not the case: viscosity is an indication of the friction between the molecules of the oil itself, so a very viscous oil makes starting difficult, wastes power, and generates extra heat.

In other words, you need to choose an oil of the right viscosity for your engine.

There are lots of different ways of measuring viscosity but, to make life relatively simple, oils are now graded according to a system of numbers devised by the American Society of Automotive Engineers, in which the higher the number, the thicker the oil. Your engine manual may specify, for instance, that it needs an oil grade 'SAE 40'.

The picture is made slightly more complicated by the fact that oils become less viscous as they warm up, so an oil that is right at normal operating temperature may

be very much too thick for easy starting in the depths of winter. To overcome this, it was once common practice to use a much 'lighter' oil in winter, and to accept increased wear as a penalty that had to be paid. SAE catered for this by introducing a second series of 'Winter' grades, such as SAE 10W.

Oil technology has advanced enormously since the SAE grades were introduced. Now, additives mixed with the oil make it much less susceptible to changes in temperature. This means that most modern engine oils can be used in summer and winter alike, and therefore have summer and winter SAE grades shown together, such as SAE 20W/50 or SAE 15W/40.

Even 'ordinary' engine oils nowadays contain a cocktail of other additives intended to enhance particular aspects of their performance. Inevitably this means that some oils are 'better' or 'worse' than others, so various bodies have introduced performance standards to identify oils that are suitable for particular jobs.

The most widespread of these classification systems was developed by the American Petroleum Institute (API), which assesses an oil's performance in each of two categories: S, for spark ignition (petrol) engines; and C, for compression ignition (diesel) engines. As time has gone by, the capabilities of the oil producers and the demands of the engine manufacturers have increased, so now there are a range of API classifications from SA/CA (the oldest and obsolete) up to SL and CM.

Most oils now meet SE/CD or SG/CF specifications, and are perfectly suitable for use in most engines, but if you are faced with an unfamiliar brand it's as well to check the quality designators printed on the can and to check, if necessary, that it is specified as suitable for a turbocharged engine.

• • • *Things to do*

Safety first

The additives that make modern oils better for your engine make them worse for you. Take care to avoid unnecessary or prolonged contact with engine oil – new or used.

1 Oil level

Check the oil level each day that the engine is to be used. It is quite normal for an engine to 'use' a certain amount of oil.

a Withdraw the dipstick, wipe it with a dry rag and then put it back, making sure it is pushed fully home. Pull it out again, and look at the oil level, which should be between the 'max' and 'min' marks. Then replace the dipstick.

b If necessary, top up the oil by pouring oil in

1b

through the filler cap – usually on top of the rocker cover. Leave the engine for a few seconds for the new oil to drain down before re-checking the level.

2 Changing the oil filter

The oil and filter should be changed at the end of each season, or after about 200 hours' use.

First run the engine up to operating temperature, then protect the area around the filter from spillages. Try to avoid contact with the used oil.

a 'Spin-on' filters are best removed by unscrewing with a strap or chain wrench.

b If that isn't available or doesn't work, drive a large screwdriver through the canister, just off centre, and use it as a lever.

c Smear the sealing ring with a thin film of fresh oil. Spin the filter on until the sealing ring just touches the filter head, then tighten it another half turn by hand. Do not over-tighten it.

d Cartridge-type filters are usually secured by a single bolt.

1a

2a

2c

3 Changing engine oil

There's no point changing the filter without changing the oil, and if your engine has a sump pump, this is a simple matter of pumping the oil into a suitable container. If not, you will have to resort to other methods:

a You will have to insert a small tube down the dipstick hole, connected to a pump, to suck the oil out.

b Replace the sump drain plug if you have removed it, taking care not to over-tighten it, before topping up with the right grade and quantity of oil.

3a

e Remove the cartridge, and replace it, making sure that the various springs and washers are replaced in the correct order, and that the filter is the right way up.

f Make sure the old rubber sealing ring isn't stuck to the filter head, and replace it with the new one supplied with the filter.

g Replace the complete assembly, making sure the filter canister is correctly seated, and tighten the retaining bolt.

h Change the oil, then run the engine at tick-over for a few minutes to inspect for leaks around the filter. Even if no leaks appear, check the oil level and top it up, because some oil will be retained in the filter.

7 Electrical System

One of the great virtues of a diesel engine is that it doesn't need electricity to start or run. Small diesels can be started by hand, bigger ones by coiled springs, and the biggest of all by compressed air or separate starter engines.

An electric motor, though, is such a convenient way of doing the job that almost all marine diesels now have an electrical system of some description.

The basic system

Diesels intended for hand starting usually have *decompression levers*, which make it a lot easier to build up momentum in the heavy flywheel by opening the valves in the cylinder head to release the pressure in the cylinder.

Even so, hand starting a diesel can still be hard work, so it shouldn't come as any surprise to find that it takes a lot of electrical power to do the same thing – especially as electric-start engines don't usually have decompression levers. Compared with any other electrical equipment on board, the amount of power involved is huge: the initial surge of current may be in the order of 1,000 amps. It quickly drops away to about 200 amps as the motor picks up speed, but it's still asking a lot to expect any battery to start an engine more than once or twice without recharging.

This means that as well as the *starter motor* itself and a switch to control it, even the most basic electrical system is likely to include a *dynamo* or *alternator* to recharge the battery, and a *regulator* to stop the battery being overcharged. For indirect injection engines, there is usually also some kind of *cold starting aid* to make the starter motor's job a little easier by warming the air in the cylinders.

No ordinary switch can cope with the sort of currents involved in the starter circuit, so the 'switch' that controls the starter motor is actually a relay or *solenoid* – a remote controlled switch operated by another switch on the control panel. The control panel also needs a warning light or buzzer to attract attention to any failure of the electrical system, so the complete system ends up looking something like that in Fig 17 (over page).

Making electricity

Generators and motors both depend on the close link between electricity and magnetism, which can be summed up by saying that if you move a wire in a magnetic field you'll create electricity, and if you pass electricity through a wire you'll create magnetism.

Fig 18A shows how this might be applied to make electricity: a coil of wire, wound around a central core, is spinning in the magnetic field between two magnets. As it rotates, the wires that make up the coil move through the magnetic field, to generate an electric current.

Fig 18B shows one way of getting the electricity out of the coil: the ends of the wire are connected to brass *slip rings*, fixed to the spinning shaft. Self-lubricating carbon *brushes* press against the slip rings to

40

Basic electrical circuit

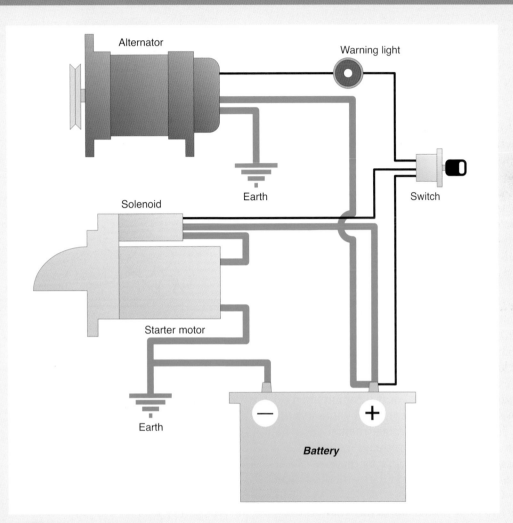

Fig 17 *Basic electrical circuit.*

Tracing an engine's wiring loom can be complicated because some wires do two or more jobs, and it is not possible to see exactly what is going on inside some components.

Here, the battery supplies power to the starter solenoid, which – when activated – passes it on to the starter. The starter returns the current to the battery through the engine block itself, shown by the 'earth' symbol.

The solenoid is activated by the key switch, which draws power from the battery through a thinner wire and feeds it to the solenoid. The solenoid current returns to the battery through the starter's earth connection.

The alternator creates current which flows straight to the battery and is returned through the engine block. A thinner wire links the alternator terminal labelled 'IND' to the warning light, which is connected to the battery through the key switch. So long as the alternator is charging, no current flows through this wire, but if the alternator fails, current flows from the battery, through the switch and warning light, and returns to the earth.

collect the electricity, and wires take it away to the rest of the system.

This is simple, but for practical purposes it has a major problem: because the coil is passing up through the magnetic field on one side, then down through it on the other, the current created in it is regularly changing direction.

Batteries can't handle *alternating current* (AC): they need a one-way current (*direct current*, or DC). One possible solution is shown in Fig 18C. Instead of a pair of slip rings there is only one, split in half along its axis. Every time the current flow reverses, the connection to the outside world reverses as well, producing an intermittent but one-way current.

Dynamos

A real dynamo looks much more complicated than the contraption shown in Fig 18, but works in exactly the same way.

Instead of a single coil of wire, it has several, each wound around its own soft iron core. This, in turn, means that the two-piece 'slip ring' of the rudimentary dynamo has to be replaced by a *commutator* made up of several segments – one pair for each coil. This produces a smoother flow of current, because as the flow generated by one coil is reducing, the flow from another is increasing.

The other major refinement in a real dynamo is that instead of using permanent magnets to create the magnetic field, it uses electromagnets. They consist of soft iron cores bolted to the casing of the dynamo, and wrapped in coils of copper wire called the *field windings*. Passing an electric current through the field windings creates the magnetism.

The virtue of using electricity to make more electricity is that it allows the intensity of the magnetic field to be varied. A separate component called the *regulator* monitors the output of the dynamo and

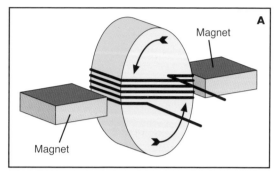

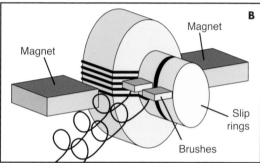

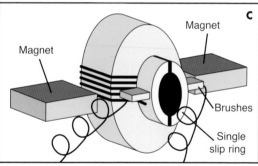

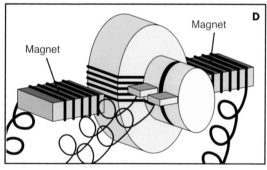

Fig 18
A *A simple generator*
B *An AC generator*
C *A simple dynamo*
D *Electromagnets allow control of output*

interrupts the power supplied to the field windings if the output rises too high, allowing the dynamo's output to be controlled without having to adjust its speed.

Alternators

Dynamos are something of a rarity nowadays, having been almost completely replaced by a more efficient kind of generator called an *alternator*.

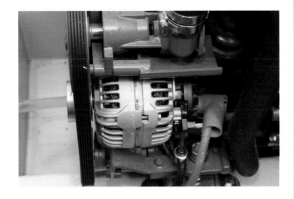

Power is generated by the alternator.

Mechanically, an alternator can be regarded as a dynamo turned inside out, with its field windings mounted on a spinning *rotor* in the middle, surrounded by a fixed ring called the *stator* which carries the generating coils.

This arrangement leaves the coils stationary, but subjected to a spinning magnetic field. Having stationary generating coils means that an alternator can't use a commutator arrangement to convert AC into DC: instead, it uses a solid-state electronic *rectifier* and regulator, usually built-in under a plastic cover at one end of the alternator body.

As well as being more efficient than dynamos, alternators are generally more reliable and require little or no maintenance. Their main weakness is that their electronic components burn out very quickly if they are kept running with

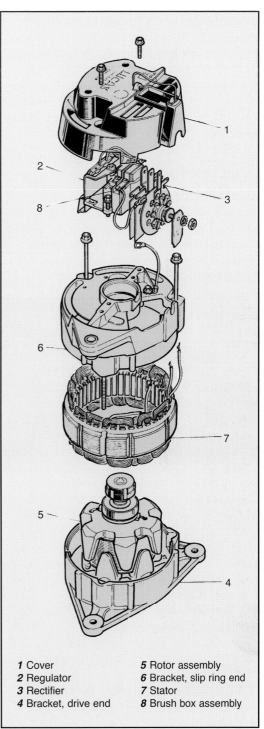

1 Cover	**5** Rotor assembly
2 Regulator	**6** Bracket, slip ring end
3 Rectifier	**7** Stator
4 Bracket, drive end	**8** Brush box assembly

Fig 19 *ACR alternator.*

nowhere for the electricity to go, so it is essential to make sure never to disconnect an alternator while the engine is running – by switching the battery isolator switch off, for instance. If your installation allows you to stop the engine by turning a key, make sure it really has stopped completely before switching the key to the 'off' position.

Starter motors

Structurally, an electric motor is very much like the rudimentary dynamo in Fig 18: it too has coils of wire mounted on a central shaft called the *armature*, and magnets bolted to the inside of the casing to create a magnetic field.

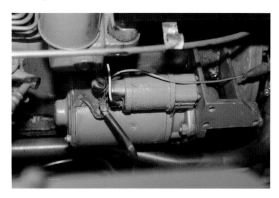

The starter motor.

The big difference is that a motor uses electricity instead of creating it! When a current is passed through the armature coils, it creates a magnetic field which interacts with the magnetic field set up by the field windings in such a way that the armature is forced to rotate.

Dynastarts

A motor and a dynamo are so similar to each other that at one time there was a trend towards using a single component, called a *Dynastart*, to do both jobs. Unfortunately a good dynamo doesn't make a good motor or vice versa, so this rather neat idea has now gone out of fashion.

Batteries

We can't create energy: we can only convert it from one form into another. That is what happens inside the engine itself: chemical energy is released from the burning fuel and converted into mechanical energy. The alternator then converts some of that mechanical energy into electrical energy. Electrical energy, however, can't be stored: to achieve that effect, the battery has to convert it back into chemical energy.

There are lots of ways of doing this, including the lightweight nickel-cadmium (NiCad) and nickel-metal hydride (NiMH) batteries used for mobile phones and hand-held radios. For the time being, however, these are too expensive to be used to store large amounts of power, so boats almost invariably use relatively cheap, low-tech *lead-acid* batteries.

The working part of a fully charged lead-acid battery is a stack of lead plates, interleaved with layers of lead peroxide and porous separators and surrounded by sulphuric acid. The acid tries to convert both sets of plates into lead sulphate while converting itself into water by rearranging the electrical charges that hold the molecules together. In the process, it creates an electric current between the positive peroxide plates and the negative lead plates.

Eventually, the sulphuric acid becomes so diluted that the reaction stops. The battery is then described as 'flat'. The beauty of the lead-acid battery, however, is that the whole process can be reversed by pumping electricity through it in the opposite direction. This converts the lead sulphate back into lead and lead peroxide, while the left-over sulphate turns the water back into sulphuric acid.

Starter motor

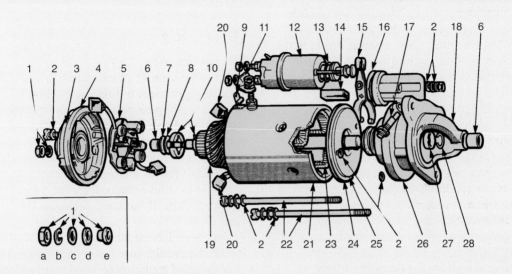

Fig 20 *The Lucas M50 starter.*

Key

1 Nut and spring washer.
2 Sealing washers.
3 Commutator end cover.
4 Sealing ring.
5 Brush gear assembly comprising earth brushes and springs. Marine version has insulated negative brushes.
6 Bearing bush.
7 Fibre washer.
8 Steel thrust washer.
9 Flexible link.
10 Brake shoe and cross peg.
11 Copper link.
12 Solenoid unit.
13 Return spring.
14 Sealing grommet which is deleted on the marine version.
15 Engagement lever.
16 Gasket.
17 Eccentric pivot pin.
18 Drive and fixing bracket.
19 Armature.
20 Insulated brushes – field coils.
21 Yoke.
22 Through bolts.
23 Field coils.
24 Sealing ring.
25 Intermediate ring.
26 Drive assembly.
27 Thrust collar.
28 Jump ring.
Inset for marine version (a) Nut, (b) Plain washer, (c) Insulated washer for outside cover, (d) Insulated bush for inside cover.

The system isn't absolutely perfect, though. For one thing, the conversion process is never 100 per cent completed: repeated charging and discharging leaves some unconverted lead sulphate on the plates, gradually reducing the battery's ability to 'hold its charge'. Eventually, the accumulated lead sulphate flakes away, to lie useless in the bottom of the casing.

Another problem is that passing electricity through water – or through a solution of sulphuric acid in water – causes a process known as electrolysis, which breaks down the water into hydrogen and oxygen. For safety reasons, this potentially explosive mixture of gases should be vented overboard, but it's important to appreciate that by doing so you're effectively discharging water from the battery, which will have to be topped up with distilled or de-ionised water from time to time.

The demands of starting an engine are very different from those imposed by 'ship's services' such as lighting and navigation equipment: the starter motor demands a lot of current for a few seconds at a time, while domestic and navigation equipment draws a relatively tiny current for hours at a stretch. Ideally, these contrasting requirements call for two different types of battery: a *heavy duty* battery for engine starting, and a *deep cycle* or *traction* battery for domestic loads. Structurally, the two types differ mainly in the number and thickness of their plates: a heavy duty battery has a large number of relatively thin plates, in order to expose as much surface area to the acid as possible, while a deep cycle battery has a smaller number of thicker plates in order to withstand the long term effects of sulphation caused by being repeatedly discharged almost to the stage of being 'flat'. *'Marine'* batteries are a half-way house, intended mainly for small boats on which one battery may have to do both jobs.

Fuses and circuit breakers

Whenever an electric current passes through a wire it creates heat – and the heavier the current or the thinner the wire, the hotter it is likely to get. Taken to extremes, this could melt the insulation around the wire, or even start a fire. To stop this happening, designers should specify cables that are big enough to allow heat to radiate away from the wire naturally.

There is still an element of risk, though, because the current could – for all sorts of reasons – increase to levels far greater than the designer envisaged. To make sure this doesn't happen, any properly installed electrical system incorporates some kind of excess current protection – either a *fuse* or a *circuit breaker*.

A fuse is a short piece of thin wire built into the system as a weak link that will heat up and break before the rest of the system suffers. The commonest type is similar to the fuse in a domestic plug, consisting of a short length of wire inside a glass tube. An increasingly common alternative is a small plastic peg with a strip of thin metal on the outside acting as the fuse. Both of these types have to be replaced as a complete unit when they 'blow'. The much rarer alternative consists of a piece of replaceable wire mounted in a porcelain carrier, similar to that in an old-fashioned domestic fuse box.

Circuit breakers are taking over from fuses because although they're more expensive, you don't have to carry spares. Essentially, a circuit breaker is an automatic switch, which uses either the solenoid principle or the heating effect to switch itself off if the current flowing through it becomes dangerously high.

Fuses and circuit breakers occasionally 'blow' for no apparent reason. Although this is a nuisance, it's essential not to give in to the temptation to replace a fuse with a bigger one, or to stop the breaker tripping with string or sticky tape! Find out why it's blowing, and cure the cause, rather than disabling your protection just when it's doing its job!

Solenoids

A *solenoid* is an electrically operated switch consisting of a coil of wire around a metal plunger. When electricity flows through the coil it becomes a magnet, and pulls the metal plunger into itself. This pulling action has all sorts of purposes on an engine: it can, for instance, be used to shut off the fuel supply, allowing the engine to be stopped from the dashboard, or to operate the heavy duty switch that allows current to flow between the battery and starter motor.

On most small petrol engines, that is all the starter solenoid does – it just allows current to flow to the motor. The physical connection between the motor and the engine is achieved by an arrangement known as a *bendix*, made up of a cog (called a *pinion*) that can slide along a spiral groove machined into the motor's shaft. While the motor is stopped, a spring holds the pinion down towards the starter body by a spring. As the starter starts to turn, the pinion takes time to catch up so for a fraction of a second it is turning more slowly than the shaft on which it is mounted. As a result, the spiral groove in the shaft screws its way through the pinion, forcing it away from the starter body to engage with a circle of matching teeth (called the *ring gear*) on the engine's flywheel. As soon as the engine starts, the ring gear drives the pinion faster than the motor is turning, so the opposite happens: the pinion screws its way back down the starter shaft to disengage itself from the ring gear.

Diesels generally have a more rugged set-up called a *pre-engaged starter*. Here, solenoid does two jobs. The first part of its travel is used to push the starter pinion into engagement with the ring gear: only when the pinion is engaged can the plunger complete its movement to allow current to flow to the motor.

• • • *Things to do*

Safety

The low voltages used in boats' electrical systems are safer than high-voltage mains electricity, but can still create heat or sparks that could start a fire. Use the isolator switch to disconnect the battery before working on or near the starter or alternator, and before physically disconnecting the battery terminals.

Never allow metal objects such as tools, jewellery or watch straps to touch both terminals of a battery simultaneously. Ideally, keep the terminals covered when working near a battery, and keep one terminal covered while you are working on the other.

Batteries give off explosive gases while being charged, so the battery compartment should be well ventilated, with the vent high up (to cope with gases that are lighter than air). Don't smoke near a battery, and avoid creating sparks.

Battery acid is highly corrosive. Use goggles and gloves, especially when cleaning battery terminals, and avoid spills. If you get splashed use plenty of water to wash it off immediately.

1 Checking or replacing drive belts

The alternator or dynamo is usually driven by a *vee-belt* from the crankshaft pulley. The same belt may be used to drive the water pump, so if it is so loose that it slips, the engine will overheat. If it is too tight, it will put a sideways load on the alternator and water pump bearings, causing increased wear and making the belt itself more likely to break.

a Once a season or after every 100 hours' running, inspect the belt for cuts, fraying or oil, and check the tension by pressing firmly on the middle of the longest section of the belt: it should deflect by approximately half an inch.

b Adjust the belt if necessary by loosening the bolts that hold the alternator on to the engine, without removing them altogether. Then slacken the bolt holding the supporting bracket to the engine, followed by the one holding the support on to the alternator. Use a short piece of wood such as the handle of a hammer to lever the alternator away from the engine until the belt is tight enough, then tighten all four bolts in the reverse order.

c To replace a worn, greasy or broken belt, slacken all the alternator bolts, and swing the alternator so that it is as close to the engine as possible. Use a degreaser such as Gunk or Jizer to clean the pulleys and remove any rust by rubbing with wet-or-dry abrasive or wire wool.

d Fit the new belt over the crankshaft pulley, water pump and idler wheel (if there is one),

1a

1b

1d

then up to the alternator. Guide it into place as best you can, then use a spanner on the crankshaft pulley to turn the engine while easing the belt into its groove in the alternator pulley. Adjust the belt tension, and check it again after a few hours' running.

2 Looking after your battery

All electrical connections need to be clean and tight, but one of the commonest causes of starting problems is corrosion around the battery terminals.

a Slacken the clamp that secures the cables to the battery, and twist it to remove it from the terminal post. Flush off any white or cream-coloured 'fur' – acidic crystals of electrolyte – with plenty of very hot water before cleaning the terminals and posts with a wire brush or emery cloth.

b Lightly smear the terminal posts with petroleum jelly, and wipe off any excess before replacing the terminal and tightening the clamp. Finally, smear the whole terminal with petroleum jelly to keep out moisture.

c Over time, electrolysis and evaporation remove water from the battery, which has to be replaced by pouring distilled water into each cell of the battery until it just covers the top edges of the plates. Some modern batteries have specially designed fillers intended to minimise the loss of electrolyte. Instructions for these are usually given on the battery casing.

d If a battery is to be stored or left unused for more than a month or when there is any risk of freezing, it should be left disconnected and fully charged: a voltmeter connected between the + and – terminals should read no less than about 2.1 volts per cell, so a 6-cell, 12-volt battery should show at least 12.5 volts.

2a

2b

2c

... *Things to do*

General maintenance and fault-finding

The majority of electrical problems are caused by poor connections or defective wiring, so fault-finding is made very much easier if you have a wiring diagram, and if the wires are either colour-coded or labelled.

A lot of preventative maintenance, however, involves no more than inspecting the visible wires and connections to make sure that connections are clean and tight and that the wires show no sign of fraying, breaking or corrosion. Look particularly carefully wherever the wires are free to move, or where they bend around a hard object such as the edge of a hole or duct.

Having the right kind of wire helps enormously: 'flex' made up of lots of thin strands is much less liable to break than 'cable' made up of one thick one, but matters can be improved still further by making sure the wires are well supported, and that where a wire emerges from a connector it is cushioned, stiffened and protected by a blob of silicon rubber sealant.

Don't be tempted to use electrical measuring equipment on an engine's electrics unless you know exactly what you are doing: some instruments (especially ohmmeters and 'meggers') produce sufficient electricity themselves to damage modern engine electrics if you apply the voltage in the wrong direction or mistakenly short circuit the wrong terminals.

8 | Gearboxes

The overwhelming majority of engine-driven craft use propellers to convert the power of the engine to useful work. There are plenty of alternatives which may have advantages for specific applications, but propeller systems are good all-rounders that are reasonably cheap, simple, reliable, efficient and easy to use.

They suffer, however, from one potentially significant drawback, which is that a large slow-turning propeller is generally more efficient than a small, fast-spinning one. Even on small pleasure craft, where the maximum size of propeller is often limited by hull shape, the optimum shaft speed is usually in the order of 1,000 rpm

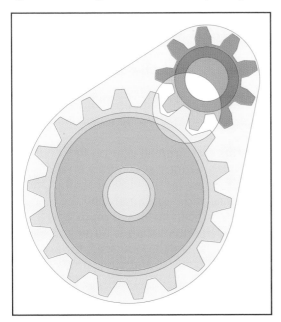

Fig 21 *The principle of gears.*

– only a half or a quarter of the speed of the engine. Running the engine more slowly isn't the answer, because you'd just lose most of the power you've paid for by buying it in the first place. What you need is something that will reduce the shaft speed but increase its *torque* (turning effort).

It's also very useful to be able to reverse the direction of rotation, to provide astern power to stop the boat or make it go backwards, or to fit counter-rotating propellers on a twin-screw boat. Again, there are alternatives such as variable-pitch propellers whose blades swivel on the hub, scoop-like deflectors, or even engines that can be stopped and restarted in the opposite direction, but by far the most popular arrangement is a reversing gearbox.

Basic principles

The diagram (Fig 21) shows two gearwheels, whose teeth mesh together so that as one turns, the other has to turn as well. The smaller gear has 9 teeth, so if it is turning at 1,000 rpm, its teeth are moving at 9,000 teeth per minute. The larger wheel is twice the size, and has 18 teeth, so although its teeth must also be moving at 9,000 teeth per minute, that means only 500 rpm. Notice, too, that if the smaller wheel is turning clockwise, the larger wheel must be turning anticlockwise.

Now imagine that you're using a spanner a foot long to turn the smaller wheel. If you apply an effort of 10 lb to the end of the spanner, you're applying a torque of 10 lb/ft (10 lb at a radius of 1 ft). The gearwheel is much smaller – let's say it has an effective radius of 1 in. That means its teeth must be pushing on the teeth of the other wheel with a force equivalent to 120 lb (120 lb at a radius of $^1/_{12}$ ft = 120 x $^1/_{12}$ = 10 lb/ft). The larger wheel has an effective radius of 2 in, so a force of 120 lb to its teeth corresponds to a torque of 20 lb/ft (120 x $^2/_{12}$ = 20 lb/ft).

In other words, by using a 9-tooth wheel to drive an 18-tooth wheel, we've:

- halved the speed
- doubled the torque, and
- reversed the direction of rotation.

A simple gearbox

Real gearboxes look more complicated, but depend on exactly this principle. In fact, the main difference between the simple gear train in Fig 21 and the Volvo MS2 shown in Fig 22 is that the MS2 uses cone-shaped bevel gears, so that although the input shaft is horizontal, the central driven shaft is vertical.

The motive for this is that it provides a simple way of achieving a choice of ahead or astern gear.

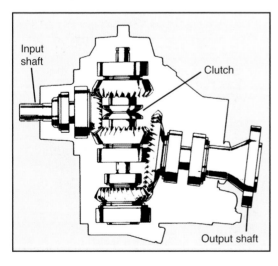

Input shaft

Clutch

Output shaft

Fig 22 *Volvo MS2 gear train.*

The bevel gear on the input shaft turns two slightly larger bevel gears that spin freely on the vertical shaft. One is driven by the top of the input gear and the other by the bottom of it, so they rotate in opposite directions, but they are the same size as each other so they turn at the same speed.

Between the two gears is a sliding clutch assembly, shaped like two shallow cones mounted base-to-base on the shaft. Ridges called *splines* on the shaft and matching grooves in the clutch ensure that it can easily slide up and down, but can't turn without turning the shaft as well. Moving the gear lever slides the clutch up or down so that one of the cones engages into a matching hollow in one of the spinning gears, which locks that gear on to the shaft.

At the bottom of the shaft, a relatively small bevel gear engages with a much larger gear on the output shaft, to give a horizontal output, at a much lower speed of rotation.

Layshaft gearboxes

Although the MS2 and its derivatives are common on Volvo engines up to about 200 hp, it's somewhat unusual in using a vertical shaft. A more widespread arrangement is the *layshaft gearbox*, like that shown in Fig 23.

In this case, a small gear on the input shaft turns a larger gear on the *layshaft*. Like the gears on the vertical shaft of the MS2, this is free to spin around the layshaft, but can be locked on to it by a clutch. If the input shaft is turning clockwise and the clutch is engaged, the layshaft turns anticlockwise and more slowly. At the other end of the layshaft a smaller gear meshes with a large gear on the output shaft, driving the output shaft clockwise and even more slowly.

Astern gear is achieved by a second

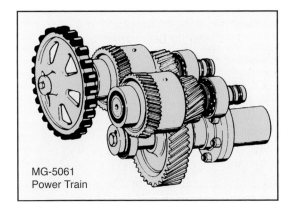

Fig 23 *Layshaft gearbox.*

layshaft. It's very similar to the first, with two gearwheels, one of which has a clutch that can leave it free-spinning or lock it on to the shaft, while the other is constantly in mesh with the output shaft. The key feature about the second layshaft is that it is not driven directly by the input shaft, but by the first layshaft. This means that it's turning in the opposite direction – so if one clutch is released and the other engaged, the direction of the output shaft will be reversed.

Epicyclic gearboxes

The third alternative – renowned for its smooth operation, but now becoming less popular – is known as the *epicyclic gearbox* (Fig 24).

The central gearwheel – known as the *sun gear* – is mounted on the input shaft, driven by the engine. Around it are several smaller *planet gears* mounted in a rigid cage called the *planet holder*, while the whole assembly is surrounded by a cylindrical *ring gear* that looks rather like the hub of a trailer wheel but with teeth machined into its inner surface. The output shaft is coupled directly to the planet holder.

For ahead operation, a clutch is used to lock the planet gears so that they can't

turn. In effect, this means that the input shaft, ring gear, planet holder and output shaft are all locked together so the whole assembly turns as though it were one piece.

For astern gear, the ring gear is locked to the casing, and the planet gears are left free to rotate. If the input shaft turns clockwise, this means that the inner planets have to turn anticlockwise, driving the outer planets clockwise. In order to do this, they have to run anticlockwise around the inside of the ring gear, taking the planet holder – and, of course, the output shaft – around with them.

One major snag with this is that although it provides an ahead/astern facility, it can't offer the reduction in shaft speed that is one of the main reasons for wanting a gearbox in the first place. To do that requires a second gearbox in tandem with the first - adding to the cost, weight, bulk and complexity of the whole unit. The second gearbox is usually another epicyclic unit, but with the important difference that there are no clutches involved, and the output shaft is connected to the ring gear instead of to the planet holder.

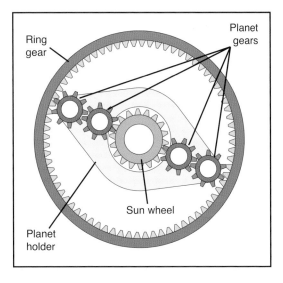

Fig 24 *Epicyclic gearbox.*

In this case, the spinning input shaft coming from the reversing gearbox drives the sun wheel, which makes the planet wheels turn, and they, in turn, drive the ring gear.

Clutches

An important characteristic of all marine gearboxes is that the gears of both drive trains – ahead and astern – are in mesh all the time, and that selection of ahead, astern and neutral is achieved by using clutches to disconnect whichever drive train is not in use.

There are two main types of clutches: the *cone clutch* used in the MS2, and the *plate clutch* used in most of the others.

The plate clutch consists of a stack of flat friction plates. Some of the plates have internal splines which mesh with matching splines on the shaft, so they have to turn with it. Sandwiched between them are similar plates which are free to spin around the input shaft but have external splines that mesh with splines on the inner surface of the clutch casing – connected to the output shaft. So long as the stack is loose, the two shafts are free to rotate independently of each other. Compressing the stack forces the plates into contact with each other so that they grip and force the two shafts to turn together.

For relatively small engines – up to about 100 hp – a hand-operated lever may be enough to operate either sort of clutch,

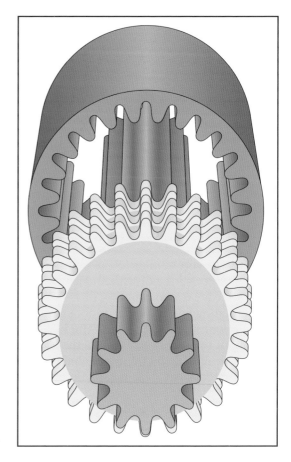

Fig 25 *Plate clutch.*

but bigger engines need more pressure to be applied. This calls for hydraulics, in which a pump built into the gearbox creates hydraulic pressure to force the plates together. All the gear lever has to do is operate a valve, diverting the hydraulic pressure to whichever clutch requires it.

••• *Things to do*

The additives that make modern oils better for your gearbox make them worse for you. Take care to avoid unnecessary or prolonged contact with gearbox oil – new or used.

Only a few teeth of each gearwheel are in mesh with each other at once, and yet the very small surfaces in contact have to transmit the entire power of the engine. When you think about a gearbox in this way, it becomes obvious that the loads involved are very large indeed, and that good lubrication is essential.

Leaks aren't always obvious, especially if they occur between the engine and gearbox, but an external visual inspection will often reveal minor gearbox faults before they develop into major problems. Look out for loose mounting bolts or control cables, as well as for oil leaks around the shaft, hoses and oil cooler.

a If the gearbox shares the engine's oil, regular oil changes are essential: the acidic by-products of combustion in old engine oil will cause corrosion and rapid wear in the gearbox.

b If the gearbox uses its own oil, the level should be checked regularly – ideally every day the engine is used. Some types need the engine to be run before the oil level is checked: consult the manufacturer's handbook for this, and to find out whether the dipstick has to be screwed in to show the correct level. Gearboxes don't 'use' oil as an engine does, so if the oil level falls it is almost certainly due to leakage.

c Having dipped the oil, top up if necessary, usually through the dipstick hole or through a separate filler cap.

Different types of gearbox need different types of oil AND THEY DON'T MIX! Check with the man-

c

ufacturer's handbook to find out whether your gearbox uses monograde engine oil, gear oil or automatic transmission fluid, and make sure you keep the right stuff on board.

Gearbox dipsticks are often rather awkward to get at, but it's important to make sure that you put it back exactly the way it came out, or it may come into contact with one of the spinning gears. Ensure that it is pushed fully home or screwed right in.

Propeller and Stern Glands

9

When you're concentrating on the engine itself, it's easy to forget that the object of the whole thing is to turn the propeller. Whilst it's true that there is little that can go wrong with a propeller, apart from physical damage such as bent, chipped or broken blades, it's worth being sure that you've got the right one for the job; a propeller needs to be carefully matched to the boat, engine and gearbox.

The science of propellers is remarkably complicated, but you can think of a propeller in any of three ways:

- as a screw
- as a pump, or
- as a foil

None of them tells the whole story, but

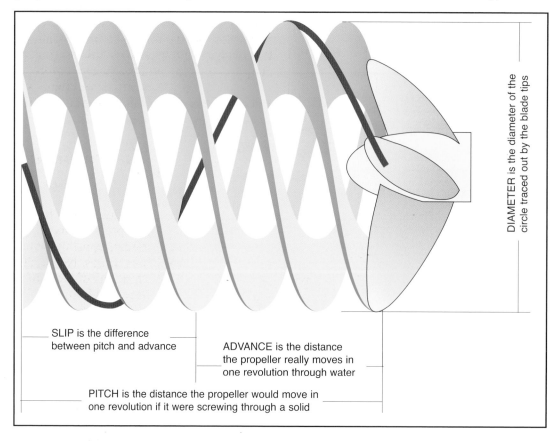

SLIP is the difference between pitch and advance

ADVANCE is the distance the propeller really moves in one revolution through water

PITCH is the distance the propeller would move in one revolution if it were screwing through a solid

DIAMETER is the diameter of the circle traced out by the blade tips

Fig 26 *Propeller pitch, advance, slip and diameter.*

between them they provide a working knowledge of a subject which could easily fill several books, each much bigger than this one.

The propeller as a screw

One theory regards the propeller as a screw, winding its way through the water like a bolt winding its way into a nut. It's not a very good theory, because a propeller

Fig 27 *Water flow over the propeller.*

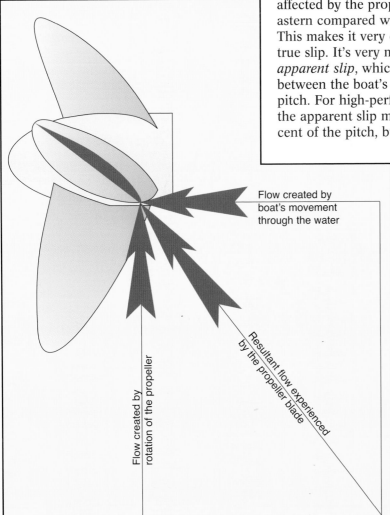

Flow created by boat's movement through the water

Flow created by rotation of the propeller

Resultant flow experienced by the propeller blade

doesn't work in a solid medium, but it explains some of the terminology.

Pitch is the distance the propeller would move in one revolution if it were screwing its way through a solid. In practice it does not move quite that far: the distance it really moves is called the *advance*. The difference between pitch and advance is called *slip*.

The picture is complicated by the fact that the advance isn't quite the same as the distance the boat moves: for one thing the boat tends to drag some water along with it, and for another, the water directly affected by the propeller tends to move astern compared with the water nearby. This makes it very difficult to measure the true slip. It's very much easier to find the *apparent slip*, which is the difference between the boat's movement and the pitch. For high-performance motorboats, the apparent slip may be as little as 10 per cent of the pitch, but for a heavy motor-sailer or workboat it can be as much as 50 per cent.

The propeller as a pump

Another theory treats the propeller as a pump, squirting water backwards. Newton's third law of motion says that for every action there is an equal but opposite reaction, so if the propeller pushes a lump of water back-wards, the water also pushes the propeller (together with the boat to which it is attached) forwards.

The amount of water the propeller can push in a given time depends mainly on the power available: a 100 hp engine, for instance, can move about 50 cubic ft per second. You can think of that 50 ft³ of water as being in the shape of a cylinder, whose diameter is roughly the same as that of the propeller, and whose length is roughly the distance the prop has moved through the water in the time. For a slow motor cruiser, moving at 10 ft/sec, that means the cylinder must have a cross-section of 5 ft², or a diameter of about 30 in. For a sportsboat doing 50 ft/sec with the same engine, the cylinder's cross-section must be reduced to 1 ft², or about 13 in.

This suggests – correctly – that the diameter of a propeller should vary depending on the power transmitted (because that determines the volume of water it can move in one second) and the speed at which the boat is moving (because that determines the length of the cylinder).

The propeller as a foil

A more recent, realistic and complicated theory regards each blade of the propeller as a foil, like a boat's sail or an aircraft's wing.

Like a sail, the blade has to be at a slight angle to the fluid flowing over it if it is to generate any useful force. Unfortunately, increasing this *angle of attack* doesn't just increase the useful thrust: it also increases the drag – which is one of the reasons why over-sheeting a sail makes it less efficient.

For a sail, the optimum angle between the sail and the air flow is about 20–25°, but for a propeller blade in water it is much smaller – about 4°.

The analogy with sailing goes on if you think about how the flow across the propeller blade is created. The 'apparent wind' flowing across a sail is made up of two components: the 'true wind' that would be felt if the boat were stationary, and the 'induced wind' caused by its own movement through the air. In the case of a propeller blade, the equivalent of the true wind is created by the rotation of the propeller, while its 'induced wind' is caused by its movement through the water.

That is why a propeller blade needs to be twisted: 'induced wind' is much the same all over the propeller, but the 'true wind' varies dramatically, because the tip of each blade sweeps around a much bigger circle than the sections of the blade that are nearer the shaft.

It also suggests that the pitch of the propeller needs to be carefully matched to the speed at which the water is moving through the propeller: a fast boat generally needs much more pitch than a slow one, in order to cope with the much greater 'induced wind'.

Choosing a propeller

What all this boils down to is that the choice of propeller depends on a mass of interrelated variables that include:

- the power available
- the shaft speed, and
- the speed of the propeller through the water

There are so many variables (even the temperature and salinity of the water have a part to play) that trying to work out the pitch and diameter of the ideal propeller for a particular boat from pure theory is almost impossible: it is invariably better to leave it to a specialist such as a propeller manufacturer who will have access to a mass of experience and information, and can probably come up with the right answer simply by tapping a few vital statistics into a computer. It's important to do so, because the wrong propeller can easily make a big difference to the boat's performance.

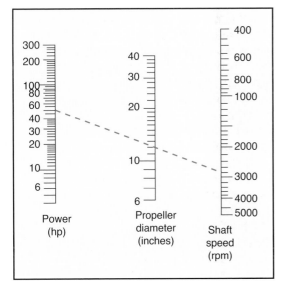

Fig 28a *Propeller selection diagram. Lay a straight edge across the two known variables to find the unknown.*

Example: For 50 hp delivered through a shaft turning at 2,800 rpm, the optimum diameter is approximately 12 inches.

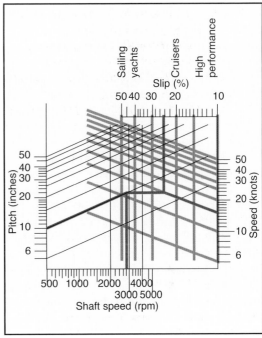

Fig 28b *Propeller pitch diagram. Estimate a likely value for slip. From that figure on the top scale, drop vertically to meet the diagonal corresponding to your estimated speed.*

From that intersection, draw a horizontal line to meet the vertical drawn upwards from the shaft speed on the bottom scale. Where these two meet gives the optimum pitch.

Example: For a boat expected to achieve 15 knots with a 50 hp engine, and a shaft speed of 2,800 rpm, the optimum pitch is approximately 10 inches.

If you want to do a quick check, however, the diagram and formula (Fig 28 a and b) provide a reasonably accurate estimate of the appropriate diameter and pitch.

Cavitation and ventilation

Although the words 'cavitation' and 'ventilation' are often used interchangeably, they are really two quite different things. What they have in common is that they can rob a propeller of almost all its grip on the water.

Ventilation is most common on sports boats and on sailing boats with outboard motors mounted high on their transoms, because it is caused by air being sucked into the propeller. A propeller designed to operate in water obviously can't work very well in air: it generates very little thrust

and suffers very little drag, so the engine speed increases while the boat slows down.

Cavitation is caused by the propeller itself. As it rotates, it creates thrust by increasing the pressure on the aft faces of its blades and simultaneously reducing the pressure on their forward faces. As the pressure falls, the boiling point of water reduces, eventually reaching the stage at which it will boil, even at sea temperature. When this happens, bubbles of water vapour form on the forward face of the propeller. The immediate effect of severe cavitation is very much like ventilation: the engine races but the propeller ceases to generate much thrust. The long-term effect of even minor cavitation is an erosion of the propeller blades known as 'cavitation burn', caused by the collapsing bubbles.

Cavitation can be caused by using the wrong propeller for the boat, such as one with too much pitch or not enough blade area, but can also be caused by damage to the propeller such as nicks in the leading edge of the blade.

Stern glands

It may be stating the obvious to say that a propeller works best in water, and that an engine (generally) works in the air inside the boat, but it's an important point because it means that somehow the shaft that turns the propeller has to pass out through a hole in the hull without letting water in. The component responsible is a *stern gland*.

Engineers have faced this problem for centuries, and one can imagine the joy of some Egyptian farmer when he discovered that his slave-powered irrigation pump worked better if he stuffed reeds around the handle to stop it leaking, or the relief felt by a Viking longship's crew when they found they got less wet if they used rags to fill the gaps between their oars and the row of shields.

Those simple discoveries were the direct ancestors of what is still the commonest kind of stern gland – the *'stuffing box'*.

Stuffing boxes

A stuffing box is basically an extension of the boat's stern tube – the tube that carries the propeller shaft out through the hull – enlarged to form an outer casing that is

filled with rings of grease-soaked packing. A sleeve around the shaft holds the packing in place, and can be tightened down to compress the packing so that it forms an almost watertight seal. A common refinement – essential for engines mounted on modern 'soft mounts' – is a short length of flexible tube between the stern tube and the stuffing box, to allow the stuffing box to move with the shaft as it vibrates.

Another is a reservoir of grease, so that the packing can be re-greased without having to dismantle the whole thing. Obviously this only works if you use it, so it makes sense to get into the habit of tightening the greaser every time the engine is used.

Even with a good supply of fresh grease, an inevitable problem with a traditional stuffing box is that if the stuffing is compressed tightly enough to make a perfect seal, there would be so much friction that the packing would get hot – drying out the grease and wearing away both the packing and the shaft. For this reason, a stuffing box should never be tightened down so much that it is completely dry: a slight leak helps cool and lubricate it without imposing too much strain on the bilge pump. This is so important that on planing boats, where the movement of the boat itself might suck water away from the stern gland, water is often pumped into the stuffing box by the cooling system.

Other shaft seals

This perceived 'problem' of essential leakage – and the rather fiddly job of re-packing – has led to the development of several more modern alternatives.

Some use a synthetic rubber diaphragm clamped to the shaft or stern tube to hold a ceramic or carbon sealing ring in firm contact against a phosphor bronze or stainless steel seat. The virtue of this is that there's nothing rubbing against the shaft,

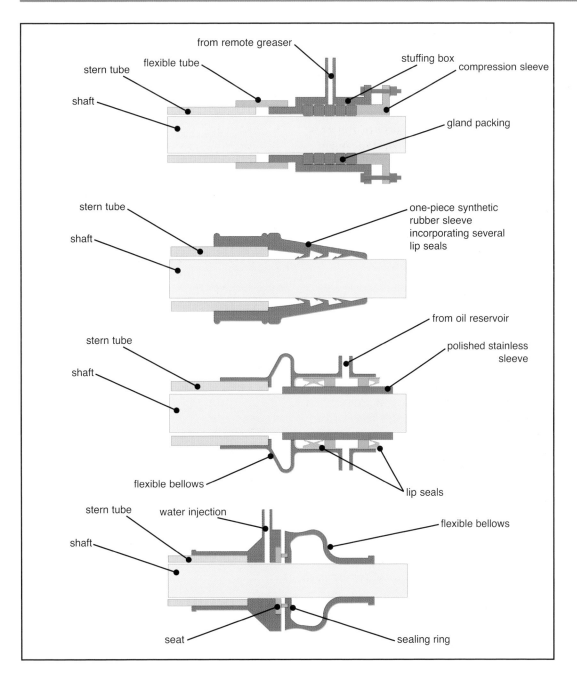

Fig 29 *Stern glands.*

and no need to mess about with grease: the only maintenance required is occasionally to pull the diaphragm away from the seat, to flush out any debris and stop the two parts sticking together if the boat is left idle for any length of time.

Another consists of a hollow rubber cone with a row of *lip seals* – similar to

61

• • • *Things to do*

Propellers

It is a good idea to remove the propeller from time to time, to stop it seizing solid on the shaft. This is particularly important in the case of outboard and outdrive propellers, which usually have either shear pins or flexible hubs that are designed to protect the engine and transmission by slipping or breaking if the propeller hits something. Unfortunately, after a period of time, these protective devices break of their own accord, so it's important to make sure that the propeller can be taken off and replaced at sea.

Removing a propeller

a Straighten out the legs of the split pin and remove it, or flatten the lugs of the tab washer that holds the propeller nut in place.

b Use a block of wood to stop the propeller turning, and undo the propeller nut.

c It should be possible to pull an outboard or sterndrive's propeller off the shaft by hand. Make a note of the order that any springs or washers come off, and which way round they go.

d The best way to remove a stubborn propeller is with a *puller*. Once the puller has been tightened, a few light taps with a hammer on the puller should make the propeller slide off.

e As a last resort, try warming the propeller boss with a blow lamp.

Repairing a propeller

If necessary, use a file to smooth any burrs or nicks from the edges of the propeller, but be careful not to remove so much metal that there is a risk of the propeller becoming unbalanced. If it is badly damaged, refer it to a propeller repair workshop.

Replacing a propeller

a Before replacing the propeller, grease the shaft with a non-graphite grease.

b Slide the propeller back on, making sure that any keys, shear pins, springs or washers are replaced exactly as they were removed, but use a new tab washer (if there was one) to hold the propeller nut in place.

c Tighten the propeller nut just sufficiently to grip the propeller, then insert the split pin (if there was one). Bend up one tab of the tab washer to hold the nut in place, or open the legs of the split pin and bend them round the nut.

Stern glands

1 Greasing a stern gland

If your stern gland is fitted with a greaser, routine greasing involves either turning the handle or tightening the cap by one turn after every few hours' running: once every four hours is about right. Eventually, this will use up all the grease, which will have to be replaced. Don't use graphite grease: its carbon content causes extremely rapid corrosion in the presence of salt water.

a Remove the top cap of the greaser. If yours is the type that uses a handle like that of a garden tap to operate a plunger, 'unscrew' the handle to return the plunger to its starting position.

b Invert the grease can, so that the hole in the plastic disc is over the greaser.

c Press the whole can downwards, so that the plastic disc slides into the can and forces grease out. You may have to stop a few times, especially when the greaser is nearly full, to allow trapped air to escape.

d Replace the cap of the greaser.

2 Adjusting a stern gland

a With the engine stopped and out of gear, turn the shaft by hand to get a feel for how stiff it is.

b Slacken off any lock-nuts holding the two parts of the stern gland together. Tighten the clamping bolts that hold the two parts of the stern gland together, or screw the sleeve into the outer casing. Don't tighten them by more than half a turn at a time, and – if yours is the type that has two or three bolts – make sure that you tighten them evenly.

c Turn the shaft by hand and check for drips: it should turn freely and leak between one and six drips per minute. If it is leaking too quickly, tighten the clamping bolts further.

2a

2b

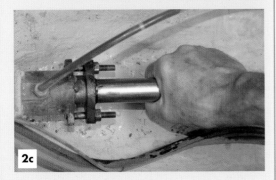

2c

those that prevent oil escaping from the engine itself – moulded into its inner surface. These need greasing once a season or every 200 hours, and have to be 'vented' to ensure that they are full of water each time the boat is launched.

A third variety keeps water out by surrounding the shaft by a tube filled with oil. Lip seals keep the oil inside the tube, by sealing against a polished stainless steel sleeve fitted to the shaft.

Outdrives and saildrives

Outdrives and saildrives circumvent the need for a stern gland altogether by – in effect – extending the gearbox right into the water in the form of a drive leg. Of course, this doesn't make the problem go away altogether: it just changes it a bit, because instead of having to seal the gap around a small rotating shaft, there's a much bigger hole to plug between the hull and the drive leg. Outdrives achieve this by using flexible rubber bellows between the transom and the leg, while saildrives use a rubber diaphragm to seal the joint between the drive unit and the bottom of the boat. Servicing recommendations vary depending on the manufacturer and model, but the importance of following them to the letter is obvious.

••• Things to do

3 Repacking a stern gland

If the stern gland cannot be tightened enough to reduce the leakage to an acceptable level without making the shaft unduly stiff to turn, then the packing needs to be replaced. THIS CAN ONLY BE DONE WITH THE BOAT OUT OF THE WATER. (Photos 3 a-b show the stern gland viewed from above.)

3a

a Remove the lock-nuts and nuts that hold the two parts together, or unscrew the two parts completely. If necessary, use two large screw-drivers or pinch-bars to prise the two parts apart.

b Remove the old packing. This will probably involve fashioning some home-made 'tools', such as a small screwdriver filed to a point, or bent coat-hanger wire.

c Use a degreasing agent (such as 'Jizer' or 'Gunk') to clean the shaft and stern gland.

d Check that the new packing is the right size: it should just fit the gap between the shaft and the outer casing of the stern gland.

3b

e Wrap the packing around the shaft, making sure that it sits squarely on the shaft, and then use a sharp craft knife to cut through the packing along the line of the shaft so as to produce several short lengths of packing, each just long enough to fit round the shaft. Use the stern gland's end cover to push each ring of packing down into the stern gland case, making sure that each one sits squarely on the shaft and that its cut ends are not lined up with the cut ends of the one before.

3c

f Reassemble the end cover and clamping bolts, but leave them finger tight. Turn the shaft several times by hand to help bed the packing rings together.

g As soon as the boat is re-launched, adjust the stern gland to the required slow drip.

3d

10 | Control Systems

A few small open workboats still have engine and gearbox controls that can be operated directly by the helmsman, but that simple system is becoming increasingly rare on pleasure craft, where it is very much more common to find some kind of remote control system.

As is often the case on boats, there is no 'standard' arrangement: push-pull cables are by far the commonest, but even these are available in several different forms and face competition from hydraulic systems – in which the remote control lever operates a pump connected by pipes to a hydraulic ram that operates the engine controls – and electronic systems that use wires to carry control signals from the wheelhouse to the engine room.

Cable systems

The cables that are used in most systems are rather like those used to work the brakes on a bicycle, with a central control cable inside a tubular outer casing. The casing is fixed at both ends, so that when you pull one end of the inner cable, the other end retracts.

Boats' control cables are usually very much bigger and more robust than those on a push-bike, but the main difference is that instead of using very flexible multi-strand wire for the inner cable, marine systems use a single strand of stiff wire that enables them to push as well as pull.

Control heads

It's easy to see how cables can be used in a *twin-lever* system, where one lever controls the engine and another operates the gearbox. Pushing the top of the 'throttle' lever forwards, for instance, pulls on the cable, which in turn pulls the lever on the engine's fuel pump.

Single-lever systems, in which engine

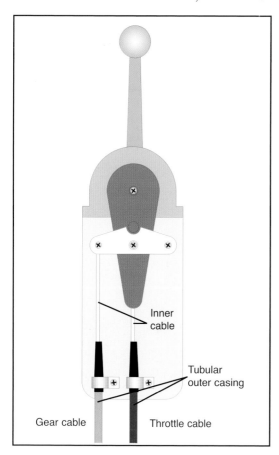

Fig 30 *Single lever control.*

Inner cable

Tubular outer casing

Gear cable

Throttle cable

and gearbox are controlled by the same lever, are generally more popular – but are more complicated because they have to achieve a positive gear shift between ahead, neutral and astern, but also offer progressive control of the engine speed.

This is achieved by connecting the 'throttle' cable directly to the control lever, while the gear cable is connected to a horizontal seesaw arrangement. A peg sticking out of the throttle lever engages in a notch in the top edge of the seesaw, so that the first few degrees of movement of the control lever is enough to rock the seesaw so that it pulls or pushes on the gear cable. The geometry of the arrangement is such that this first movement of the control lever has virtually no effect on the throttle cable. Once the seesaw has been rocked far enough to engage gear, however, the peg is clear of the slot, and the lever can move further, pulling on the throttle cable without having any more effect on the gear control linkage.

Dual Station controls

One snag with this system is that it can only be worked with the control lever:

pulling or pushing on the other end of the gear cable would have no effect whatsoever. In a boat with only one control station, this is not a problem, but on boats such as motorsailers or flybridge motor cruisers, where the engine may have to be controlled from two different places, it would make the whole system jam up if it were not for a component called a *Dual Station (or DS) unit* that isolates one control head when the other is in use.

A DS unit is based on a sheet metal frame with two curved slots cut into it. Bridging the gap between the two slots is a metal bar connected to the incoming cables from the two helm positions and the outgoing cable to the engine. The bar is held in place on the base plate by two metal pegs which pass through the slots. The clever bit about this arrangement is that the pegs are slightly further apart than the slots: the only reason the pegs can fit into both slots at once is that each slot has a semicircular cut-out. When one peg is nestling in its cut-out, the other peg is free to slide along the slot and vice versa.

If, on a motorsailer, you move the saloon control lever while the cockpit control is in neutral, the cockpit cable's peg drops into

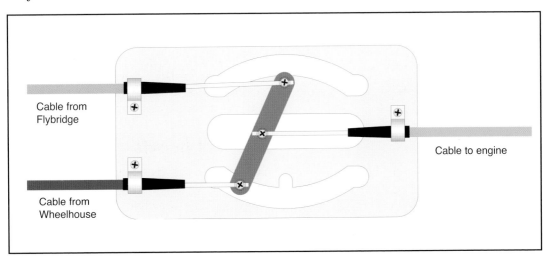

Fig 31 *Dual station control.*

its cut-out, allowing the saloon cable to move its end of the bar to push or pull the outgoing cable. When the saloon control is in neutral, any movement of the cockpit control is enough to move the bar so that its 'saloon' end drops into its cut-out, leaving the 'cockpit' end free to move – with the same effect on the outgoing cable.

Cables

Cable systems are generally reliable so long as they are properly installed in the first place and then receive a certain minimal level of maintenance. It's worth doing, because if your control system fails, you will almost certainly look foolish (bystanders never believe that a messed-up manoeuvre was caused by mechanical problems), and you may well face serious damage or injury.

When problems do occur, control failure is more often due to problems with the cable, rather than to the control units themselves:

- Internal corrosion, caused by water getting in through splits in the outer cable, can jam the inner cable.
- Wear on the inner surfaces of the outer cable allows the inner cable to slop from side to side, producing excessive backlash (free play) on the cable end: on a gear cable this may mean that there is not enough controlled movement to operate the gear lever properly.
- Bent or corroded end rods make operation stiff and may eventually lead to the inner cable stretching: again, this is particularly serious in the gear cable.
- Worn, corroded or disconnected end fittings. The split pins that secure the cable to the gearbox and fuel pump are so thin that they are particularly prone to corrosion, but look out too for the clamping arrangements that hold the outer cable in place.
- Poorly designed cable runs can make controls stiff from the outset, and give rise to a lot of backlash. Over time, this gets worse, as the bends cause increased wear and tear inside the cable: ideally cables should be dead straight, with no long sweeping bends or bends tighter than about 8 in (20 cm) radius.

••• *Things to do*

a

a Periodically – about once a season, but more often in exposed locations – inspect the cable end fittings for wear and corrosion. Replace split pins with new ones if they are corroded, or if they have been removed for any reason.

b With the inner cable in its fully extended position, lightly grease the exposed part with a non-graphite grease.

c Clean and re-grease the moving parts of control heads and DS units. Inspect the cable run, looking for splits or wear in the outer plastic sheath – often given away by rust streaks.

b

c

Tools and Working Practices

A lot of work on an engine involves removing and replacing components, so it involves dealing with a wide variety of fastenings – literally, 'getting down to the nuts and bolts'.

Bolts vary in length and diameter, but come in a number of standard sizes quoted in imperial or metric measurements. Metric measurements are now used almost universally on British, European and Japanese equipment, while imperial sizes are found on old British equipment and on almost anything intended primarily for the American market. This means that you are unlikely to come across a mixture of the two on one engine, but doesn't mean to say that you won't find imperial fastenings on the engine and metric elsewhere on the boat – or vice versa.

Even if you find two bolts of exactly the same diameter, they may not be interchangeable because there are a variety of different 'standard' screw threads which differ in cross-section as well as in the number of threads per inch (Fig 32). It's important to make sure that you match the right nut and bolt together and that you screw bolts or studs back into the holes they came out of, because although some odd combinations are compatible, the vast majority are not. Unless a nut or bolt is clearly in poor condition, it should turn smoothly and easily until it reaches the final tightening-up stage: if it starts easily but suddenly becomes stiff for no obvious reason, or if it feels unusually floppy, it's a pretty safe bet that it's the wrong one for the job.

If the differences between screw threads seem subtle, the differences between their heads certainly are not: it is obvious that you can't use a spanner to undo a bolt with a domed and slotted head intended for a screwdriver! It's surprising, though, how often DIY mechanics find themselves trying to work with spanners or screwdrivers that don't quite fit. It's important to use the right tool for the job, because although a 13 mm spanner will just about cope with a 1/2 in hexagon head, it is slightly too large. The difference is only about a quarter of a millimetre, but that is

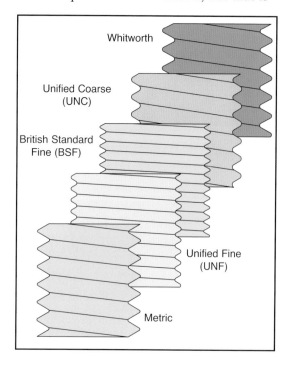

Fig 32 *Screw thread sizes.*

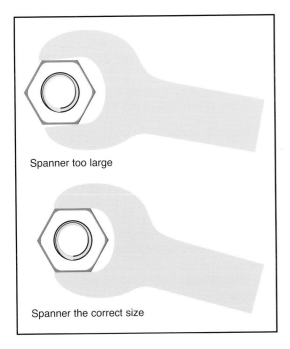

Spanner too large

Spanner the correct size

Fig 33 *Spanner sizes.*

enough to allow the nut to twist between the jaws. Instead of the load being spread across the flats of the nut, it's then concentrated at the corners, so as soon as you try to apply any appreciable force to the spanner, the nut levers the jaws of the spanner apart, while the spanner rounds off the corners of the nut.

Similar comments apply to screwdrivers – probably the most misused tools of all.

Fig 34 *Screwdriver shapes.*

Not only do you need the right kind of screwdriver – flat-bladed for slotted heads, and cross-point for cross-heads – but it should also be the right size for the job. A screwdriver that is too big won't go into the slot at all, but one that is too small will tend to twist out of shape and damage the edges of the slot. A flat-bladed screwdriver should be ground to a fairly shallow taper, so that it doesn't try to lever itself out of the slot, and have a sharp-edged square tip so that it doesn't hit the bottom of the slot before it makes contact with the sides.

The drive towards more compact engines has made engine manufacturers turn increasingly to fastenings with 'unconventional' heads. *Allen screws*, in which the head of the bolt has a hexagonal recess, are now so common that they hardly rank as unconventional. Dealing with these requires either a screwdriver equipped with a selection of appropriate 'bits' or a set of Allen keys – bent pieces of hexagonal hardened steel bar. You may need lots of them: Allen screws come in a variety of metric and imperial sizes, and a good fit between the tool and the fastening is even more important than for a spanner – not least because if you damage the head of an Allen screw it can be exceedingly difficult to remove.

Pipe fittings

Pipe fittings also come in a variety of shapes and sizes, designed to cope with pipes of different materials and different sizes, and with operating pressures ranging from partial vacuum to several thousand pounds per square inch. There are, however, only three main types that you are likely to come across.

Pipe clips are bands of thin metal designed to fit round flexible pipes. A bolt or screw joins the ends of the band so that it can be tightened to compress the pipe against the rigid spigot to which it is attached. They're found in all sorts of relatively low-pressure applications, from marine toilets to engine cooling systems and exhaust pipes.

Removing a hose clip is a simple matter of unscrewing the clip until it is loose enough to slide along the hose and then pulling the hose off the spigot. In practice, a common problem is that the hose may have glued itself to the spigot, in which case it may come free if you massage the hose to loosen the bond, and then prise it off with a screwdriver. As a last resort, a flexible pipe can always be cut, but do make sure you have a replacement available before you do so.

Replacing a hose can be more difficult, because it may be such a tight fit on the spigot that you wonder why it needs a hose clip at all. Dipping the end of the hose in boiling water may help by softening it, and a smear of washing up liquid can be used to provide some gentle lubrication. Whatever method you use, it's worth threading the pipe clip on to the hose first, so that you don't have to unscrew it completely in order to fit it on to the pipe in situ.

Fitting the pipe on to the spigot is especially difficult if the spigot has a bulge or ridge around its end, but these things are not put there just to make life awkward: they are intended to provide extra security once the pipe is in place. They only work, however, if you make sure that the hose clip is on the right side of the ridge – nearest the root of the spigot so that the pipe would have to drag the pipe clip over the ridge in order to pull itself free.

Compression fittings are used on rigid pipes, or occasionally on flexible pipes with a rigid insert. There are two types, but both look like an unusually deep nut with the pipe sticking out of the middle.

One kind, used mainly on relatively low-pressure applications such as domestic plumbing and sometimes on the low-

pressure side of the fuel system, uses a straight-ended pipe with a brass or plastic ring called an *olive* threaded on to it. The end of the pipe fits into a recess in the spigot, but the olive rests on top. Then, when the nut is tightened down on to the threaded spigot, the olive is compressed between the 'nut' and the spigot, to grip the pipe and form the seal.

The only cause for concern when working with this type of pipe fitting is that over-tightening it can distort or split the olive.

High-pressure pipes, such as injection pipes, use a development of this principle in which the pipe itself is shaped to form the olive. Making the joint in the first place requires special equipment, but once the pipe has been shaped it forms a secure and leak-proof joint that is as easy to do up or undo as a nut and bolt. Perhaps the biggest danger is the temptation to treat these kinds of joint as though they are flexible: they're not, so don't try to bend or move the pipe without slackening the unions that hold it in place.

The third kind of pipe union is called a *banjo bolt* – so-called because one part of it is supposed to look like a banjo. The 'banjo' is a metal fitting that has to be brazed or soldered on to the pipe, and which then forms a hollow channel right around the central bolt. The 'bolt' part looks exactly like a conventional bolt, except that its head is often rather larger and thinner than you might expect, and its shaft is a hollow. A hole in the side of the bolt allows liquid to flow from the pipe, around the circular channel formed by the banjo, and down through the hollow bolt. Brass, fibre or nylon washers form a seal around the upper and lower edges of the banjo to stop leaks: be careful not to lose them when undoing a banjo bolt, and make sure that they go back when you replace it.

Seals and gaskets

Other joints in an engine, such as those between the face plate and casing of a water pump or between the injectors and the cylinder head, are just as important as the joints in the 'plumbing' that surrounds it. It's difficult to get a good metal-to-metal seal over a wide area, especially as the parts concerned may be expanding and contracting at different rates when the engine warms up and cools down. To overcome the problem, these kinds of joint usually include a *gasket* of more resilient material.

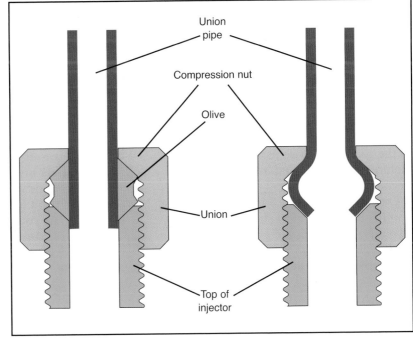

Fig 35 *Pipe fittings.*

Some gaskets, especially cylinder head gaskets, are quite sophisticated components in their own right, including layers of different materials and inserts to withstand particular stresses or to help them stay in shape, but the majority of gaskets are relatively simple sheets of steel, copper, cork, rubber or paper.

Copper gaskets are used in small, highly stressed joints such as between an injector and its seat, and usually look much like an ordinary washer. Ideally, a copper gasket should only be used once, because it loses its resilience once it has been fitted. If necessary, though, it can be renovated by heating it over a gas ring until it turns blue, and then immediately dropping it into cold water.

At the other extreme are *cork* or *rubber*

gaskets used in places such as the joint between the rocker box cover and the cylinder head. There are no great stresses involved here, but the rocker box cover is so thin that it would easily distort if it had to be bolted down very firmly to achieve a seal. The only snag with these is that the gasket almost invariably sticks to one or the other of the two components: if part of it sticks to one and the rest of it sticks to the other, you may need to peel it away very carefully with a thin knife to make sure it comes away in one piece.

Paper gaskets are less resilient than cork or rubber, but they work well and are so cheap that although it's almost impossible to salvage one once it's been used, there's no excuse for not using a new one every time. If you can't get a ready-made replacement, it's easy to make your own from a sheet of gasket paper. In a real emergency, it's even possible to use writing paper or a cornflake packet as a stopgap!

The first step in the process of replacing a gasket is to remove all traces of the old gasket from the surfaces. You may need to use a scraper, but be careful not to scratch the machined surfaces – if you must use a screwdriver for the job, file the corners off first! Then, if you're making a new paper gasket, smear one of the mating surfaces with a little oil, and press it down hard on to the gasket paper so as to leave a clear picture of its shape and any holes that are needed.

Once you've cut out the new gasket, use another smear of oil to stick it temporarily to one surface, and make future separation of the joint easier. Then reassemble the joint and tighten all the bolts evenly.

Tools

The standard advice about tools is 'buy the best you can afford'. All too often that advice goes with a list of 'essential' tools and spares that would not disgrace a professional workshop, but would go a long way towards sinking a small cruising yacht!

There's no doubt that high-quality, high-price tools such as those made by Britool, Gedore and Snap-On are virtually indestructible and a pleasure to use, but unfortunately they sink just as quickly as any others if they get dropped overboard or in the bilges, rust nearly as quickly once they've been exposed to salt water, and are exceptionally prone to being 'borrowed'.

Very cheap tools, such as many of those imported from India and China, will let you believe you've got a full tool kit until you try unscrewing a tough nut in an awkward spot. That's when you find out that the reason they are cheaper is because they don't fit as well in the first place, and that they get worse once they start to bend under the strain.

Fortunately there are plenty of mid-range tools made by companies such as Stanley and Kamasa, which are nearly as good as the front-runners but are a fraction of the price.

Tool kit

A set of *open-ended spanners*, of the right sizes – imperial (AF) or metric – is essential, and if you have a very old boat or engine, you may need the now obsolete Whitworth sizes, too.

Ring spanners are better if you need to use much force or work in an awkward position, but can't be used on pipe fittings or lock-nuts. As you need two spanners of the same size to undo a nut and bolt anyway, it makes sense to have one set of rings and one of open-ended.

Combination spanners have a ring on one end and open-ended jaws on the other, but as both ends are usually the same size, you will still need two sets!

Socket spanners make life much easier, and are the only way of getting at some of the less accessible fastenings on compact modern engines, but it's debatable whether they are essential for basic maintenance. They're nice to have, but no substitute for conventional spanners because there are some fastenings they can't cope with. Whitworth socket spanners are very hard to come by, but a set of tubular box spanners is a reasonable (and economical) alternative.

Few professional mechanics would admit to using *adjustable spanners* on an engine, because they are inevitably less rigid than proper spanners, and more likely to damage the nut or bolt as a result. Every boat, however, has at least one fastening somewhere that is an odd size. When you find out which one it is, a good adjustable will get you out of trouble. Anything less than the best is a waste of space.

Much the same applies to *Mole-Grips* or *Vise-Grips*. Few mechanics will admit to using them, but few would be without them!

The most useful *pliers* are the square-ended 'general purpose' type, about 6–8 in (15–20 cm) long. 'Needle-nose' pliers are less versatile, but are a cheap and worthwhile addition to a tool kit, especially if your boat has much electrical equipment on board.

You'll inevitably need several *screwdrivers*, including a couple of cross-point screwdrivers and three or four flat-bladed ones, including a small 'electrician's' and a long-shafted 'heavy duty'. Handle shapes are a matter of personal choice, though the oval handles of 'carpenter's' screwdrivers may allow you to exert more force than the round handles of 'mechanic's' screwdrivers.

Allen keys (or a screwdriver with a selection of hexagonal bits) are becoming more and more important.

A *hammer* is a nasty thing to threaten an engine with, but a light ball-pein 'engineer's' hammer is worth having, as is a soft-faced hammer with a weighted nylon head instead of a lump of hardened steel.

Finally, there are cutting tools: a small *hacksaw* and some spare blades; a *craft knife* or large scalpel, and perhaps a small, flat-bladed scraper.

Tricks of the trade

The possibility that you might take an engine to pieces and not be able to put it back together again is probably the mechanic's worst nightmare. The best tip for avoiding it is to be scrupulously and relentlessly methodical: lay the bits of your engine down in the order they were removed, and keep the fastenings with the relevant part – don't tip all the nuts and bolts into one box, because it may then take hours of trial and error to find the right one, and don't complicate matters by taking things apart that you don't have to.

It almost goes without saying that you should refer to the manual for any job that is not completely familiar to you, but if you do find yourself working without a manual, don't be afraid to make notes or sketches of the order in which things came apart or what went where. Look carefully at any component before you remove it, and try to figure out what it does, which bolts hold it on, and which hold something inside it.

Seized fastenings make life difficult, but are a common feature of many boat engines. Before applying brute force, it's important to bear in mind that conventional spanners are designed to apply the right amount of leverage for the fastenings they fit, and that if you lengthen a spanner to unscrew a bolt that is already weakened by corrosion, you may make it shear off completely.

The first stage is to make sure that you are working efficiently:

- Try to give yourself as much room and light as you need by removing any covers or hatches that are in the way.
- Keep your hands and tools clean so that you can get a good grip.
- Pull on the end of a spanner: you are less likely to get hurt if the spanner slips when you are pulling than pushing, and the end gives you more leverage.
- Use a ring spanner if possible, rather than an open-ended one.
- Turn the nut rather than the bolt.

If that doesn't do the trick, it's worth trying to tighten the offending fastening to break the bond between the threads, and penetrating oil can work wonders so long as it is left alone for long enough to penetrate.

More drastic measures include lengthening the spanner with a length of pipe; and shock treatment by tapping the spanner with a hammer while applying steady pressure by hand.

For a really stubborn fastening, you may have to resort to more destructive methods such as using a cold chisel or a gadget called a nut splitter (like an oversized ring spanner, but with a blade which can be screwed in to break a seized nut) to split the nut, or a hacksaw to cut the side off it. Bolt heads that have rounded off can be carefully filed down to take the next size of spanner, or can have a slot hacksawed in. Most drastic of all, but often quickest, is to cut through the bolt completely.

Destroying a nut and bolt isn't too frightening because it can always be replaced, but the idea of cutting or snapping a stud or bolt that has seized into a casting is more worrying. Even so, it's not the end of the world.

Once the load has been removed from the broken stud, it may unscrew relatively easily, particularly if it has been well soaked with penetrating oil. This is where mole-grips come in handy. Alternatively, you could try cutting a screwdriver slot in the remains, or screwing two nuts down on to it. Once the second nut has been tightened down hard against the first, a spanner applied to the lower nut can be used to unscrew the stud.

If the stud has broken off flush with the casting, it should be possible to drill a hole down the centre of it in order to use a tool called a *stud extractor*. This is a tapered rod of hardened steel with a very coarse thread cut into it. The stud extractor's thread is in the opposite direction to that of a conventional bolt, so as you screw the stud extractor into the stud, it first grips the side of the drilled hole, and then unscrews the stud.

If this doesn't work, it may be possible to drill out the stud altogether, and then use a device called a tap to recut the thread in the hole. Taps, unfortunately, are quite expensive, so it's hardly worth having a full set in hand to cope with the occasional mishap, and it may be worth referring the job to a professional.

The ultimate sanction is definitely a professional's job because of the equipment required, but it's worth knowing that it is possible to drill out the hole oversize, and put in a completely new thread known as a *helicoil insert*.

12 | Fault-finding

Even though the individual processes that make a diesel engine run are basically simple, there are so many of them, and so many individual components involved, that trying to trace a particular fault can seem an almost impossible task. It can be done, though!

The first stage is to establish exactly what the symptoms are, and how they developed. Was the engine OK the last time you used it, but playing up now? Have you done anything in between which may have caused the fault to develop? Did it develop suddenly, or gradually?

Armed with this information, the daunting-looking fault-finding lists that follow can be whittled down to a more manageable size.

Suppose, for instance, that we're faced with an engine overheating. The fault-finding list offers a wide range of possiblities, ranging from a faulty gauge to wrong valve timing. Working through all of them could easily take a professional mechanic a full day or more, so it's important to establish what is *likely*, as opposed to what is *possible*.

Assuming you haven't done anything to change the valve timing or fuel pump timing, it's most unlikely to be either of those. Suppose, however, that you shut the seacock in order to check the raw water filter, and the engine overheated quickly the next time you started it. In that case, it's a fair bet that you may have forgotten to open the seacock again!

Having narrowed down the possibilities, it's then time to work through them in a logical order. Try to avoid making random changes or adjustments to your engine: don't do anything without a good reason, and always remember (or write down) what you've done so that you can undo it if it doesn't solve the problem or makes it worse.

Most important of all, though, remember that common, simple problems, such as a blocked fuel filter or leaky pipe, are much more likely than more obscure or complicated ones such as a sheared fuel pump drive.

 ## Starting problems

The starter won't turn the engine fast enough to start ... or at all:
- Battery charge low
- Electrical connections loose, dirty or defective
- Engine in gear
- Oil of wrong grade
- Starter faulty
- Starting procedure incorrect

Cont

Starting problems

The engine turns over but will not start:
- Air in fuel system
- Air filter blocked
- Cold start aid (if fitted) faulty
- Compression poor
- Engine in gear
- Fuel contaminated by water (or ice)
- Fuel filter blocked
- Fuel lift pump faulty (or sucking air through leak on suction side)
- Fuel of wrong grade or quality
- Fuel pipes blocked or leaking
- Fuel tank empty (or nearly so)
- Fuel tap shut
- Fuel 'waxing' (caused by using 'summer' fuel in low temperatures)
- Injection pump drive broken
- Injection pump faulty
- Injection pump timing wrong
- Injector(s) faulty
- Starting procedure incorrect
- Stop control faulty

The engine is hard to start:
- Air in fuel system
- Air filter blocked
- Cold start aid (if fitted) faulty
- Compression poor (see page 84)
- Exhaust pipe blocked
- Fuel contaminated by water (or ice)
- Fuel filter blocked
- Fuel lift pump faulty (or sucking air through leak on suction side)
- Fuel tank vent blocked
- Fuel of wrong grade or quality
- Fuel pipes blocked or leaking
- Fuel tap shut

Cont

Starting problems

The engine is hard to start:
- Fuel 'waxing' (caused by using 'summer' fuel in low temperatures)
- Injection pump faulty
- Injection pump timing wrong
- Injector(s) faulty
- Starting procedure incorrect
- Stop control faulty

 ## Problems shown up by the gauges

The engine overheats:
- Air filter blocked
- Cold start aid (if fitted) faulty
- Cooling water low
- Cylinder head gasket faulty
- Exhaust pipe blocked
- Gauge faulty
- Heat exchanger blocked
- Injection pump faulty
- Injection pump timing wrong
- Injector(s) faulty
- Raw water filter blocked
- Raw water pump faulty (eg impeller worn or broken)
- Raw water system blocked or seacock shut
- Thermostat faulty
- Valve timing incorrect
- Valves leaking
- Vee-belt on water pump broken, loose or greasy

The oil pressure is unusually low:
- Bearings worn
- Gauge faulty

Cont

Problems shown up by the gauges

- Oil cooler clogged
- Oil filter clogged
- Oil level low
- Oil of wrong grade
- Oil pressure valve faulty
- Oil pump faulty

The oil pressure is unusually high:
- Gauge faulty
- Oil of wrong grade
- Oil pressure valve faulty

Smoke

The engine produces black or grey exhaust smoke:
- Aftercooler clogged
- Air filter blocked
- Cold start aid (if fitted) faulty
- Compression poor (see page 84)
- Excessive load caused by dirty hull or too much weight on board
- Excessive power losses due to internal friction in engine or transmission
- Exhaust pipe blocked
- Fuel of wrong grade or quality
- Injection pump faulty
- Injection pump timing wrong
- Injector(s) faulty
- Inlet manifold leaking
- Leak-off pipe blocked
- Propeller damaged or wrong size
- Thermostat faulty
- Turbocharger faulty
- Ventilation to engine room inadequate

Cont

Smoke

The engine produces blue or white exhaust smoke:
- Air filter blocked
- Cold start aid (if fitted) faulty
- Crankcase breathers clogged
- Compression poor (see page 84)
- Oil level too high
- Oil of wrong grade
- Thermostat faulty
- Turbocharger oil seals worn

 ## Unusual noises or behaviour

The engine misfires:
- Air filter blocked
- Air in fuel system
- Cold start aid (if fitted) faulty
- Compression poor (see page 84)
- Fuel filter blocked
- Fuel lift pump faulty (or sucking air through leak on suction side)
- Fuel pipes blocked or leaking
- Injection pump faulty
- Injection pump timing wrong
- Injector pipe(s) distorted or broken
- Injector pipe(s) leaking
- Injector(s) faulty
- Overheating

Engine is unusually noisy, with a hammering or knocking sound:
- Bearings worn
- Cold start aid (if fitted) faulty

Cont

Unusual noises or behaviour

- Engine mountings loose or broken
- Fuel lift pump faulty (or sucking air through leak on suction side)
- Fuel of wrong grade or quality
- Injector(s) faulty
- Oil level low
- Overheating
- Piston rings or cylinder bores worn
- Shaft coupling loose
- Valve clearances incorrect
- Valve spring broken
- Valve timing incorrect
- Valves sticking

Engine runs unevenly, 'hunts' or surges:
- Air filter blocked
- Air in fuel system
- Cold start aid (if fitted) faulty
- Control system faulty
- Compression poor (see page 84)
- Fuel filter blocked
- Fuel lift pump faulty (or sucking air through leak on suction side)
- Fuel pipes blocked or leaking
- Fuel tank empty (or nearly so)
- Fuel tank vent blocked
- Injection pump faulty
- Injector pipe(s) distorted or broken
- Injector(s) faulty
- Stop control faulty

The engine vibrates excessively:
- Air filter blocked
- Control system faulty
- Compression poor (see page 84)
- Engine and shaft out of alignment

Cont

Unusual noises or behaviour

- Engine mountings loose or broken
- Fuel of wrong grade or quality
- Injection pump faulty
- Injector pipe(s) distorted or broken
- Injector(s) faulty
- Propeller damaged or wrong size
- Propeller or shaft bent, broken or unbalanced
- Shaft coupling loose
- Shaft misaligned

The engine lacks power:
- Air in fuel system
- Air filter blocked
- Control system faulty
- Compression poor (see page 84)
- Excessive load caused by dirty hull or too much weight on board
- Excessive power losses due to internal friction in engine or transmission
- Exhaust pipe blocked
- Fuel filter blocked
- Fuel lift pump faulty (or sucking air through leak on suction side)
- Fuel of wrong grade or quality
- Fuel pipes blocked or leaking
- Fuel tank vent blocked
- Fuel 'waxing' (caused by using 'summer' fuel in low temperatures)
- Injection pump faulty
- Injection pump timing wrong
- Injector(s) faulty
- Inlet manifold leaking
- Overheating
- Propeller damaged or wrong size
- Thermostat faulty
- Turbocharger faulty
- Ventilation to engine compartment inadequate

Cont

Unusual noises or behaviour

The engine uses more fuel than usual:
- Air filter blocked
- Cold start aid (if fitted) faulty
- Control system faulty
- Compression poor (see below)
- Excessive load caused by dirty hull or too much weight on board
- Excessive power losses due to internal friction in engine or transmission
- Exhaust pipe blocked
- Fuel of wrong grade or quality
- Injection pump faulty
- Injection pump timing wrong
- Injector(s) faulty
- Inlet manifold leaking
- Leak-off pipe blocked
- Thermostat faulty
- Turbocharger faulty

 ## Compression poor

- Cylinder head gasket faulty
- Piston rings or cylinder bores worn
- Valve clearances incorrect
- Valve guides in cylinder head worn
- Valve spring broken
- Valve timing incorrect
- Valves leaking
- Valves sticking

13 Winterizing

A few months of idleness over the winter can do far more harm to an engine than any amount of hard work.

Oil that has done its cleaning job throughout the season lies in the engine, contaminated by the acidic by-products of combustion, while the upper part of the engine, now dry of oil, is exposed to the damp and possibly salty atmosphere. Things that are supposed to be flexible, such as vee-belts and pump impellers, may become stiff; mice and spiders hibernate in air filters and exhaust pipes; and if you're unlucky, the air temperature may fall low enough to freeze the water in the cooling system, to crack the engine block or cylinder head.

Winterization, then, is primarily about protecting the engine against corrosion and cold. It's also an opportunity to do a lot of routine maintenance jobs.

It's important to plan what you're going to do, and when and how you're going to do it: some jobs are best done afloat; others can only be done with the boat ashore, and although some can be left until spring, others should really be done in the autumn. The exact process will vary between different boats and circumstances, but the following routine is fairly typical:

 ## Autumn: before lifting out

- If possible, fill the fuel tank to reduce the air space in which condensation can form (but check that this won't take the boat over the weight limit for the crane or boat-lift).
- Drain the fresh water cooling system. It's often easiest to do this by disconnecting a hose from the circulating pump. Then shut any taps or drains or reconnect any hoses, and refill with a strong solution of fresh antifreeze.
- Drain off any water and sludge from the fuel pre-filter, and change the fuel filter(s).
- Run the engine to operating temperature.
- Change the oil and oil filter while the engine is warm.

Autumn: after lifting out

- Clean the raw water filter.
- Flush the raw water system. There are various methods, but this is one of the most widely recommended:
  - Remove the thermostat.
  - Disconnect the raw water inlet hose from the skin fitting or sea cock, and extend it with an additional length of hose if necessary so that the end can be immersed in a bucket of water. Support the bucket at or near the boat's normal waterline, and arrange for it to be kept topped up by a constant supply of fresh water from a hose.
  - Start the engine and let it run for a few minutes to flush the system. Tip anti-freeze solution into the bucket, turn off the hose, and switch off the engine just before it empties the bucket.
  - Re-connect the hose to the skin fitting.
- Remove the raw water pump impeller. (Put it in a plastic bag and hang it on the engine controls or tie it to the keys so that you don't start the engine without it!)
- Remove alternator and water pump drive belts.
- Change the air filter, and seal the air intake with oiled rags and/or a plastic bag.
- Seal the exhaust pipe with oiled rags or a plastic bag.
- Inspect the gearbox/saildrive/outdrive oil, and replace it if it looks grey or milky.
- Remove the propeller and grease the shaft (not necessary for shaft-drive boats).
- Either remove the batteries to storage ashore or clean and grease their terminals and arrange for them to be charged once every 6 weeks or so. *All lead acid batteries lose their charge over time, and a flat battery can then be irreparably damaged by freezing.*
- Spray the backs of switchboards, instrument panels, and other electrical connections with water-repellent oil.

Spring: before launching

- For Saildrives: inspect the rubber seal around the drive leg, and replace in accordance with the manufacturer's instructions (eg every 5–7 years).
- For outdrives inspect the bellows between the drive leg and transom shield, and replace in accordance with the manufacturer's instructions (eg every 2 years).
- Test and re-fit the thermostat.
- If your raw water cooling system includes zinc anodes, inspect them and replace if necessary.
- Check that all plugs and drain cocks in the cooling system are shut.
- Re-fit the raw water pump impeller with a new pump gasket.
- Inspect all hoses: replace any that are visibly cracked or which do not feel pliable.
- Check hose clamps for security: tighten any that are loose, and replace any that are corroded.
- Re-fit the alternator and water pump drive belts, and adjust them.
- Unblock the air filter and exhaust.
- Check the oil level in the gearbox/saildrive/outdrive.
- Grease the propeller shaft and re-fit the propeller.
- Reconnect the batteries.

Spring: after launching

- Inspect for leaks.
- Check the engine oil level.
- Grease or bleed the stern gland as appropriate.
- Run the engine to operating temperature, inspect for leaks, and check oil and water levels.

Appendix 1

The RYA Diesel Engine Course

Aim of Course

To give an awareness of the main systems of a marine diesel engine so that the yachtsman can take simple measures to prevent mechanical breakdown at sea and rectify defects which do not require workshop support. No pre-course knowledge is required.

Course Syllabus

1 Introduction
Principles of the diesel engine

2 The four stroke cycle
- Naturally aspirated engines
- Turbocharging
- Intercooling/aftercooling

3 The fuel system
- The basic system
- The tank
- The water separating pre-filter
- Fuel lift pump
- The engine fine filter
- Injection pump
- Injectors
- Bleeding the system

4 The Cooling System
- Seawater cooling
- Freshwater cooling
- Temperature control
- The thermostat
- The seawater impeller pump

5 The air systems
- The airway in
- The airway out

6 Engine electrical systems
- The basic system
- Battery capacity and care
- Drive belts
- The alternator

7 Spares and tool requirements
- Basic spares and tools

8 Importance of winterisation and servicing
- Engine lubrication
- Transmission lubrication
- Winterisation and servicing
- Service schedule
- Winterisation

9 Fault-finding

Course Requirements

The minimum duration of the course is six hours. A diesel engine (not necessarily in working condition) will be provided for practical sessions. (No more that six students to one engine.) Instructors will have attended an RYA Training Course.

Enquiries to: Royal Yachting Association, RYA House, Ensign Way, Hamble, Southampton SO31 4YA. Tel: 023 8060 4100 Website: www.rya.org.uk

Index

"Really? It's been thirty years and we've never had a program announcement that let us move to trial?" she said.

She had seen this sort of scientific sea change before. As a clinical immunologist, Klimas had worked early in her career treating HIV patients during the 1980s. That field of researchers started small with, at least at first, everybody knowing everybody else. One year there might be 500 attendees at the annual HIV research meeting at the Hilton in Washington, D.C. The next year, perhaps 800. But then the NIH invested massively in the research, and 10,000 people showed up at the conference.

You couldn't move your arm in the crowd without spilling someone else's drink. "Everybody in the room had coffee stains down their shirts," she laughed. "We were all standing with our elbows tight against our sides, moving through posters and exhibits with our coffees and our teas. Everyone looked like they had their coffee thrown at them." Of course, a little extra for a dry-cleaning bill was a tiny price to pay for catalyzing interest in solving the AIDS pandemic. But through the 1990s and 2000s, as Klimas focused her immunology career on a different set of acquired immune deficiency syndromes, there was less of a need to fight crowds. Her research team was among only a handful of teams in the country that routinely pulled down grants from the NIH to study ME/CFS and its cousin, Gulf War syndrome. Though they protested that the research field would grow directly if the funding levels grew, the message from federal agencies always seemed to be that funding levels should stay low because most scientists just weren't interested. It was a chicken or egg problem. But now the egg was finally cracking.

With Long Covid funding approaching major league levels, the interest from researchers at an annual meeting might again fill a large conference space, buzzing with new scientists spilling coffee on each other…assuming in-person meetings become

nomic measures, biologic workups, and immune panels, comparing people who regained their health with those who remained ill, looking to determine the overall epidemiology of the disease and general profiles of who gets Long Covid. Their team, based in Fort Lauderdale, Florida, built a system to specifically recruit patients from the major healthcare systems in south Florida.

Deeper into the pandemic, in the winter of 2021, the mysteries were compounding. Were there any discernible differences in a person's Long Covid risk among the Delta, Omicron, and the original Alpha strain of the coronavirus? And while it was clear that vaccines and boosters were protective against severe illness and death, there weren't yet definitive answers on how well they could guard against Long Covid, given that most long haulers got sick following a mild infection.

One UK study showed that vaccinations could cut the risk of contracting Long Covid in half. That's good news. But when the virus is spreading in massive waves of up to a million cases per day in the U.S.—as it was in December 2021—there's little consolation in that data.

"Long Covid prior to Delta was not predicted by the severity of infection. We're seeing that over and over and over again," Klimas said. If the general rate of long-term symptoms is usually cited in a range between 10 percent to 30 percent in most studies, then halving the risk still means the rates of possible long-term illness might tally 5 percent to 15 percent. It's a mass disabling event, with a virus that can cause memory loss in young people wildly on the loose.

Breakthrough cases weren't uncommon during the Delta wave. And throughout the Omicron wave, vaccines largely prevented severe disease, but mild breakthrough cases were rampant. During the first wave, any Covid infection had some risk of triggering long-term symptoms. The same true is with Omicron, and subsequent waves of infection thereafter. Some of the most important—and most basic—questions about Long Covid proved unanswered even two years into the pandemic.

"It's going to be awful. There's going to be a lot of people sick for a long, long time because we already have a million people ill with ME/CFS, and we don't know what to do with post-infectious ailments," she said. "The potential that Long Covid is a likely second pandemic is extremely alarming when there is a political policy response right now that is arguing for herd immunity, letting everybody get infected. Certainly in my state that is widely said out loud."

BUILDING A FIRMER FOUNDATION

While Klimas was launching her epidemiology study with the CDC, the National Institutes of Health's RECOVER Initiative was starting to enroll thousands of patients around the country. Many Long Covid patient activists worried that that RECOVER Initiative might just rediscover the same types of post-viral abnormalities that Klimas and the coterie of neuroimmune experts had been finding for years, rather than launching off from the base they had so painstakingly assembled "on a whisper and a prayer." However, the base of knowledge—useful as it was for informed patients comparing notes in online communities—had never grown strong enough to truly fly the nest into the mainstream of medical practice.

"I have no problem with learning it all over again," Klimas said. "That's not a problem, particularly with this very well-funded group with a cohort of 15,000 people." As a leader in the post-viral field, she knew the prevailing themes in how patients could present with a range of immunological abnormalities, how

persistent infections could often be at the root of the problem, and how imaging studies had shown neuroinflammation in the brains of those with ME/CFS. Despite the thousands of published research articles, though, most of the studies over the past thirty years were underpowered, conducted using small cohorts of a few dozen patients. A big study, by ME/CFS standards, might have 100 subjects in it. The studies were underpowered because they were underfunded, and it became impossible to repeat them at the larger scale needed to rewrite the medical textbooks. When researchers received funding, it was usually incumbent on them to show how their research might innovate in the field, forge new ground, rather than to go back and validate an earlier finding.

So Klimas was elated to see how the NIH's call for research proposals had prompted hundreds of applicants from nearly every major university and health system. Teams were falling over themselves to submit grant applications to study Long Covid made her recall how when bank robber Willie Sutton was asked why he robbed banks, he replied, "That's where the money." The same was now true for post-viral illness. The urgency to study the massive health crisis required narrow deadlines, just twenty days between the application releasing until the it was due, a process her team usually would have needed months to accomplish. "When they put aside enough money to fund a small nation, then all of a sudden everybody went and had a deep burning interest in what was going on in long-term ill Covid patients," she said.

And it wasn't just for the observational research delving the underlying biology. Klimas was heartened that by late the NIH opened applications for researchers seeking funding clinical trials to treat Long Covid. That stood in stark contrast the titanic struggle to which she was accustomed with M advisable again. "It's an exciting and wonderful thing that this huge amount of money is going to be spent on this important study. I'm really behind it," Klimas said. "I'm just bemoaning the fact that it took a pandemic to get the interest in post-viral illness to the point where there's sufficient funding."

She had a wish list of drugs that she had been using with patients off-label for years and which could easily be slotted in for drug trials.

First, it was a chance to finally use antivirals in a definitive way. Some antivirals could work on both herpesviruses and coronaviruses, so even if the exact underlying mechanism wasn't clear, patients still might feel better and that was fine with her. "I'm sure it would be more mechanistically pure if you used a very, very specific coronavirus antiviral or very, very specific herpesvirus antiviral to try to discern these things," Klimas said. But overall, a drug might show efficacy even if it was closely, if not perfectly, targeted. From there, it would be important to try specific immune modulation drugs that could enhance cytotoxicity, the ability of immune cells to kill off invaders. Researchers ought to also try cytokine therapies that inhibit proinflammatory cytokines, such as Enbrel and Humira. Those three categories of therapies, she explained, had all shown some amount of success in ME/CFS in early phase clinical trials but hadn't received funding to move forward into the larger trials necessary to gain FDA approval.

Another broad area is drugs that repair patients' bioenergetic pathways. They would carry the virtue of being very safe and fast launching points following a "first, do no harm" philosophy. And those types of treatment studies could be launched inexpensively and remotely, without needing patients to come into the clinic, or live anywhere near the site.

Assuming sleep is distorted in Long Covid in the same way that it's disrupted in ME/CFS, then it follows suit that people have adrenaline surges at night that keep them up and have trouble balancing the sympathetic and parasympathetic nervous systems. "Restorative sleep is a very reasonable target and a very easy thing to survey to see if people are waking up feeling rested or not," Klimas said. "It's something that we routinely do in our clinic-based population and something we are doing in our CDC study. We should know a little bit more about the nature of sleep in this post-Covid illness and then interventions can be applied."

Ultimately, it would amount to a moonshot mission to cure the disease(s), and not just manage the symptoms.

CORONA WITH A TWIST OF LYME

Mark Twain reputedly said, "History doesn't repeat itself, but it often rhymes."

The notion is at once comforting and disturbing—that we're part of some unfolding song, that deeper patterns direct the uncertainty of our existence, that everything new in our collective experience resonates with something that's come before.

With each expert and patient I spoke to, I couldn't help thinking of how diagnosing and treating Long Covid felt so similar to controversies in the history of Lyme disease. It surfaced many of the same nagging questions. Were chronic cases driven by a persistent infection? Did symptoms emerge from a permanently altered immune system? How could people get so sick, and yet their underlying signs of disease be so difficult to detect? Could the infection reach into the brain? And why did this happen more commonly in women?

The fundamental questions pulled at me because in one version of events, my entire history of relapsing symptoms revolved around the tick-borne illness and the contested science around it. Growing up with one foot always in the woods, I'd constantly been exposed to ticks, regularly picking the little arachnids off the skin of my beloved black Labrador, Jenny. They showed up on my own skin as well.

But one bite haunted me. During a weeklong Boy Scout summer camp at age fifteen in Kentucky, I'd stopped by the little first aid hut with a tick stuck at the base of my left buttock. I couldn't twist far enough down to get a good look at it and remove it myself, so I asked the nurse to pry it off with tweezers.

"I got most of it," she told me. "But I couldn't remove the head."

I felt a little pang of panic in the pit of my stomach. Leaders constantly preached to Scouts the need to fully remove a tick—head and all. I knew those facts like a religious dogma, and violating them felt wrong. But the nurse was an authority figure and I just assumed it wouldn't matter.

For me, taking huge risks and testing rules was the point of camp in the first place. I instigated other boys in ramming sailboats until they submerged in the lake, and we occasionally sparked balls of fire in the air when cooking with propane stoves. So, taking a risk with a fragment of a bug—even one that caused a disease I was supposed to be afraid of—felt less ominous than a more obvious tragedy like a mishap on the shotgun range. Knowing little else I could do, I shrugged off the botched tick removal by the end of the week.

The bite site stayed red and inflamed for the next year. When all-consuming fatigue forced me to stop attending school, I showed the bite site to each doctor in the failed parade of diagnosis toward chronic fatigue syndrome. Each agreed it looked inflamed but my skin didn't match with the classic bullseye rash—a red splotch with a ring around it—characterizing most Lyme infections. And their blood panels showed I was negative for Lyme, according to the CDC's surveillance definition for the disease, which tests for specific antibodies to the infection.

Two years later, I found Dr. Bullington—my current doctor—and she ordered a more specific test offered through IGeneX, a California-based laboratory specializing in tick-borne diseases. Through its more expanded threshold for bands of detectable antibodies, I came up positive.

She explained to me that the mainstream methods for detecting Lyme may miss more than half of cases, according to one study.

From there, at least part of the strange years-long illness shifted into a clearer focus, potentially traceable to a discrete event in space and time.

Bullington added a course of long-term antibiotics to my already robust treatment plan. But because I was prescribed so many drugs and supplements at the same time, it's hard to know whether it was the antibiotics or prescriptions for other symptoms and abnormalities that had the greatest effect in my recovery. My health trended overall toward stability. Outside of torturous flare-ups here and there, the overall treatment plan built space for the pursuits that fulfilled me: I joined a college intramural soccer team, challenged myself academically with advanced astronomy and Mandarin Chinese, pursued love, and built a life.

After the antibiotic course, we drew blood for a Lyme culture test, which seeks to grow the bacteria in a lab over a period of weeks. Though it hasn't yet gained mainstream acceptance, the culture test, I was told, could definitively determine whether bacteria still existed in the blood, looking beyond whether the patient was capable of mounting an immune response.

At the time, I knew little about the decades of controversy around Lyme and tick-borne diseases, learning as much science as suited me through doctor's appointments, books, and Internet searches. But my own body was nothing if not a single data point in a vast scientific debate, one which lent yet another tantalizing lens through which to examine how we contend with the Covid and its long shadow.

Lyme disease is named for a cluster of cases in children and adults that appeared around the town of Lyme, Connecticut in 1975. Six years later, researchers linked the infections to the *Borrelia burgdorferi* spiral-shaped bacteria, or spirochete, which is carried by ticks. However, the disease has likely circulated for thousands of years. Researchers discovered parts of the *Borrelia* genome in the prehistoric mummy Ötzi, also called Ice Man, who was preserved in the Alps between Austria and Italy after likely being murdered some 5,300 years ago.

In the days or weeks after a tick bite, acute Lyme most often appears with the bullseye rash alongside fever, chills, fatigue, and muscle and joint aches, according to the CDC. It has reached epidemic levels, and today the agency estimates there are 300,000 new cases—or possibly even more—of Lyme each year in the U.S., with 10 to 20 percent of those infected remaining ill after treatment.

Lyme has been the subject of decades of heated debate, with so-called "Lyme-literate doctors" and chronic patients on one side fighting a pitched battle against the medical establishment, exemplified by the Infectious Disease Society of America, over the underlying cause and therefore treatment of chronic symptoms in some Lyme patients.

Lyme-literate doctors argue that patients' ongoing symptoms may be driven by the *B. burgdorferi* bacterium, or other tick-borne infections, stealthily persisting in the body's tissues, evading the body's immune response. If so, then the infection can be eradicated by long-term courses of antibiotics, not unlike the plan my doctor prescribed. However, most academic specialists argue that there isn't evidence of the bacteria persisting in the human body after the standard course of a few weeks of antibiotics, and many doubt whether chronic Lyme is a real disease at all. Regimens of antibiotics for months or years could do more harm than good, the IDSA argues. And a handful of placebo-controlled clinical trials haven't borne substantive evidence that long-term antibiotics are appropriate.

Given the controversy of this disease, patients with post-treatment Lyme disease syndrome are often left desperately fumbling through a medical underground of contested science and alternative practitioners. Unproven or even bizarre treatments become vastly preferable to a mainstream that tells them their disabling symptoms are psychosomatic, and don't have a basis in objective fact.

Lyme is part of a class of "great imitators," a designation given to diseases with wide-ranging or non-specific symptoms that overlap with other diseases. For great imitators, which can include fibromyalgia, multiple sclerosis, and lupus, there's a high chance for misdiagnosis. Just as in Covid long haulers, Lyme can begin with an acute infection that apparently resolves, but then later produces long-term fatigue, pain, and cognitive dysfunction even though patients appear to come up normal on routine lab tests.

The symptom presentation in post-treatment Lyme disease syndrome and Long Covid patients is "remarkably similar," said Dr. John Aucott, director of the Johns Hopkins University Lyme Disease Research Center. He was amazed at early studies of Long Covid patients with bar graphs showing the prevalence of major symptoms. If you placed those charts alongside self-reported symptoms of Lyme "long haulers," it was almost like they were mirror images of each other.

That suggested to him perhaps the best corollary to Long Covid came from previous insights in ME/CFS and POTS, disorders marked by decreased blood flow to the brain, and associated with inflammation in the autonomic nervous system, the part of the nervous system that directs automatic functions of the body. The autonomic nervous system tells the heart to beat at seventy beats per minute while sitting at rest or the lungs to breathe faster while running sprints—tasks that don't require active thinking. So even though organs themselves weren't damaged in Lyme or Long Covid, the heart or lungs or GI tract didn't work properly because the part of the nervous system that controlled them was affected.

One way that autonomic nervous system disruption could be explained is by altered function of your vagus nerve, Aucott explained to me over the phone one afternoon in the fall of 2021. "Maybe you're not getting enough blood to your brain because of altered autonomic control of your blood pressure and pulse, which is triggered when the vagus nerve is inflamed or triggered by the infection," Aucott said.

"That's one hypothesis that ties it all together," he said. "It seems to explain why all the symptoms look the same in chronic fatigue and long haul Covid and Lyme, because maybe they all share that same mechanism. They're seeing tons of autonomic dysfunction in long haul Covid."

And few doctors fully understand the underlying mechanics because there's limited teaching about autonomic nervous system disorders in medical school.

There are plenty of other hypotheses to explore for why Lyme triggers long-term illness. But progress in studying the profoundly life-altering condition has plodded along with poor funding. To be sure, NIH funding levels have slowly ticked upward from $20 million in 2013 to an estimated $50 million in 2021. So far though, there haven't been enough resources to get a solid handle on the different possible underlying mechanisms of the illness. But even though mainstream medicine couldn't agree on the exact nature of the fire, the smoke looks very similar to Long Covid.

"From Lyme disease, I think the lesson may be more that infection can trigger persistent inflammation. That is the potential mechanism for why the patient doesn't get better," Aucott said. "To what extent post-treatment Lyme is just classic autoimmunity versus just persistent inflammation, that's still not clear."

Another lesson from Lyme could come in evidence that the pieces of the *B. burgdorferi* bacteria could be triggering long-term illness, just as fragments of SARS-CoV-2 might be doing the same for Covid patients.

"There actually is some intriguing data in Lyme disease that the proteins that make up the cell walls of the bacteria may linger in the tissues, and perpetuate inflammation," Aucott told me. "Even after the viable organisms are gone and dead. But there are pieces or bits of protein that are lying around triggering ongoing inflammation." During fifteen years of research, Aucott and his research team at Johns Hopkins have published studies showing a range of ways that Lyme appeared to cause persistent inflammation, rewiring neural networks in a way that became self-perpetuating even if the original infection truly had been eradicated.

The team had found elevated levels of a cytokine called CCL19, which stood out among dozens of inflammatory markers in long-term Lyme. They also found that gene regulation patterns are highly abnormal in post-treatment Lyme disease syndrome patients. In essence, while doctors would expect that genes regulating an immune response would be active for a few weeks during the acute phase of an infection, Aucott's team showed they were significantly altered six months after infection. That helped build a picture similar to other Lyme studies of the metabolome—the full spectrum of metabolites and other small molecules in the body—showing that the metabolic processes were altered for long periods of time and didn't return to normal after they were treated.

Similar to Covid, if the original pathogen was no longer detectable—at least through conventional means—then doctors were left to treat the symptoms, working with patients to manage their sleep, pain, and fatigue issues with existing drugs even though they couldn't solve the underlying problem outright. Proving definitively whether human Lyme infections could persist or enter the brain was difficult partially due to the few available autopsy studies on subjects with Lyme. Researchers can get ethics approval to poke around the brains of infected mice that they've sacrificed ahead of time. Since Lyme is rarely deadly, there was limited opportunity to repeat the same studies in humans. However, even if Lyme doesn't kill people directly, plenty of people with Lyme die from other causes, so these types of studies could be done by setting up established biobanks for human biopsy and autopsy tissues from Lyme disease patients.

"There is some evidence in animal models for sequestered hidden infections where the bacteria—even after antibiotics—may be hiding in a kind of dormant state in privileged sites in which the immune system can't get rid of them," Aucott said.

A similar problem presented in Covid, due to ethical and practical difficulties of performing brain autopsy studies in human subjects. Early autopsy studies by the NIH hadn't found SARS-CoV-2 in the brain, although a German study of patients who had died of Covid suggested otherwise, finding viral proteins in isolated cells in the brainstem. It was an early clue there could at least be a possibility that Covid brain fog was driven by virus infiltrating part of the brain. It wouldn't be until December 2021 that scientists from the NIH released preprint results, prior to peer review, of a more robust autopsy study that definitively found persistent SARS-CoV-2 in the brain and throughout the body.

One of the best ways around those issues is through the increased use of more sophisticated brain imaging techniques in recent years, offering a chance to "dissect" the brain of a living creature without physically cutting into it.

In a 2018 neuroimaging study, Aucott's group had demonstrated neuroinflammation from Lyme using positron emission tomography (PET) scans, the same type of imaging used to show proof of brain damage in living former NFL players. In that study, they found post-treatment Lyme patients had activated glial cells, a type of immune cell in the central nervous system. That type of PET scan isn't readily accessible for practicing physicians, but they point to a real underlying biology for the hellish aftermath of Lyme.

Beyond new technologies, the pandemic might be forcing a cultural shift, exposing whole new swaths of the health profession and society at large to rethink post-infectious, or para-infectious diseases, bringing them into the light.

"Covid is actually exciting because it's gotten people's attention on this at a much bigger scale. I think that's helpful for us," he said. "It's not as easy to deny Long Covid because of the scale of the issue."

Those similarities prompted researchers from Stanford University to adapt another set of new technologies to design a way to see into the daily lives of patients. In October 2021, they launched a two-year "Crash Course" study comparing people with ME/CFS, Lyme, and Long Covid to learn how and why they all experience the trademark post-exertional crashes common in each condition. These dynamic "continuous sensing" side-by-side comparisons of all three diseases might reveal common characteristics across each of them. The researchers gave each participant a wearable Fitbit device to keep track of daily heart rate, step count, sleep, and other variables. Each participant would collect sixteen blood samples over the course of a three-month period using an innovative at-home blood draw device called a Tasso. Some would be baseline measures, and others would specifically show how they felt on a good day versus on a crash day.

THEORY OF EVERYTHING

FOR MORE THAN A CENTURY, physicists have been feverishly searching for what scientists call the "Theory of Everything." A theory so flexible and all-encompassing that it would unite all the laws of the universe. Albert Einstein contributed a huge piece of the puzzle when he first described the phenomenon of general relativity, the rules that governed large scale physics like space, time, and gravity. Around the same time, another concept was emerging known as quantum mechanics, which is the study of very, *very* small matter, like atoms and their sub-particles, and the laws that they abide by. With these two grand theories, both big and small, it may come as a surprise that the puzzle of "everything" did not fit together. Quantum mechanics and the theory of relativity are ultimately incompatible. The rules of one did not hold up when applied to the other. What huge puzzle piece were physicists missing? Despite the genius of the subsequent generations, physicists have not yet been able to synthesize the laws of physics into an overall single theory to explain them all. And yet we know that some explainable order of the cosmos has to exist.

The field of human biology is a tricky science to design perfectly repeatable experiments around, as it usually proves hard to control the plethora of confounding variables. However, when it comes to disease, the need for a Theory of Everything is just as urgent as in the cosmos and the particles. Study after study has shown us an abundance of abnormalities across many systems in diseases like ME/CFS, Long Covid, and Lyme. Some researchers have been looking at the smaller cellular level examining mitochondria, blood vessels and endothelial cells, natural killer cells, and cytokine disruptions. At the same time, other researchers have taken a more biological systems approach and focused on characteristics of the gut microbiome, connective tissue, autonomic dysfunction, the vagus nerve, mechanical instabilities, and the brainstem. And in an arguably even more global approach to the body, some scientists focus squarely on patient symptoms like post-exertional malaise and cognitive issues to guide their research into post-viral illness. But it seems just when we have our hands around the castle, it turns to sand. Is it possible, just as in physics, as we look at the same problem from different angles or maybe even more importantly *at different time points*, that the problem shape shifts, evading a unifying theory?

"Unless we follow these things from the beginning, we won't be able to tie those things together. There's lots of information that we're already starting to see in Long Covid. It's a post-viral syndrome, it's got all these immune abnormalities," said Dr. Lucinda Bateman, the Chief Medical Officer at the Bateman Horne Center of Excellence in Salt Lake City, Utah . "There's a lot of neurological symptoms. There's actually quite a bit of mitochondrial dysfunction as well. It'll be interesting to see if the story of Long Covid pulls all those together to see how they relate to each other."

Maybe Covid is our Big Bang. We have to start at the beginning.

Is it also possible that most accepted and well-described diseases behave according to a theory of everything but are not subject to this level of scrutiny and doubt from the medical community and society at large? Perhaps it's because most of these conditions have a definable and agreed upon biomarker that is readily testable. For example, if you have a pattern of specific lesions in the brain, you may be diagnosed with multiple sclerosis. However, when you look at the biology of patients with MS, it is clearly a complex disease, with abundant red flags across multiple systems. Without the biomarker, MS might just be as confusing as ME/CFS seems now.

For now, the primary physical reaction to an infectious agent like Covid or Lyme that eventually sets off the chain of events that often leads to a new stubborn homeostasis of disease is stumping the scientific community. Maybe the infection hits multiple systems at once. In fact, is it preposterous to zoom farther out and assume all diseased states within the body are long-standing effects of assaults from viruses, bacteria, vaccines, parasites, and the like? In cases like multiple sclerosis or Alzheimer's, we don't know yet who walked in that room and flipped that switch, though some hypothesize it might've been a virus. At least in these diseases, however, we know quite a bit more about which switch it was. Sometimes we know the switch *and* who flipped it, like with HIV/AIDS.

What is clear is that at some point, the infection-associated diseases such as Long Covid and ME/CFS look like a circular merry-go-round from hell, with no way to know what came first or what is perpetuating what between vagus nerve damage, leaky blood vessels, connective tissue fragility, etc. And worst of all, it's not clear how to get off the ride. And maybe by the time you have had it for long enough, it doesn't matter what came first. You're stuck. A growing body of research points to some sort of switch getting flipped, throwing people into a long-term state of illness. Interestingly, in the case of Long Covid, we know *who* flipped the switch: it was SARS-CoV-2.

"One of the problems is that it's a hypometabolic state," Ron Davis, professor of genetics at Stanford University, told me during a wide-ranging conversation about the many avenues of dysfunction in the disease and the quest to neatly sum them all up. In a hypometabolic state, the body's metabolic processes are suppressed and normal activities are suspended.

"For ME/CFS there's a lot of metabolites that are very low level, probably because the mitochondria have been partially shut down," he said. "We're looking at some of the pathways in mitochondria in great detail. Mitochondria are clearly involved in this in some way and that needs to get explored."

THE PUZZLE SOLVER

It's been nine years since I first searched the name "Ron Davis" in a Stanford dorm room before interviewing him in 2013, and I learned about his career earning dozens of patents as a pioneer of the technology that drove the Human Genome Project. At the time, he had just dropped his entire research agenda to focus on ME/CFS after his son developed a severe case of the disease, becoming bedridden for a decade and unable to eat or swallow solid food. Davis vowed that for as long as he lived, he would fight on behalf of his son and the millions around the world with the same disease.

Over the past decade, he injected new vigor and rigor into the field, recruiting new researchers with a pitch that ME/CFS is the "last great disease left to conquer." He joined a National Academy of Medicine committee convened by the federal government, which reviewed the full body of thousands of peer-reviewed research studies. It published the 2015 report that suggested a new name for the illness, "systemic exertion intolerance disease," based around its foremost clinical sign. It was the consolidation of everything known to date about ME/CFS, and called for a new way forward for research, clinical care, and medical education, recommending dramatic increases across each area. Davis built a network of dozens of scientists and several collaborative research centers around the world, including at Stanford, Harvard, and Uppsala University in Sweden. The Open Medicine Foundation, where he is the lead scientific advisor, raised more than $30 million for research.

All the while, Davis and his wife, Janet Dafoe, arranged each aspect of their daily lives toward responding to their son's needs. Multiple times each day, they sat outside Whitney's room, head bowed, waiting for their son's signal that it's all right to come inside his room. They hook up IV drips for hydration, wash his feet, and clip his toenails. For years, they wore plain shirts without lettering because even the sliver of energy it takes for Whitney to process a word could cause him to crash, triggering severe stomach pain that made it impossible to put more food into his feeding tube. Caring for Whitney, monitoring his every bodily signal, was one of Davis' central ways of generating new ideas to test out and new drugs to try. With a port in his chest, Whitney was an easy source of blood draws, and often served as an initial guinea pig for studies. Whitney had the starkest form of ME/CFS, and cases like his might serve as a benchmark for the trajectory in which the illness could progress in some cases. The OMF funded a study of severe ME/CFS, believing that whatever was wrong at a fundamental level would be most clear or apparent for those with the direst cases. Whitney's symptoms represented the most extreme reality for sufferers of post-viral illness, like Long Covid. Where the disease is paints the body in its boldest and most destructive colors, its individual brushstrokes might be most discernible.

And those brushstrokes, Davis believes, are most likely rooted at the molecular level. He and his team designed an ultrasensitive "nanoneedle" device that could test for that molecular signature from a single drop of blood. In 2019, they published initial findings in the journal Proceedings of the National Academy of Sciences showing that in a study of forty patients and healthy control subjects that their nanoneedle could distinguish each time whether the person had the illness or not. Patients' blood responded to a stressor—in this case, salt.

"What we don't know is whether other diseases show the same thing," Davis said. "And it doesn't prove anything until we can do a number of other infections."

Getting the nanoneedle to work at scale might mean a biomarker for the disease and could eventually lead to creating a blood test to diagnose the condition quickly and easily. From there, they could compare the marker to a catalog of drugs already approved by the FDA which could be repurposed to treat ME/CFS.

As the beginning of the pandemic took shape, Davis saw another opportunity to deploy advanced techniques such as systems biology, genome sequencing, and metabolomics to observe the likely beginnings of the ME/CFS and try to learn if and how a switch gets flipped, transitioning the person into a chronic illness. They enrolled Covid-19 patients in a new study so they could collect regular samples over a period of years and monitor which people developed a longer-term post-viral fatigue syndrome. Having data on patients from the beginning of an illness like Covid and observing them longitudinally over time as the illness progresses gives Davis and his team a unique opportunity to capture the disease process and increases the likelihood of discovering the molecular Holy Grail.

Davis had prominence, a prestigious collaborative network, and significant headway into understanding post-viral conditions. As expert patient leaders living with Long Covid began meeting with planners of the NIH's big initiative to study long haulers, Ron Davis's research agenda—and of a dozen others established in the field—appeared to be obvious and relevant to their ongoing plight. At the same time, a different Davis, the Patient-Led Research Collaborative's Hannah Davis, was so worried that RECOVER Initiative planners might not take prior post-viral research into consideration with Long Covid that she gave them a presentation in the summer of 2021 highlighting more than a dozen current clinicians and scientists who had spent their careers working on these complex syndromes, who might have the most relevant experience and most promising leads within a field that conventional medicine had consistently bobbled for decades. She highlighted their ongoing lines of research: Michael VanElzakker and his work in neuroinflammation, Nancy Klimas and her career in post-infectious immunology, and Avindra Nath and his ongoing intramural study within the NIH itself.

Hannah Davis included Ron Davis among those high on the list that she and patients hoped would be included in the RECOVER Initiative. The PLRC leader thought his team's nanoneedle technology might provide the basis for eventually discerning a biomarker in the blood for Long Covid.

The genome pioneer felt the same way, linking ME/CFS and Long Covid.

"I'd be surprised if they're actually different," Ron Davis said. Symptomatically, the basic differences between ME/CFS and Long Covid disappear in the months after the acute infection. "They're different in one way, in that ME/CFS was ignored and Long Covid was not."

His team applied for two grants to study Long Covid, but both were rejected on the grounds that he was collecting molecular data. Other longtime post-viral researchers whom the patients recommended didn't make the cut either, for one reason or another. He was in fundamental disagreement with the pieces of feedback he received in his rejection.

"One of them specifically said that I couldn't run any of the data, I had to archive it. I would have to collect blood samples, and then freeze them, but not study them," Davis said. The initiative intended to set up a biorepository of samples so that many teams of researchers could study them for their different projects.

For him, those kinds of logistical considerations were a huge problem in designing the careful experiments required to tease out the source of the disease. The Stanford Genome Technology Center's nanoneedle device—which might hold the key to discovering a biomarker for ME/CFS and therefore Long Covid—didn't work on frozen blood samples. "We've tried and tried and tried to find a way that preserves them, but we haven't found that. Just that fact alone says that changes are occurring in the blood when you freeze it. We don't know what is changing but we know something is changing. And that could be key to what's actually happening in the immune system and cause people to miss it."

The Open Medicine Foundation found an initial $1 million in funding at the beginning of the pandemic to study post-Covid patients, starting with post-ICU patients they had access to through their center in Sweden. While they had a small amount of private money available to study long haulers, the bulk of the organization's funding came from private donations earmarked for ME/CFS. Running their tests on both sets of patient communities in comparison groups side-by-side was almost assured to garner the most useful results but wouldn't be fair to the patients who'd originally donated to study their own disease.

"I am very resistant to taking donation money from patients that suffer with ME/CFS to study Long Covid. It just seems unethical to me," he told me. "There's lots of money for Long Covid, hundreds of times more money than for ME/CFS. And why should the ME/CFS patients pay for trying to understand Long Covid?"

Such is the dilemma of siloes. The private scraps available for one disease were in one pot, and the large public outlays for its nearly identical twin were in a different pot out of reach.

Davis and his team are working to prove or disprove whether patients' cells enter a "metabolic trap" that disrupts the molecular process for energy production. The science is a complicated two-step involving a pair of genes. The first gene, IDO1, works to process the amino acid tryptophan into compounds involved in regulating the immune system, reducing inflammation in the brain, and producing the energy molecule ATP. If there's too much tryptophan in a cell, IDO1 can get overwhelmed and can't produce the compounds that underpin healthy immune functioning and energy production. A major insult to the body, such as a viral infection, can increase tryptophan and overload IDO1. There's a backup gene, IDO2, ensuring the body keeps producing energy as normal. But 65 percent of the human population has a mutation there. That's not a problem if the first system never gets overwhelmed, but if exposed to a powerful virus such as SARS-CoV-2, it could be enough to flip the switch.

"One way to study this is that we would like to put a cell into a trap, which we can do in yeast and human immune cells to see how to get the cell out of a trap with a drug," he told me. "We have completed our screening of all the FDA-approved drugs for yeast. We have a number of compounds that will get yeast out of the trap."

If the metabolic trap is proven, it might be a keystone helping hold together the myriad of symptoms and far-flung clinical observations in the disease.

Davis didn't want to get too excited about certain Long Covid drugs that generated a certain amount of early buzz. For a desperate patient community, directing too much hope to a hot new treatment too early can lead to disappointments, especially when they might only work well for a small subset of patients or if the positive effects proved fleeting. New findings garner headlines and generate glimmers of hope in patient communities. However, the research process is slow and may or may not bear the kind of fruit that ultimately results in drugs reaching the finish line for FDA approval. Beyond that, many new drugs and interventions can be overly expensive or lack a financial model by which the treatment can be distributed widely and equitably. The ideal solution would be repurposing a drug already on pharmacy shelves, rather than bringing a brand new compound to market, a process often cited as requiring about a decade and at least $1 billion to complete. In order to reach the greatest number of people, research findings would have to be reproducible across multiple trials, and treatments would ideally be fairly inexpensive.

Berlin Cures, a pharmaceutical company in Germany, generated fanfare by successfully treating several patients in the summer of 2021 with a new compound called BC 007, which was originally developed to treat heart disease. Administered in a little over an hour by IV drip, the drug acts to improve blood flow and may reduce autoantibodies circulating in the body long after Covid infection. By early 2022, the company was enrolling dozens more patients in a clinical trial. Davis was keen to collaborate with them.

"I don't know if it's going to be a cure or not. But it could be a treatment, which could be great," Davis said.

But he warned that the trail of clinical research is often littered with disappointments, so keeping a judicious eye on the big picture mattered. Many long haulers get thrown into the murky backwaters of experimental treatments, desperately seeking anything that might get their lives back beyond just trying to manage their symptoms.

PUZZLE PIECES IN LONG COVID RESEARCH

Pieces of the puzzle continue to emerge, with a stream of studies confirming the persistence of SARS-CoV-2 in the body along with inflammation, autoantibody activity, and deterioration of the endothelial cells that line blood vessels.

So far, there's no simple equation or theory of everything to describe the underlying disease, and there's no simple protocol to follow in treating it. But it hasn't stopped brilliantly determined investigators like Amy Proal, a microbiologist at the PolyBio Research Foundation, from trying. The perpetually crumbling sandcastle is beginning to congeal.

As mentioned in chapter eight, Proal worked with her colleague Mike VanElzakker to review the research from the first two years of the pandemic—as well as the history of science focused on infection-associated chronic diseases. She neatly folded them into a unified framework for thinking about Long Covid. She sees seven major factors driving cycles within the body that lead into the persisting illness, which provide the basis for the many teams of researchers working to understand, treat, and eventually cure the disease.

First, at least some of the long-term disease in Long Covid can be directly attributed to a measurable organ injury such as lung, heart, or kidney damage. But a standard echocardiogram or blood test can usually see that right away. From there, though, things get much more interesting.

The vast majority of patients may have a set of underlying pathologies that require robust judgment and attention from doctors to discern. Additionally, the field needs innovation in diagnostics so that the most relevant abnormalities could stand out. According to Proal's analysis of the ongoing research in the field, Long Covid manifests as a combination of some or all of the following: persistence of the SARS-CoV-2 virus, reactivation of other persistent pathogens, dysregulation of the patient's microbiome or virome, blood coagulation, extended autoantibody production, and disruption of vagus nerve signaling to the brainstem. Because the disease is heterogenous, the exact version of those factors would manifest differently depending on the myriad of complexities of a particular body.

Your average nasal swab or blood test won't pick up on persistent virus after the acute stage of the infection is over, a fact that has complicated the understanding of lingering viral loads. Rather, residual virus can hide out in tissues. Studies have increasingly shown that SARS-CoV-2 is *capable of persistence*. Researchers from the NIH performed forty-four autopsies. All had been infected with SARS-CoV-2. Some had been asymptomatic while others had died from Covid. The results, posted as a preprint in December 2021 ahead of a publication in the journal *Nature*, offered definitive evidence that the virus could dwell in the brain. In early January 2022, it was top of mind for Dr. Anthony Fauci when Sen. Tim Kaine—who regularly made a point to ask about Long Covid—posed a query to the expert about the NIH's progress helping long haulers during a Senate health committee hearing. He explained that an individual could test negative for the virus via nasal swab while the virus persisted in anatomical sanctuaries throughout the body, including the cardiovascular, gastrointestinal, renal, endocrine, and reproductive tissues. In one case they found the virus lasting in tissues for up to 230 days, the full length of the study. The autopsies showed that the virus could likely enter the brain by crossing the blood-brain barrier, and lodge itself in the brainstem. It was the most high-quality study to that point proving widespread SARS-CoV-2 viral reservoirs.

The next puzzle piece—*reactivation of persistent pathogens*—highlights how some of the dysfunction in post-infectious illness stems from older pathogens in the body that are newly emboldened to cause damage again. "Under conditions of health these viruses are kept in check by the immune system," Proal says. "The immune system has defenses that keep them in a largely dormant or inactive state. But, and this is a well-known phenomenon under conditions of stress, the same viruses can reactivate and begin to drive symptoms." Most humans accumulate a range of viruses throughout their lifetimes, including multiple strains of herpesviruses. Many people with Long Covid experience reactivations of latent herpesviruses, which can manifest in cold sores or as shingles. That phenomenon, long established in the literature of chronic illnesses, isn't new in Long Covid. In one study of Long Covid patients, some two-thirds showed Epstein-Barr virus reactivation, compared with just 10 percent of controls.

The human body contains trillions of organisms, the sum total of which make up what's called the microbiome. Another area of Long Covid is *dysregulation of host microbiome*, Proal explains. Similar to how Covid-19 leads to virus reactivation, it can also tip the balance in the microbiome, shifting the homeostasis characterizing normal function.

Those phenomena together help lead into the category of *endothelial cell damage, platelet hyperactivation, and blood coagulation*. While it is clear these mechanisms are implicated in symptomatology during acute Covid infection, researchers are finding persistent dysfunction across these areas in Long Covid patients as well. These anomalies could help link multiple factors together. Each reactivation of virus and bacteria can cause inflammation and sometimes direct infection of endothelial cells, the cells lining the blood vessels. As platelets in the blood—which contribute to the dysfunction in more ways than one—react to these microvascular injuries, they clump together into microclots. If the blood becomes clotted because of Long Covid, it makes it harder for oxygen and nutrient-rich components to perfuse tissue throughout the body, and that can contribute to small fiber neuropathy, a kind of nerve damage. The clots could be a major contributor to the post-exertional malaise most long haulers feel. In addition, as endothelial cells maintain the integrity of tissue barriers and also mediate both innate and acquired immunity, injuries to these cells can cause increased permeability in the membranes throughout the body, including those in the gut and the brain. Even here, you can start to get an appreciation of the snowball rolling down the hill, gathering weight, mass, and speed as each assault builds on the previous one and sets the stage for a new dysfunction.

In a study, Harvard's Dr. David Systrom used a process called invasive cardiopulmonary testing to find abnormal blood flow throughout the body, including blood flowing to the brain. In that test, researchers insert a catheter into a subject's vein with a tiny balloon in it that can take measurements of factors in their blood while they ride an exercise bike. They brought ten people with Long Covid into their process used for studying exercise intolerance in ME/CFS and a range of diseases. Sure enough, they found that each of the ten long haulers demonstrated impaired oxygen extraction. And the reduced blood flow to the brain could be a primary driver of the brain fog so many patients report.

Notably, of the four types of tissue in the body—connective, epithelial, muscle, and nervous—connective tissue is of particular interest to some researchers. Connective tissue, a cohesive structural tissue that supports organs and other bodily tissues and includes cartilage, fat, bone, blood, and connective tissue proper, has been implicated in a number of post-pathogen disease states. Proal added, "it would be strange if connective tissue would be sterile." As mentioned above, blood, a type of connective tissue, is significantly affected by Covid-19. It's possible the virus degrades other connective tissue as well. After all, Proal states, a pathogen like "*Borrelia burgdorferi*—the bacterium found in Lyme disease—is a known connective tissue degrader." There are many diseases and disorders of connective tissue, such as Ehlers-Danlos syndrome. Some are genetic, while others are acquired, or epigenetic, coming from an interaction between genes and the environment.

There is an abundance of ways diseases of connective tissue can show up, and many look very different from each other. One common outcome is when connective tissue fails to provide adequate support in ligaments, joints, and skin. The results can be a plethora of structural instabilities that cause painful and disabling neurological symptoms, many of which have been noted in patient accounts of those suffering from ME/CFS and POTS. These instabilities are caused by weakened structural connective tissue. For instance, craniocervical instability, or CCI, is associated with diminished connective tissue around the craniocervical area that holds the head and spine in proper position. Weak ligamentous connections around the base of the skull or in other spinal regions can lead to pressure or stretching as internal elements compress or stretch important anatomy including the spinal cord and deep brain areas, including the vagus nerve. The resulting symptoms become disabling and serve as one more example of the myriad ways in which a particular syndrome has a web of possible underlying causes. In the case of CCI, a surgery might repair the underlying problem and set the patient back toward good health.

Finally, Proal's model relies on *disruption of vagus nerve signaling*. The widely branching nerve has major receptors that innervate every major organ in the body, and a disruption of the vagus nerve was proposed by Michael VanElzakker as a major explanation for ME/CFS in 2013. It's also a direct highway to the dorsal brainstem. Under ideal conditions, the vagus nerve can maintain immune homeostasis and regulate autonomic and metabolic function. Under conditions of possible persistent infection, like those seen in Long Covid, the balance is upset. If there is a SARS-CoV-2 reservoir, a reactivated virus, a disrupted microbiome, or structural compression, then the vagus nerve can sense inflammation and send a signal to the brainstem, triggering neural cells that cause what's known as a "sickness response." And it's not just a signal and a subjective feeling of illness, the vagus nerve can elicit neuroinflammation, disrupting vital signals throughout the brain. VanElzakker's PET scan studies in ME/CFS have shown a kind of brain inflammation that likely contributed to brain fog and are now being rolled out in Long Covid. Proal points out, "no one gets this sick without the brain involved."

The model distills many areas of complex and emerging science into a set of themes, which can vary person to person. Long

Covid probably isn't one-size-fits-all. Any particular patient might have any individualized version of the mix of factors that Proal outlines.

Proal ran through a few different scenarios depicting how the various factors could play out in a particular individual. In one scenario, the SARS-CoV-2 virus could have formed a reservoir in a person's intestines, resulting in inflammation that triggers the vagus nerve to send a proinflammatory signal to the dorsal brainstem that resulted in the person feeling sickness, pain, nausea, and autonomic symptoms. Simultaneously, proteins from the virus could leak into the blood, leading to distortions in coagulation and the vasculature as well as low oxygen levels in tissue.

In another scenario, a patient might have totally cleared SARS-CoV-2 from every part of the body. But then the Epstein-Barr virus, lying dormant up to that point, could have seized on the opportunity of a temporarily weakened immune system to reactivate. In Proal's example, this patient also has significant gut dysbiosis, in which the diverse microbial ecosystem in the GI is disordered. The patient's Epstein-Barr reactivation and gut issues then trigger a similar proinflammatory signal up through the vagus nerve and the dorsal brainstem set off the same feelings of sickness, pain, nausea, and autonomic symptoms. This person could also be a Covid long hauler, with the virus setting off a chain of events even after leaving the body. Rather than persistent infection, this person might be the victim of a hit-and-run.

Still, a third person might have similar symptoms, but a third set of underlying factors to their Long Covid. In this storyline, SARS-CoV-2 sets up shop long-term in lung tissue in a person who might already have had an enterovirus infection in the stomach and oral microbiome dysbiosis. This person, with Covid-19 being just one of multiple hits to their system, becomes even sicker through the same process of the vagus nerve signaling a three-alarm fire of systemic sickness response throughout the body.

The examples could go on and on, of course, substituting different underlying infections, different host sites for SARS-CoV-2, and different routes of disruption.

MOVING FORWARD BY LOOKING INTO THE PAST

Proal's own life experience of nearly dying from microbial infection would inspire a lifetime researching the roots and triggers of chronic illness. She grew up in Mexico City, and as a young girl she was hospitalized for a series of measles, rubella, scarlet fever, and pneumonia infections. She barely survived. Her slew of encephalitic infections appeared to quiet down, and she grew into a successful high school athlete, later captaining the school's tennis team. While an undergraduate at Georgetown University, though, some sort of illness began to plague her. The illness left her bedridden for eight months, unable to tolerate light or sound. Doctors at the school's health center couldn't figure it out, and she barely pulled off graduating.

"I just started, when I could, to read about infections and slowly, slowly try to understand if any of the infections that I'd had might have contributed to my case because I didn't know what could have happened," Proal said.

She began reaching out to longstanding researchers studying infections and launched into a series of experimental treatments supporting her immune system along with pulse antibiotics to wear down bacterial infection and "a huge number of antivirals." She got herself back up and functioning and was eventually the lead author of a paper in *Immunologic Research* on immuno-stimulation in the treatment of ME/CFS. That experience propelled her to pursue her PhD in microbiology and polish the lens through which she observed the infectious roots of complex illness.

She formed the PolyBio Research Foundation with Harvard neuroscientist Michael VanElzakker, who had a close friend with a similar story to Proal's. Their constant observation of symptoms—of close friends and those in patient networks—helps them generate new hypotheses. "One of these things that both Mike and I do is we actually just listen and talk to the patients that we know in our lives and on Twitter. That's a huge part of how we come up with what we're going to study."

In 2019, *before* the pandemic, Proal reached out to South African scientist Resia Pretorius, a leader in the field of blood clotting who had conducted research into how clotting was connected to diabetes and related conditions. Proal was impressed by Pretorius' work showing how platelets activated in response to bacteria and viruses. So, she wanted to study how proteins from enteroviruses and herpesviruses activated platelets and contributed to clotting in ME/CFS patients' blood.

"While we were working to get that off the ground, Covid started. So Resia's team started to look at clotting in acute Covid and Long Covid, and I just jumped in pretty quickly," she said. "Ironically, that Long Covid data was out before the ME/CFS data, but they just started to find *clear* microclots in the blood of basically every Long Covid subject analyzed, which is pretty rare, and puts them in the mind of some researchers as potentially the first bio-marker for Long Covid."

Pretorius and her team found the microclots by looking at long haulers' blood under a fluorescence microscope, using techniques not widely available in conventional medical settings.

Under normal circumstances, blood should form clots if you cut your finger. The clots would soon break up via a process called fibrinolysis. But in many Long Covid patients, they found, the tiny clots didn't break up, and inflammatory molecules were trapped inside them, where they could avoid detection in routine blood tests that made deeply distressed patients come up looking healthy. The molecules that help break down clots were stuck inside the clots themselves.

"A regular doctor or clinical center is not going to be able to see the clots, so you have to go through a series of steps to make them show up in your sample. They published that in their paper, so teams can replicate that now," Proal explained.

The next step involved training other research teams to find the clots in a variety of different ways, for instance using the lab technique called flow cytometry, which filters the blood down and measures characteristics of the sample, and some groups showed success in detecting the clots that way in addition to microscopy.

"If you know how to find them, it's not very hard," Proal told me. "So it's not a dream that you could go to a Long Covid clinical care center and that they could have a little lab where they could look for the clots."

The sticky blood has more trouble flowing throughout the body. The South African researchers found a strong signal in those with post-Covid symptoms who improved after a month of treatment with a protocol that included antiplatelet and anticoagulant drugs, as well as proton pump inhibitor. That also led the team toward looking into apheresis treatments, a process similar to dialysis, which clears out harmful molecules from the blood. The apheresis process is expensive and would require continual visits to a clinic with the right equipment for patients to continue experiencing positive effects, but if the initial case studies lead to positive results in randomized control trials, it could become a more mainstream option.

But it's not just the here and now Proal and researchers like her worry about. The brain damage in long haulers could lead to dramatic increases in dementia, Alzheimer's, and Parkinson's, fitting an emergent consensus about the infectious roots of many brain diseases. "The idea that the brain is sterile and that it's not infected is falling. It's just crumbling," Proal said. Now that we know SARS-CoV-2 infects the brain directly and is persistent in tissues long after the acute illness is over, this fact opens the door to other questions about what happens to infection in the brain long term.

What was once a fringe theory that viruses might contribute to devastating neurodegenerative diseases like Alzheimer's is now gaining mainstream traction. In 2018, scientist Leslie Norins offered $1 million to any scientist who could demonstrate that Alzheimer's disease was caused by a germ. "There's all kinds of connections between existing virus and neurodegenerative disease," Proal said. After all, no one believed *Heliobacter pylori* triggered stomach ulcers and many could not have guessed that Epstein-Barr virus was a precursor for multiple sclerosis, two facts we now accept. In the case of Alzheimer's disease, which accounts for 60 to 70 percent of all dementia, the "amyloid beta hypothesis," which postulates that toxic plaques consisting of amyloid beta protein and noxious tangles of tau proteins damage neurons and cause widespread brain inflammation, accounting for the devastating symptoms. While there was generally a consensus around this hypothesis for years, the field has stumbled in its efforts to break apart the plaques and tangles in a manner that significantly relieves symptoms of the disease, leaving the cohort of researchers scratching their heads.

As interest in what's known as the "infection theory" has grown, many researchers are beginning to understand that the two theories are not mutually exclusive. "Overall, amyloid beta seems to act as part of the innate immune response toward infection in brain tissue and is highly conserved, which usually means it's been selected for and it's continued to occur because it has a function," says Proal. One group of experiments led by Ruth Itzhaki, now an emeritus professor at the University of Manchester in the UK, in the 1990s hypothesized that repeated reactivation of a herpesvirus, HSV-1, was causing the buildup of amyloid plaques in patient's brains. The researchers found that the viral infection *and* the presence of the APOE4 gene variant led to a significant increase in Alzheimer's risk. One without the other: not so much. Although originally met with suspicion, this finding has been replicated many times over.

Although no single lab won the $1 million reward for identifying the sole microbe implicated in causing Alzheimer's disease, Itzhaki's group split the prize with seven other researchers who identified six different infectious agents in the brains of Alzheimer's patients. With six different microbes identified in the brains of these subjects, it's possible multiple agents can cause what we refer to as Alzheimer's disease. If this is the case, Alzheimer's might come to be known as an "umbrella" term, indicating an infection in the brain. Much like pneumonia or diarrhea, the condition might be treatable in its symptomology as well as at its infectious origin. Interestingly, a large study in 2018 showed that treatment with antivirals was associated with a reduced risk of dementia in those carrying the herpes simplex virus. Other studies have found that a herpes zoster infection (also known as shingles) is associated with increased risk of dementia, and that the bacterium associated with gum disease, *Porphyromonas gingivalis*, may trigger the accumulation of

amyloid beta. Coronaviruses, including SARS-CoV-2, are neu-
rotropic, meaning they are capable on infecting the nervous system. So is not a far stretch then to wonder if SARS-CoV-2 could
predispose a population of survivors to increased dementia risk.
"Why wouldn't SARS coronavirus be one of those viruses?"
Proal pondered. The tide is undoubtedly turning, at least in
scientific circles. An international consortium, made up of the
Alzheimer's Association and representatives from more than
twenty-five countries, are exploring the long-term consequences
of SARS-CoV-2 on the brain. With technical guidance from the
World Health Organization, this large team of interdisciplinary
researchers will examine the underlying biology that may contribute to Alzheimer's and other dementias.

EVOLUTIONARY CUES

Underneath all of it, though, there's the ever-present hope that
many principles might be distilled into one, that there might be a
singular way to conceptualize the magnificent assault on our bodies. In many ways, Long Covid and these types of infection-associated chronic diseases haven't been solved because of how and
where we are looking. The right observations haven't been performed to build the foundation of the scientific house yet.

"The problem is that the scientific method is not 'hypothesis, test' which is what the NIH does," Ron Davis says. "The
actual scientific process is 'observation, hypothesis, test.'" Charles
Darwin didn't come up with the theory of evolution by sitting at
his desk: "He went around and observed things, saw evolution
actually happening, and then began to ask why. So that's why you
don't want to sit and come up with a hypothesis in a very abstract
way. You'd like it to be based on an observation, and sometimes

the observation can be the nature of the disease, and ME/CFS affects so many different things. But you want to go deeper than that, and the best way to do that in my opinion is by collecting molecular data. Then ask why in the world is this high or low? Then you can begin to explore."

Starting something completely new is much harder than piggybacking off an existing research agenda—for instance, the data generated by ongoing cancer research offers fodder for future cancer grants. Incremental science is possible when there's a foundation from which to build. But the Human Genome Project had been different. It propelled a revolution in biology, stemming from a soaring strength that it didn't have a hypothesis. The giant data-gathering endeavor almost by definition had to be nothing more than an exercise in observation. There was no past agenda to build on. It was all brand new. With a map of every gene in the human body, scientists could later systematically discern what each of them might do.

Through the lens of genetics and molecular biology, diseases like Long Covid and ME/CFS take shape a bit differently as we tip into the substantial question of "why?" Genetics research begs to understand questions around evolution and selective pressure or why certain organisms have either a survival benefit or disadvantage. At first glance, this presents a paradox for disease states, especially ones where behavior is so greatly affected. Afterall, how could someone who is bedbound—unable to care for themselves let alone bear children—survive and successfully pass their genes onto the next generation? Perhaps the genetic mistake that allowed for an ME/CFS-like state to survive 100,000 years in humans doesn't manifest before childbearing age, therefore one might successfully pass their genes onto the next generation before succumbing to one's illness.

On the other hand, what advantage might chronic diseases give people in terms of survival?

Ron Davis suggests the disease state witnessed in conditions such as Long Covid or ME/CFS could have been caused by an organism needing to rest. He is convinced that there may be a set of genes that can trigger ME/CFS. From one point of view, there's an evolutionary basis that the sickness behavior triggered by an infectious agent is a signal for an organism to rest and allow the immune system to kick in and heal the organism. However, rather than serving as a temporary adaptive state, the system could shift for some reason into permanent dysfunction. Other animals, like bears, bees, and snakes, exhibit hibernation behavior and retreat into a power-down mode where only the essential bodily functions are maintained for long periods of time. This mode of operation allows the animal to survive extremely harsh conditions. University of California at San Diego researcher and Davis' collaborator Robert K. Naviaux found that people with ME/CFS show markedly slowed metabolism and suggests that this state is similar to a "dauer state" seen in nematode worms exposed to life-threatening conditions like starvation or toxins.

Although some animals bear resemblance to one another, Davis is suspicious of one transforming into a meaningful model of the disease. "I don't know if we'll ever find an animal model that is a decent model for ME/CFS. If a mouse comes down with ME/CFS it's only probably a matter of hours before it gets eaten," Davis said. In most cases, given an atmosphere in which only the fittest survive, natural selection would weed out those with disabilities who couldn't easily survive solely on their own. "We're a tribal sort of organism," he explained. "We'll take care of one other. That's been one of our strengths. We populated the world because of this intelligent way to take care of people, with a moral standard that we have to take care of everybody."

One thing is clear, despite our genes or because of them, humans are in a unique position to lean into our prosocial behavior as it surrounds the more vulnerable in our society. As Long Covid leaves millions with potentially lifelong physical and cognitive disabilities, it requires building out the social systems that take care of disabled people.

Chapter 14

A NEW EPIDEMIC OF DISABILITY

WITH MILLIONS OF PEOPLE EXPERIENCING long-term complications from Covid-19, the disease could cause decades of strain on our healthcare system, insurance industry, and federal safety net programs.

Figuring out exactly how Long Covid warps the economy and the labor market is a complex set of questions, which economists are only beginning to determine. The answer will be a function of how many people are sick, how sick they are, how long they stay sick, and the cost of medical interventions, assuming there are treatments that work. Finally, there's the cost of subsistence for families when Long Covid makes the primary wage earner too disabled to work. We do have some comparisons about the effect at scale. A 2015 study cited ME/CFS as causing an annual $17 to 24 billion impact on the U.S. economy in lost wages and inability to work.

In March 2021, the Body Politic's Fiona Lowenstein co-wrote a *New York Times* opinion piece with the PLRC's Hannah Davis. They argued that Long Covid could represent "one of the largest mass disabling events in modern history." The piece culminated what could be considered a trilogy of agenda-setting op-eds by Lowenstein, beginning with the piece telling the story of being hospitalized with Covid-19 at age twenty-six and the second article published a month later with the chronicle of prolonged recovery. This third essay, timed as the second year of the pandemic was getting underway, was prescient as well. Davis and Lowenstein benefitted from daily conversations with chronically ill patients whose lives were upended and could articulate a stark reality before it dawned on others. Public health authorities constantly reported on case counts, hospitalizations, and deaths. However, public dashboards displaying all kinds of pandemic data did not have any way of keeping track of how many people were failing to fully recover, the pair explained. The CDC didn't directly track that type of record.

For reference, polio was disabling about 35,000 people per year in the 1940s in the U.S. at a time when parents feared letting their children outside during the summer months. As of late April 2022, an estimated 81 million Americans had tested positive for the coronavirus, per the CDC's tracker. If a conservative 10 percent had symptoms lasting more than three months, that would mean nearly eight million had a chronic illness. If only 1 percent of them became disabled, that would indicate 800,000 Americans had been disabled within two years of the virus first being identified in China.

But the CDC knew from the PLRC's published study of Body Politic Slack group members that a large number of their members reported they hadn't been able to return to work, and many were being denied disability benefits.

British statistics offered a more detailed snapshot. Across the pond, British scientist Nisreen Alwan, an associate professor at the University of Southampton, had been campaigning with a similar pitch, expressed in the Twitter hashtag #CountLongCovid.

More than one in ten respondents reported symptoms twelve weeks after testing positive for Covid, according to a study by the nation's Office of National Statistics.

In its effort to track the post-acute sequelae of Covid, the American Academy of Physical Medicine and Rehabilitation eventually released its own PASC dashboard. On any given day, you could set the parameters on its dashboard for a given long-term symptom percentage rate. The algorithm then spits out how many new Covid long haulers were generated that day. If the total U.S. case count was 148,000, and the rate was 10 percent, then there were going to be 14,800 new Long Covid cases. But such a tool was a far cry from actionable information with its inputs based on estimates rather than a real-world count. Public health officials were largely blind because doctors and public health departments had no way of officially reporting Long Covid cases.

In June 2021, Davis and McCorkell presented the PLRC findings to a meeting of the White House Covid Health Equity Task Force. Among their recommendations was creating a federal short term disability program. A year of volunteer advocacy appeared to be paying off when the federal government recognized that Long Covid could be considered under the Americans with Disabilities Act.

"Many Americans who seemingly recover from the virus still face lingering challenges, like breathing problems, brain fog, chronic pain, and fatigue," President Joe Biden said in a Rose Garden speech, marking the thirty-first anniversary of the ADA.

"We're bringing agencies together to make sure Americans with Long Covid, who have a disability, have access to the rights and resources that are due under the disability law," he said.

In coordination, a host of executive branch agencies, including the Health and Human Services, the Department of Justice, and the Department of Labor, released their own guidance and resources supporting long haulers. This ensured that employers would be required to provide accommodations such as modified equipment or work schedules.

Biden touted the initiative as the "first of its kind" to address the new disease, designed for long haulers "so they can live their lives in dignity." The policies were largely a reiteration of existing law, but still the public acknowledgment from the White House was powerful, prompting a statement from Body Politic praising the move.

Lisa McCorkell, the public policy expert in the Patient-Led Research Collaborative, noted in the Body Politic statement that the official buy-in from the federal government would help reduce the "self-advocacy burden" long haulers felt in navigating access to accommodations and services.

Approval to receive full disability benefits through the Social Security Administration in the U.S. is a tall order. While some medical conditions offer instant approval, many aren't so easy. Proving that you qualify for disability means showing that your health condition has made, or is expected to make, it impossible to work for twelve months. Most applicants are denied on their first attempt. The U.S. doesn't offer a federal program for short-term disability benefits. Most European nations offer universal paid leave policies and more generous healthcare policies.

Absent a wonder drug, the most effective therapy for Long Covid and similar conditions is rest. Profound rest. That's not easy if you have to work in order to pay rent, care for elderly parents, or have young mouths to feed.

That's why McCorkell and the PLRC included a federal short-term disability plan in their presentation to the White House Covid Equity Task Force. Because exertion can worsen symptoms and lead to disability, essentially all the patients I spoke to for this book felt that those who had the relative privilege of resting for as long as possible—rather than being forced back to work—had at least a better shot of trying to prevent some of the worst harms the illness could inflict.

When physicians make a diagnosis they must plug in an insurance code, which all hail from the International Classification of Diseases (ICD). The system holds immense power because whether or not a doctor is willing to make a diagnosis can hinge on whether an insurance company will pay for a particular appointment or treatment. The specificity of the codes can get a bit absurd. For instance, there's the code W55.41XA, for "bitten by a pig, initial encounter." If you're struck by a duck, your doctor can file that under W61.62XD, and there are other codes if the offender is a cow or a macaw. If you happen to be injured in a spacecraft collision, that's V95.43XS. You're covered by a separate code if you get hit by a roller skater on the street. And it's hard to imagine what prompted the creation of a code for "burn due to water skis on fire, subsequent encounter," but your doctor's office can file a claim for you if it happens to you, too.

There were codes for suspected Covid exposure or for the rare multisystem inflammatory disease in children, but for more than a year, long haulers existed in a kind of bureaucratic no-man's land. On October 1, 2021, the ICD-10 code U09.9 went live, enabling reimbursement for "Post-Covid-19 condition, unspecified." The tweak vastly simplified the process by which patients navigated the labyrinthine insurance system and helped protect them from unexpected bills. Lisa McCorkell, from the Patient-Led Research Collaborative, ran point on representing Long Covid patients' interest in the discussions with the WHO and CDC.

Less than a week after the ICD-10 code rolled out, the World Health Organization published its case definition for "post-

Covid conditions," criteria which could be used universally for diagnostic or research purposes to identify who had the disease. This distinction matters, injecting authority and clarity into the pandemic fog of war. The WHO unified around a list of symptoms, including cognitive dysfunction, fatigue, and breathlessness, which lasted more than three months after the initial onset and had an impact on everyday functioning. Seventeen global experts had served on the WHO's working group, including the PLRC's Hannah Davis, filling the agency's new expert category of "patient-researcher."

Disease case definitions formalize whole scientific fields, ensuring everyone is referring to the same illness in the same way. When the definition was approved, some had lived with the symptoms fitting the criteria for fifteen months, a seeming eternity. But in the history of disease, the mobilization and consensus was lightning-fast. By contrast, a similar process for HIV/AIDS had required nearly four years, with the first human immunodeficiency virus case being identified in June 1981, researchers coalescing around the name of "acquired immune deficiency syndrome" in September 1982, and the WHO's AIDS case definition being released in October 1985.

AN UNREADY SAFETY NET

Patient advocates could shine a light on the new disease and help implement changes to healthcare systems, but the deterioration of their own bodies defied what bureaucracies were even capable of addressing.

For instance, after nineteen months without an income, Karyn Bishof, a co-founder of the Long Covid Alliance, was denied disability coverage for her Long Covid case at the end of September 2021.

The terse notice from the Social Security Administration stated, "While you are not capable of performing work you have done in the past, you are able to perform work that is less demanding." The single mom from Boca Raton, Florida disagreed. Given the variable nature of her unyielding symptoms, it was impossible to schedule a reliable hour or two in which she could work a job. Even if she could, she worried that attempting to work while so chronically ill would drive her health down below the basic motherly requirements of caring for her twelve-year-old son Jayani. There was no way of predicting when she would have physical ability or cogent thoughts. She hadn't been healthy enough to work for more than a year and a half after falling ill with Covid in the first wave. The timing of her illness was particularly cruel, coming after Bishof had completed two years of training to become a firefighter and paramedic. She had envisioned 2020 as a culmination of a lifelong dream that she'd put off for years as she raised her son. But it was not to be.

Prior to Covid, she worked out five days a week doing high-intensity interval training. Now she needed to spend as many as twenty hours a day in bed. She relied on her son to take their dog out, and to sweep, mop, wash dishes, and help with grocery shopping. Jayani was proud to contribute.

"Originally, before Covid, I did a fair amount, but I feel like I have a lot more responsibility now," he said. "I have to step up."

With Bishof's POTS symptoms, it was a titanic effort to walk upright for more than ten minutes before her heart rate skyrocketed and she had trouble staying conscious, so she and her son divided grocery store aisles between the two of them when they bought food. Some days she had to stay in the car while he made the rounds for her.

"I fight so hard so that I can also get better. But I'm really fighting for my son to have his mom because it really is just me and him in this whole world," she told me.

Bishof had thrived in the intense environment of firefighter training, pushing through injuries to graduate. But Long Covid was a vastly more brutal test of the body and soul. Among her dozens of symptoms were debilitating migraines that left her hiding under blankets for a day, insomnia that limited her sleep to a few hours each night, and inexplicable rashes on her arms. Constant nausea made it difficult to down her meds or eat more than one meal a day. When Bishof went out for doctor's appointments, she packed blankets and pillows in the car so she could rest before the drive home.

She couldn't earn her $55,000 salary. And she couldn't qualify for unemployment checks, because the program require certification that one is *capable* of working. She wasn't. With no one else to turn to, Bishof had to make do with food stamps as well as temporary cash assistance from the state of Florida that amounted to $158 per month. The cash assistance was still a few dollars short of paying the monthly power bill, and was thousands of dollars less than their other monthly expenses. Despite managing to raise a little over $2,000 online with a GoFundMe campaign, it wasn't enough, and being denied for disability meant falling one step further toward homelessness. In the coming months, there could be a lien on her house. It wasn't hard to envision the water or power being turned off, and she worried that child protective services might intervene to take her son.

"When I turn fourteen, I'm looking for jobs that I can do over the summer," Jayani, a seventh grader, told me. "I've been waiting to do a grocery store job where I'm a bag boy—I would be a really good bag boy—to just earn a little bit of income for us, because we don't get much income. No income at all really."

He played on a travel team where he'd met most of his closest friends, and he said he dreamed of becoming a professional soccer player. Given how high his civics grades were, and how much he liked reading history, his mom thought he ought to be a politician.

"You got to hope whoever's in charge of this actually wants to help," Jayani told me. "The long haulers aren't really being listened to. They all want this to be researched because it might be the key to getting rid of most of their stuff. I don't think there's going to be a cure for all of Long Covid, but I think there are going to be ways to bring it down so it's not as severe and there are ways to get people back to their normal lives."

If he did run for office one day, telling his mother's story of fighting through bureaucracy might carry the poetry of a stump speech that could win votes. There was heartbreaking irony in how Bishof, herself a national leader in the long hauler advocacy community, was falling through the cracks in the social safety net. That voluntary work, informed by her background studying health promotions and exercise science in college and fueled by a sense of desperation to get her own life back, carried the promise of benefiting millions of people.

Shortly after falling ill, Bishof created the Covid-19 Longhauler Advocacy Project. Later, she co-founded the Long Covid Alliance. Among her extensive list of contributions, she helped seed online support groups all over the country, built a comprehensive care guide for patients and medical providers, provided input to Congress for legislation to help long haulers, and consulted with the NIH as it designed its research initiatives for post-Covid conditions.

"I have a unique position in both being a patient, but also having health care experience and research experience. My background allows me to kind of take the best of both worlds—

the messaging of both worlds—and relay them to the other side," she said.

Knowing the long odds, Bishof had tried to be strategic, waiting to file her disability application until April 2021, once she could document a full twelve months of disability. She couldn't list all of her diagnoses in the online form, but she included her post-Covid conditions as postural orthostatic tachycardia syndrome, myalgic encephalomyelitis/chronic fatigue syndrome, fibromyalgia, chronic migraines, autoimmune disease, post-traumatic stress disorder, and Ehlers-Danlos syndrome. The notice from the SSA showed that the agency had received documentation from seven out of the more than twenty doctors Bishof had seen.

Because of the multisystem nature of her conditions, she needed care from a complex list of specialists—a rheumatologist, an endocrinologist, a migraine specialist, a geneticist, and a motility specialist, to name a few. Some had waiting lists as long as eight months. Her physicians collectively had made no progress in developing treatment plans. The delays in arriving at adequate care and the mounting medical bills left her under severe financial stress while she ate through her savings and her health worsened. She was caught up in a vicious cycle. She needed an attorney to be able to fight her case and win her appeal for disability with the Social Security Administration. But because she couldn't work, she couldn't afford to hire a lawyer. All of her energy for a whole day might be sucked up by a single phone call or one appointment. And even with an attorney, if her case required a hearing, that might mean waiting another year to get through the backlog of cases. Meanwhile her expertise within patient, medical, and policymaker communities didn't offer any tangible direction either.

"I don't know one person—one long hauler—who's been accepted for disability post-Covid," she said.

Unfortunately, it's not a surprise that Bishof and other long haulers like her would be denied the coverage. The program's eligibility criteria are notably stringent. The rolls are kept tight by design. The Social Security Disability Insurance program, created in 1956 under President Dwight Eisenhower, is funded by payroll taxes taken out of workers' paychecks each month. Applicants are required to have worked for at least a quarter of their adult lives and at least five of the last ten years. They must have medical documentation that they've already been disabled and incapable of gainful employment for at least twelve months or expect to be. And they must then endure a waiting period of another five months before receiving their determination. Decisions are based on medical documentation of an individual's functionality, regardless of diagnosis.

To be accepted, applicants must show that they can't perform "substantial gainful activity," meaning they are unable to hold down a job earning $1,350 monthly, or $16,200 annually. And still, those who do qualify aren't winning a golden ticket: Nine in ten beneficiaries receive $2,000 or less per month, consigning them to a life below the federal poverty level and short of affording market rate rent. Those criteria—which put the U.S. among the strictest of developed nations—mean that just 34 percent of applicants ultimately win benefits, either on their first try or on their appeal, according to the Center on Budget and Policy Priorities.

Further, poverty rates and ill health are still high among those denied coverage, according to a 2014 analysis published in the *Journal of Disability Policy Studies*, a fact that reinforces how strict the requirements truly are. Most people who do end up qualifying for benefits are so significantly disabled that they'll stay on the program for life. So far, Bishof felt like she was just a statistic in a larger tidal wave of disability threatening to overload the system.

"I wish that I could say that it would happen sooner rather than later. But I think it's gonna come years down the road when they start realizing how so many people unable to work affects the economy," she told me. "And I think that they're going to unfortunately only care about Long Covid when it comes down to the numbers versus the experiences of those people."

If a substantial number of Covid long haulers don't recover and return to work, the sheer size of their population represents a substantial risk to the workforce. In 2020, just over 8 million U.S. workers were Social Security disability beneficiaries. With the median age of Long Covid occurring around middle age, the heart of the disease burden falls on people at the prime of their working lives.

LONG HAULERS DISRUPT THE SYSTEM

"Covid long haulers represent the largest influx of new entrants to the disability community in modern history," according to Rebecca Vallas, a senior fellow at the Century Foundation. "Evidence suggests that between three million and ten million Americans may now have Long Covid. These are just wildly, wildly large numbers for a system that is already not handling the existing population seeking to access these benefits. This is a system that wasn't prepared even before the pandemic."

Vallas began her career in the 2000s as a legal aid attorney in Philadelphia representing people who had been denied disability benefits right out of law school. The job left a mark on her. She had to counsel her low-income clients that being denied on the first attempt was part of the system. "The human consequences are absolutely dire," she explained. Without an income, disabled people often exhausted their savings, lost their homes when they couldn't pay mortgages, and could be reduced to living out of their cars.

"Thousands of people die every single year when they are waiting for disability benefits," she said. "Those are statistics that might be a gut punch at one level when you hear them in the abstract, but I saw this firsthand more times than I can count—and certainly more times than I would like to remember—during my legal aid days because I was representing someone who didn't have enough resources to meet human survival needs."

Those experiences motivated her to become an advocate working on public policy reform in Washington. Working for the Center for American Progress, she helped launch the think tank's Disability Justice Initiative, and frequently testified in front of Congress about disability and poverty issues, working to defend the SSA from budget cuts.

"I can tell you we have made it incredibly, incredibly difficult to access what are literally survival benefits," she told me. "We make people jump through a maze of Kafkaesque hoops and fill out a mountain of paperwork that honestly is complex even for lawyers. And all of that is to access incredibly modest benefits."

Add to that the fact that during the pandemic, the SSA's 1,200 field offices were closed—blocking access for on-demand or walk-in services of particular need for those with low incomes, no incomes, mental health issues, or limited English proficiency needing to file applications and fix bureaucratic errors. It contributed to historically unprecedented declines of 25 percent fewer people receiving benefits across all disabilities.

For Covid long haulers, though, the process could seem even more impossible. Some people did present with specific, concrete, anatomical damage that could be verified with objective medical documentation. But there wasn't a basic blood test for Long Covid that could furnish that type of objective proof to SSA's satisfaction. Even if patients could find a specialist who understood the condition, they were often jam-packed and overbooked.

"One of the opportunities of this moment is a paradigm shift when it comes to how our society understands the concept of disability. That's true in the disability system as we're talking about how many are wrongfully denied because they don't fit into the Social Security Administration's mold for how they recognize disability," Vallas told me. "But that's true even more broadly, given that we have for so long portrayed disability as a person in a wheelchair or with a physical disability. Now we've got chronic illness in the spotlight in a way that has not happened in quite some time, if ever, at this scale. And we have a paradigm shift away from disbelief and gaslighting. We should move away from a program that's designed to deny people and been so defined by the 'makers, takers, fakers' mythology towards one that is intended to be there for people in their time of need, and, dare I say, that is actually accessible."

One way Vallas and disability advocates hoped to improve access was through setting up a "navigators" program to help people find their way through the byzantine system, similar to those created by the Affordable Care Act for buying health insurance in the marketplace. Another area of low hanging fruit for reform would be to pass legislation eliminating the mandatory five-month waiting period to receive SSDI benefits and the additional twenty-four-month period recipients must wait before they can obtain health coverage through Medicare. And even adjusting programs for inflation—and tagged to the federal poverty level—would be a step up from the status quo. If people could get approved from day one, without needing to wait years to win an appeal at a hearing, then they could dodge at least some of the descent into poverty and have a better shot at a dignified life.

As many as 1.6 million jobs in the U.S. could be unfilled due to Long Covid, according to an analysis by Katie Bach, a non-resident senior fellow at the Brookings Institution. After a year and a half of pandemic, hordes of workers quit their jobs, in a steady mass migration seeking out new opportunities that would become known as the Great Resignation. The result was a historic U.S. labor shortage, an unusual economy characterized not by too few jobs, but by too few workers. Many were pursuing better working conditions or seeking out new dreams.

But 31 million working-age Americans were likely somewhere on the spectrum of Long Covid, either with some lingering symptoms or a more intense disabling illness. Therefore, about 15 percent of the ongoing workforce problem could be due to long haulers unable to continue working or who needed to work fewer hours due to their illness or disability, she argued, citing the PLRC's peer-reviewed research showing that about a quarter of long haulers in their study were no longer working. To be conservative, Bach assumed that a third of Long Covid patients stayed sick for about three months, such that as many as 4.5 million long haulers were sick at any given time during the pandemic. If about a quarter of them couldn't work, that meant that at any point some 1.1 million Americans were not working due to Long Covid. Further, another study had showed that 46 percent long haulers had needed to reduce their hours at work, enlarging the impact to 1.6 million full-time equivalent workers.

Getting an accurate snapshot of the actual labor impact is a question encumbered by the instruments that economists use to collect data. Just as there are limits in how quickly biomedical science can ask the right questions and publish quality literature about a new disease, economists also have their hands tied in trying to immediately characterize the sheer mass pall that condition casts across individual lives and fortunes. Building those questions into surveys is the most robust way to ensure long haulers get counted from a labor perspective. The most responsive tool is the U.S. Census Bureau's Household Pulse Survey, a twenty-minute online questionnaire, Bach explains. Its question structure asking about employment status doesn't carve out a space to specifically capture Long Covid as the reason for not working, giving respondents an option to say they were sick with coronavirus symptoms, or that they are sick or disabled with something other than the coronavirus. The average Long Covid patient would likely feel that either of those categories didn't apply to them. The Census Bureau's monthly Current Population Survey, a more rigorous assessment, has a similar issue in that long haulers might fall through the cracks.

Bach advocated for the Census Bureau to work with the NIH research teams and patient advocacy groups to write questions that could meaningfully collect information on the number of people disabled by Long Covid, the average time not working or needing reduced hours, the workplace accommodations they would need to get back to work.

"Until we have data from a representative sample that accurately capture the extent of the impacts to the labor force, economists and policymakers are likely not going to consider Long Covid an economic issue or recognize it for the mass disabling event that it is," Lisa McCorkell said.

In April 2022, a team of researchers organized by the Solve Long Covid Alliance published a white paper with the most thorough estimate yet of Long Covid's economic impact to the U.S. It based its assumptions off data that between 7 million and

14 million Americans, amounting to 2.3 percent and 4.4 percent of the population respectively, had experienced or were experiencing disabling Long Covid through January 2022. If so, the total impact to the U.S. economy ranged from $386 billion to $511 billion, as the disease prevented many from returning to the workforce as their previous selves.

The researchers argued that the mass disabling event highlighted the a "need for changes to the structure of U.S. disability benefit programs as demand exponentially increases." Postviral disability was not an immutable state. The disability caused by Long Covid was waxing and waning, such that employees might be capable of working one day and incapable the next. They called for disability benefits systems to recognize partial disability. Further, they called for systems to drop caps on earnings, which counterproductively can create barriers preventing those who are capable of working from entering back into the workforce part-time or with accommodations during periods in which their symptoms were less severe. Creating a stable post-Covid workforce meant providing incentives for employers and employees to work together to support rehabilitation of workers with post-Covid health conditions and to accommodate the large number of workers likely to be experiencing disabilities.

That number of workers affected was jaw-dropping, in part because it was in range with the total number of workers, 8 million, who had lost their jobs during the lowest parts of the Great Recession in 2008. If the totally amount of disability veered toward the higher end of their projection, then the resulting socioeconomic impact would be "seismic" in scope.

Chapter 15

THE EPATIENT REVOLUTION AND CROWDSOURCING RESEARCH

SUSANNAH FOX WAS ONE OF the people most stunned by the resilience and resourcefulness of Long Covid patients.

"We are watching patients, caregivers, clinicians, researchers, and policymakers move through the stages of peer-to-peer health innovation at a fast clip," she wrote in a blog post about Long Covid patient activism in January 2021. "Faster than I've ever seen in my twenty years of tracking this phenomenon."

She is the type of person you'd want to impress, as someone who is uniquely qualified to spot patients changing the world. From 2015 to 2017, Fox had led health innovation efforts as the Chief Technology Officer for the U.S. Department of Health and Human Services. She rose to that position after a career charting the ways people diagnosed with life-altering diseases had built and leveraged online communities to share hard-won wisdom not available anywhere else, track symptoms, pool their data, and generally take back control of their own destinies.

She was used to seeing a specific storyline across diseases. Patients began with feeling isolated and alone. Then they discover a group, develop a sense of identity or pride with their new community, and then eventually spearhead a project to fix what they perceive as broken in a health system. Here, she was seeing a group innovating before the world even knew the condition existed.

During her time in the federal government, Fox had been impressed by the work of the Cajun Navy, an informal group of volunteers and boat owners who banded together to rescue people stranded in their homes following devastating flooding in the aftermath of Hurricanes Katrina and Harvey. Credited with saving thousands of lives, they served in areas where the government's emergency response was spread too thin. Their heroism prompted the Federal Emergency Management Agency to coordinate with them as part of a whole community approach to disaster response.

As Covid-19 tore through society and misinformation became rampant, Fox wondered if a digital health version of the Cajun Navy could activate in support of pandemic response, particularly with a citizen brigade who could help aid not just in disseminating accurate scientific information about the virus, but also in building tools to help patients track symptoms, pointing people in the right direction to get care, and even organizing the science themselves. Just as the Cajun Navy blurred the line between citizen and first responder, she thought there could be a similar model for tapping into people's existing skill sets to enlist them directly in public health. In particular, those who had been infected themselves might have the most useful firsthand experience to offer others newly getting sick. The answer was in organic peer-to-peer health communities, and the PLRC was the most effective version she had ever seen.

Fox's life story made her perfectly poised to understand the significance of what they had accomplished. A self-described "Internet geologist," Fox was instrumental in creating the original website for *US News and World Report* in 1995, eventually working her way up to becoming its lead online editor. She then spent a decade and a half with the Pew Research Center, helping start its Internet and American Life Project focusing on health and technology.

Early in that role, around the turn of the millennium, she met Dr. Tom Ferguson, a Yale-trained physician who believed in the power of patients to contribute not just to their own well-being, but to scientific discovery as well. Though he had never practiced medicine, he wrote prolifically, serving as the medical editor of the counterculture magazine *Whole Earth Catalog* and representing a strain of self-sufficiency within the hippie movement. Its articles focused on how to build your own house, plant your own garden, and nurture your own health to prevent disease. Once you were diagnosed with a serious disease, self-reliance became less possible because doctors had a huge information advantage in the days before the Internet. Ferguson championed a more equal doctor-patient relationship. He felt doctors ought to collaborate with patients, rather than command them. He coined the term "e-patient" to describe empowered or expert patients who didn't just take greater control of their own healthcare but who actively built new platforms or communities or devices that could change the larger system.

HANGING OUT WITH COWBOYS AND REBELS TO SEE THE FUTURE FASTER

Ferguson's concepts would come to fuel the rest of Fox's career. Her research leveraged the power of Pew's research methodology to get a broad view of the national population. That data outlined details such as the number of households with Internet access or which types of people searched for health information online. She combined that with field work in which she interviewed members of early online patient communities.

"I would go into a certain patient community and spend time interviewing people, in order to stay in touch with what was being created, what was being built by these pioneers, by these rebels," she told me. "They were often left out of the mainstream conversation about health care because they were living with something rare or life-changing."

She got to know a host of digital health pioneers, including the founder of Psych Central, the first mental health website.

"I began generating reports focused on the evolution of the digital health culture and market every two years. And Tom [Ferguson] was my guide," she told me. "What Tom taught me is that if you hang out with the cowboys and rebels and pioneers, you will see the future faster."

Many of those people weren't typical tech geeks. They plunged into online communities out of sheer desperation. Some of the most avid early adopters of technology were those who were trying to save their own lives or the lives of their children.

"I would learn from these radical patient communities, and I would bring that back and ask questions to start tracking the trends," she said. "It's through them that I saw the real future of healthcare, which is bringing it back into the home, allowing people who are kitchen table innovators to contribute to science and to contribute to medical and assistive device innovation."

As the Internet matured, patients and caregivers developed increasingly sophisticated ways to use digital technology as a tool to share real-world knowledge about treatments and accelerate research or even self-organize their own studies. One key step in the unfolding of the ePatient movement was the launch of the site PatientsLikeMe, founded in 2005. Brothers Jamie and Ben Heywood started the platform in honor of their brother Stephen who was diagnosed with amyotrophic lateral sclerosis in 1998, at the age of twenty-nine. The neurodegenerative disease, commonly known as ALS, famously afflicted baseball great Lou Gehrig and astrophysicist Stephen Hawking, and it can begin with a muscle twitching or weakness in the limbs. It leads to full-body paralysis, affecting the muscles needed to eat, speak, breathe, and eat. It has no known cure and results in death.

Desperate to save or at least prolong Stephen's life, the brothers became citizen scientists, consuming every bit of research and literature they could find about ALS. One of the best resources that could serve their purpose, though, didn't really exist yet. They wanted to mine insights from a trove of data about the lived experiences of others with the disease. For the brothers, that meant building a set of tools on the PatientsLikeMe site— as well as a community of patients using them—to crowdsource that information themselves.

"What PatientsLikeMe offered was an opportunity to at least track data so that the ALS patients together could start to understand the trajectory of the disease in ways that no clinical registry gave them access to," Fox said.

In one example, a small trial in Italy in 2008 showed that the drug lithium carbonate might have an effect on slowing the progression of ALS. That glimmer of hope prompted patients from all over the world to use PatientsLikeMe to self-organize a larger observational study using self-reported data from 348 users on the site. After twelve months the trial ultimately did not show that lithium carbonate was effective in combating the disease, but the way in which the patients had rallied toward finding an answer became a parable for how exasperated patients, who did not have time to wait for traditional scientific methodology, could take research into their own hands. If you're going to be dead before scientists can deliberate about a new standard of care, you've got to invent a new process.

Today, PatientsLikeMe boasts a community of more than 850,000 users representing nearly 3,000 different health conditions, and a track record of generating more than 100 peer-reviewed papers for patients with various diseases.

Another one of the "cowboys" in patient-led innovation was Dave deBronkart, a fifty-six-year-old Boston man working in tech marketing, who was diagnosed with stage IV kidney cancer in 2007. The condition carried a median survival time of just twenty-four weeks. His doctor "prescribed" him an online patient community, the Association of Cancer Online Resources, at ACOR.org, a story deBronkart tells in his 2011 TEDx talk. When he joined the group, he met patients who told him about an uncommon treatment, high-dosage interleukin, not offered in most hospitals and for which there wasn't any information available through government websites. The therapy had only a slim chance of helping, but for deBronkart, that was still vastly preferable to the alternative. He didn't want to ask his daughter and her boyfriend to get "married prematurely, just so you can do it while dad's still alive," he explained to the crowd. The patient experts on ACOR sent him the phone numbers for a few physicians in his area who could prescribe the treatment. It worked: the tumor sizes shrank dramatically when he received the treatments, each two months apart. DeBronkart witnessed his daughter's wedding a year and a half later. He is alive today in 2022 because of a patient community.

But his story accelerated from there. DeBronkart believed that his own experience could serve as part of a greater hive mind and be used to benefit others. If he and other patients could aggregate their anonymized data together, then smart software could comb through it to find patterns that could help lead to early detection or treatments for diseases, including the cancer that had nearly killed him. DeBronkart authorized his hospital to transfer his data to Google Health, which was experimenting with a project by which users could volunteer their health records from various sources to create a central health profile with all their conditions, medications, and lab results in one place. But when he downloaded his electronic health record from the hospital that had saved his life, he found it rife with errors, because the hospital transferred the billing codes rather than his clinical data. That brought up a more fundamental question of whether patients could fully entrust their health to any institution. If medical record data came from patients' own bodies and was collected to further their own health, should they be allowed to have sovereignty over it? DeBronkart's story ended up on the front page of the *Boston Globe* in April 2009.

The ensuing attention catapulted him into a prolific new career as a cancer blogger, speaker, and patient rights activist. That summer, when the organizer of the Medicine 2.0 conference called to ask him the theme of his keynote later that year, deBronkart said, "Gimme my damn data, because you can't be trusted." That phrase became a rallying call for greater patient engagement in transforming the health system. He was elected co-chair of the Society for Participatory Medicine. Known affectionately as "e-Patient Dave," he became one of the most recognized figures in the e-patient movement, evangelizing a mantra that patients are the most underused resource in healthcare.

A few years later, in 2012, another crowdsourced medical platform, called CrowdMed, was formed. As the name suggests, CrowdMed crowd sources knowledge from both health professionals and self-proclaimed citizen "medical detectives" to diagnose challenging and rare disease cases. After debuting its beta testing in Washington, D.C. at TEDMED in 2013, CrowdMed has gone on to raise $2.4 million from investors and worked on more than 1,000 cases. A patient can choose one of three packages and upload their own story, including how the disease has affected their life holistically. Medical detectives might be medical students, curious doctors, patients, or other interested parties. The top three diagnoses are chosen and the detectives can be up-ranked by patient feedback and previous correct diagnoses. The company points to its relatively cheap access to medical knowledge and its self-serve, patient-centered interface as innovations. While some worry about the reliability of the suggested diagnoses being provided, satisfied patients and founder Jared Heyman maintain that when looking for a diagnosis to a challenging or rare disease, many heads are better than one.

Fox explains that getting society to accept a new idea means first fighting back against a prevailing belief that the idea is radically crazy, borrowing a concept from *Wired* magazine co-founder Kevin Kelly's essay "The Natural History of a New Idea." First, the idea is outright wacko, then it's simply odd but unproven. If it has staying power, people begin to see it as true, but insignificant. Finally, in the fourth stage, an idea is simply *obvious*, something all of us knew all along. The framework can be applied to virtually an infinite number of phenomena, from the laws of gravity and the existence of the Americas, onward to the abolition of slavery and the rise of the most recent presidential candidate. The notion that Covid-19 could cause long-term illness might follow a similar rise into the public and scientific consciousness. In this case, Fox said, the progression would be "Crazy. Crazy. Long Covid. Obvious."

She took note of how Body Politic and the Patient-Led Research Collaborative were helping the whole health ecosystem respond quickly to what seemed to many to be a new post-viral syndrome. She reached out to get in touch and help however she could.

"They're super conscious that they're standing on the shoulders of giants, that so many people built things that they are benefiting from," Fox said.

They were a perfect embodiment of how she conceived a peer health innovation pipeline, beginning with a person afflicted with new symptoms and feeling isolated and alone. Finding an online patient community led to connection with others experiencing the same roadblocks and then brainstorming with them about what to do in spite of those issues. Pretty soon the groups were tapping into their existing skills as entrepreneurs to build a solution. Companies, researchers, and government agencies could then partner with the self-organized communities to amplify their signal or scale up a product or process that seemed to support sufferers or treat the disease.

DESIGNING A PATIENT-CENTERED FUTURE

I had first become aware of Fox after I produced *Forgotten Plague* and was selected as an "ePatient Scholar" to attend the Stanford Medicine X conference in 2014. I had no idea of the tradition into which I was entering. On stage, she told stories of how she had led health innovation efforts at the top level of the federal government. I was a barely employed twenty-four-year-old, not long out of college, trying to tell the story of a disease most people had never heard of. Like many, I was managing a flare up of my illness that made it hard to sit through many of the sessions. I spent hours laying in the conference's "wellness" room, which was specifically designed with the knowledge that many of the patients needed that space in order to attend at all.

But I was thrilled to find my tribe of other idealists from across the spectrum of disease attempting their own piece in what the community touted as the "patient-centered revolution" in healthcare. There was Emily Kramer-Golinkoff, in her thirties with late-stage cystic fibrosis, who has now raised $10 million to support potentially life-saving research into her rare form of the disease and been named a White House Champion of Change. Another ePatient, Hugo Campos, also received that honor for his effort to claim ownership of the data in the device embedded in his heart for hypertrophic cardiomyopathy, which delivers a life-saving electric shock if (and when) the disease sends him into cardiac arrest. I also met Julie Flygare, who developed narcolepsy in law school before going on to write a memoir about the condition and build a non-profit organization that awards scholarships to students with narcolepsy. Their stories, too numerous to list, filled my cup, spurring me into a bolder vision.

Our group of several dozen ePatient Scholars was given reserved seating in the front rows and the majority of the priority speaking slots, which were staged with all the majesty and vulnerability of a TED event. Each ePatient was doing seemingly impossible work to rebuild or reform medicine in ways that centered and celebrated the human experience of illness.

Susannah Fox had been one of the earliest voices driving the creation of the Medicine X conference and the dynamic community it would come to foster. I came to believe the values invigorating its collective spirit carry tremendous power in forging the future of medicine.

At the core of Medicine X was a vision of Everyone Included™. This trademarked leadership and design framework embodies the notion that implementing change requires co-creation with patients, caregivers, providers, technologists, and researchers. So much of medicine can falter when it is siloed across huge institutions, and when stakeholders can't join the same conversation to brainstorm, build, and execute together. A tech company could build the most beautiful symptom-tracking app but it wouldn't matter if patients found it burdensome to input data or if it collected data that researchers couldn't use. Everyone Included is a moral acknowledgment of inherent human rights. Patients deserve a co-equal role in designing every aspect of the healthcare experience.

Distilled into ten design principles, Everyone Included means:

> *Be a rebel.*
> *Value each person.*
> *Be human.*
> *Be human-centered.*
> *Co-design.*
> *Facilitate connections.*
> *Treat with dignity.*
> *Provide a stage.*
> *Be beautiful and tasteful.*
> *Create magic.*

The Med X community radiated with "design thinking," a methodology for creative problem solving that celebrated radical collaboration. It has deep roots in Silicon Valley, particularly through the IDEO design firm, which built the first computer mouse for Apple. Design thinking prizes human-centered thinking, collective idea generation, rapid prototyping, and continuous testing of ideas to refine solutions to complex problems. Design thinking suffused the university through Stanford's "d School" (officially the Hasso Plattner Institute of Design), which exists to teach creative design principles to graduate students from across all of the university's disciplines, unlocking creative potential in everyone, whether they be journalists or engineers or educators or doctors.

The process begins by empathizing with the problem through stories to get to the emotional heart of the problem and define what needs to be solved. For instance, I participated in one design workshop over three days where the question was, "How might we improve access to pulmonary rehab for those with chronic obstructive pulmonary disease?" My view of the problem pivoted after being moved by long conversations with COPD patients participating in the program who explained how the disease altered the fabric of their daily lives. Then in the ideation phase, we, as designers, suspended judgment while brainstorming bold ideas regardless of their cost, absurdity, or even simplicity. Each little group in the workshop used black markers to write out ideas on yellow sticky notes as fast as possible. Next, the prototyping phase involves role playing or drawing up a storyboard with stick figures in a cartoon scene. In the COPD example, we explored how pulmonary rehab is the gold standard for treating the disease. But at a time in which rural hospitals are closing, centers offering the expensive service aren't reimbursed enough to be able to stay open. One solution we came up with was to create a national certification program whereby LA Fitness or Gold's Gym might offer the service. Another idea the dozens of us in the workshop fleshed out was to explore setting up pulmonary rehab in Walmart stores, similar to how the retailer offers optometry at its locations. From there, you test out the prototype, take extensive feedback, and assess how to iterate.

This was the tradition that the Patient-Led Research Collaborative was stepping into when they collectively produced the first research into the long-term effects of Covid-19. Their contribution could set the standard as a model for patient innovators to follow for other diseases as well. In June 2021, the group received a quarter-million dollar grant from the Patient-Centered Outcomes Research Institute, a federal agency created as part of the 2010 Affordable Care Act. PCORI was tasked with helping ensure patients and the public have information they can use to make healthcare decisions. In conjunction with the Council of Medical Specialty Societies, the PLRC was to explore how to bring their approach to other diseases, showcasing how to integrate patient-led research into clinical registries and formal research, building an ecosystem directly around the questions and treatment outcomes that mattered most to patients.

In their grant, they argued their model would light the way for a new paradigm in how patients could "move from research contributors to leaders of survey and research design."

And in April 2022, the PLRC received another shot in the arm in their mission to flip the script and forge a new future patient-centered care. They won a $3 million grant from Balvi, a fund created by Vitalk Buterin, the founder of the cryptocurrency Ethereum. Balvi sought high-impact Covid projects that could enable key research to be fast-tracked, and to end the pandemic. The new funding allowed the PLRC to fund full-time positions for its team of multi-disciplinary volunteer researchers who up to that point had needed to work unpaid or outside of their normal jobs for two years in order to press the international cases that Long Covid presented a severe public health problem. And it enabled the group to set up a Long Covid biomedical research fund led by patients, designed to accelerate knowledge of the underlying causes and treatments for Long Covid. They aimed to run a study on Covid reinfections, a quality of life study in a middle-income country, a phenotyping project, and a quarterly publication of patient-generated hypotheses shared in the public domain for Long Covid researchers to pursue.

Their mission to prove that patients were the experts in their own care was starting to look like it had staying power.

Chapter 16

EXPECTANT HOPE

DURING THIS SECOND COVID WINTER, I've retreated again to my parents' house to write. A year ago, I was sick in their basement fending off phone calls from disability insurance representatives, cycling through treatments, and desperately trying to carve out time to "recover." But even when I went back to work two months later, many of the residual symptoms remained. Within a few weeks, I was assigned to write a story exploring the early social media reports last spring that long haulers were improving after receiving the vaccine. As I began my research, I scheduled my first vaccine appointment immediately, hoping the shot might cure me as well. Riding up an escalator to the vaccination center within Atlanta's Mercedes-Benz Stadium, the atmospherics of an NFL game felt like a triumphal end to sickness. Yet the shots didn't wipe away the remaining symptoms—I still felt the strange buzzing sensations, the lack of energy, the loss of my usual ability to focus. I was well enough to travel to Colombia and Mexico with friends in the saddle period between waves when it seemed the virus' grip on our lives might be receding. However, other parts of me have yet to return. Each time I try going for a run or long bike ride, I feel sick for days afterwards. The classic post-exertional malaise thwarts my ability to exercise and quiet my anxiety in a world gone mad.

But as long as I don't push it, my dad and I can go on long walks to discuss scientists I'm interviewing and to hash out the next round of edits. My mom watches medical lectures with me about the latest research discoveries, and we play a nightly game of ping pong. Writing this book has fulfilled few of my writerly fantasies of living like Henry David Thoreau in a cabin at Walden Pond, communing with a world spirit. I feel trapped. I'm mortally afraid of reinfection, knowing viscerally the pain that awaits if I go out for dinner with the wrong person or attend a party at times when it can sometimes seem that every other person is a carrier. With my body's low natural killer cell function, I worry that the next hit, if it happens, might be as bad, or worse, than the last. At least for now, taking shelter in this expansive house has been a refuge away from the dystopian timeline unfolding just outside.

Omicron and its lineage and sublineage variants have triggered massive new waves of Covid all over the world, and they will not be the last. We'll likely live with more waves for many years into the future. Though this most recent strain is perceived as "mild," its transmissibility is far beyond its predecessors. Its relative mildness is little consolation when hospitalizations are again overwhelming an already burned-out healthcare system and Long Covid most frequently stems from those with mild cases that never needed hospitalization in the first place. The first U.S. Omicron cases were identified during the first week of December 2021. By March 2022, there's little formal data to show how many people are getting sick with Omicron and developing long-term symptoms. But in late December 2021, Dr. Anthony Fauci reiterated that the proportion of those infected to those who develop Long Covid, 10 to 30 percent, is likely to remain steady. And every expert I've spoken with tells me that the new variant is only going to lead to another large wave of long haulers. Several leaders of online Long Covid support groups told me by early 2022 they were already seeing surges of new members into their communities. At least now some of the pioneering work has already been done. The virus has punctured modernity, and the continuous game of cat and mouse between variants and vaccines remains a birthing ground for long haulers.

Nearly every week, substantive new research findings are released, building an ever-stronger set of insights into the pathophysiological basis for Long Covid. We now have good evidence that Long Covid is more likely in individuals who create low levels of antibodies after the infection or who have autoantibodies, Epstein-Barr virus activation, or a history of type 2 diabetes.

In the U.S., Amy Proal, Akiko Iwasaki, and David Putrino have partnered in a global effort with Resia Pretorius of South Africa, Dr. Asad Khan in the UK, and Dr. Beate Jaeger of Germany to chase down the microclot story. This gives a convincing picture of at least one key facet of Long Covid.

"We're seeing a biomarker, the microclots, that is present in all of the patients we've tested so far," Putrino said. "Everyone has microclots that we've tested in varying degrees, and we're seeing measures of microclot load correlate with Long Covid clinical symptoms that I'm measuring, which is the first time that I've seen that very cleanly. I can correlate your cognitive scores with your clot scores."

So far, those studies have been small and needed to be repeated in much larger proportions. And removing the clots through an apheresis technique doesn't eliminate the underlying cause. Patients tested for the clots again after forty-eight hours show evidence of the clots reforming. Although the clots correlate with symptoms and may be causing the symptoms, some other upstream source is contributing to the clots. But still, the strength of the ongoing research gives him confidence that the apheresis technique could advance toward a randomized control trial and eventually multi-site studies.

"In the meantime, everything we're doing on the apheresis side is very much patient-led and patient-sanctioned, so we have people with Long Covid every step of the way telling us the way to do things that is appropriate for their population and their community," Putrino said. "My mantra hasn't changed since pre-Covid which is 'fail fast' on all these interventions. I want a quick yes or a quick no. Should we move on to the next phase or un-sentimentally start all over again?"

In other preprint studies, they found that specific cytokines correlated with particular symptoms, for instance the chemo-kine CCL11 being strongly associated with patients who complained of brain fog. But many of the markers so far are person-specific or symptom-specific, so they require a personalized medicine approach. And large quantities of virus were found in the GI tracts of individuals with GI symptoms in the acute phase of Covid, showing that SARS-CoV-2 was in fact capable of infecting the GI tract. For those with Long Covid whose illness is directly driven by persistent viral infection, those sorts of findings could offer the cleanest explanation. Trials to test out Pfizer's coronavirus antiviral Paxlovid in Long Covid could be a promising area of research to knock out viral reservoirs.

There will likely be better answers, perhaps even before this book is released. In the meantime, learning to forge a new life in spite of the hardship—inside of its limits—becomes not just its own kind of medical intervention, but actually a philosophical one as well.

HONING RESILIENCE

Apart from receiving an actual successful biomedical treatment, one of the most important principles for managing or healing from a new chronic illness is radical acceptance. Many people have a hard time getting better because they don't fully acknowledge how sick they really are. It can require a full stop in life, and a total reappraisal of the magnitude of the shift in our abilities. Allowing for a period of profound rest, as contrary as that may be to our modern obsession with productivity, is likely going to pay dividends years later if you can stop the disease's progress early in its tracks. Further, you must pursue an aggressive, and holistic, set of treatments that take into account how Long Covid, or any post-viral illness, has affected many different systems of your body rather than just one.

Forgive yourself if you're not able to do work or go to activities that used to be part of your life. Let yourself rest if you need it.

In a world where the science is changing or even the mere existence of one's disease is contested, self-advocacy becomes the one true north star. There are principles that you can follow to understand how to direct your own care or be the empowered expert in your own disease. Doctors don't have time to process every new study on Long Covid, and they obviously will not have learned about the disease in medical school. But by being a responsible student of the scientific literature, you can engage with your medical care in ways that doctors appreciate. Rather than conceiving of the doctor-patient relationship as paternalistic, you can strive to work with your doctor as a co-equal partner in your care.

Karyn Bishof assembled a list of resources on the Covid-19 Longhauler Advocacy Project site to help long haulers and their medical providers "work as a team in an attempt to get the patient back to good health and regain quality of life." Know that getting the outcomes you or a loved one need means partnering not just with physicians, but with whole healthcare ecosystems of nurses, social workers, and insurance representatives. Simply committing to staying organized with all the medical paper-work and insurance claims can make a huge difference in getting results smoothly to improve your health.

To best help busy health providers do their jobs, Bishof recommends building a binder to "pre-load" your doctor with information ahead of time. This can tell your story chronolog-ically so that the whole appointment isn't spent reviewing lab work. Include a list of all your symptoms in order by severity of which affect your daily life most significantly. Compile a spread-sheet stating all your symptoms and activities over a two-week period, and paint a vivid picture of your quality of life or level of disability. Have a list of which additional tests you'd like ordered and which treatments you'd like to try. Get a friend to help you compile the info.

Make sure you take detailed notes during your appointment. If you're too sick, have a healthier friend, relative, or patient advocate accompany you to the appointment to listen and advo-cate for you. If you're not getting the care you need, fire your doctor and find a better one.

Long hauler Sandhya Kamphampati advised keeping track of all your data in a spreadsheet, which was her natural inclination as a data journalist. That way "I always had a log of everything I needed to track, especially my heart rate and oxygen, which, as a Long Covid patient, are helpful markers to share with my doc-tor," she wrote in the *Los Angeles Times*.

When the disease is loosely defined or research is scarce, you ought to bring supporting information such as studies, news articles, info posters or other resources to appointments. When the CDC released its interim post-Covid treatment guidelines in June 2021, it was essentially creating resources that patients could print out and show their doctors in order to direct them toward the recommended tests, procedures, or specialty clinics. For post-Covid patients who don't have a positive PCR test, the most useful part is the official word that Long Covid clinics shouldn't use any particular lab test as a make-or-break admission ticket to a clinic, providing coverage for a vast swath who might not otherwise have been able to get care.

One early stop can be the Job Accommodation Network, which offers free and confidential guidance on issues related to disability and employment. Accommodations can vary widely depending on the job. For instance, with remote work cultures becoming more accepted during the pandemic, it may be much easier to request arrangements to work from home or to lie down while working. There are basic adjustments that can ease some of the stress of working with a disability, such as using an ergonomic keyboard or dictation software, as well as regular breaks for rest, food, or to use the restroom. To reduce eye strain or cognitive overload, it might help to install a blue light filter on your computer screen.

Those with complex chronic illness in college can usually qualify for services designed to grant those with disabilities equal access to education. That can mean extended time for exams, being able to take a test in a quieter environment or a testing center with fewer distractions, or having a notetaker take class notes for you. After an initial letter from a doctor, the university's disability services sends an accommodation letter given to a student's professors each semester, and there's no need to disclose any uncomfortable medical information to the faculty.

In her 1969 book *On Death and Dying*, psychiatrist Elisabeth Kübler-Ross put forth her famous theory of the five stages of grief, which begins with Denial, proceeds toward Anger, Bargaining, and Depression, and ends with the ultimate goal of Acceptance. Just as learning to accept the death of a loved one is a vital part of the grief process, the loss of a version of oneself, whether temporarily or permanently, follows a similar process of grief. That's why it can be useful for those with complex chronic diseases to seek care with a therapist to complement their multidisciplinary medical care with a cardiologist, rheumatologist, or perhaps many others. Adjusting one's expectations can be a path toward finding joy in a new life, which harnesses newfound limitations rather than fighting against them.

In her book *The Phenomenology of Illness*, philosopher Havi Carel examines an idea from the philosopher S. Kay Toombs, explaining that with chronic illness we have five major losses: the loss of wholeness, certainty, control, freedom, and familiarity. These losses, residing inside the concept of *illness*, cannot be contained in the medical or clinical definition of a disease. Disease is the bureaucratic language of lab tests, specialist referrals, insurance reimbursement. What is or is not reported on a medical chart cannot define us. Illness is our own first-person subjective experience, our own life as directly lived.

Carel herself was diagnosed with a Lymphangioleiomyomatosis (LAM), a rare lung disease that leads to respiratory failure. Following the diagnosis, she wrote, "My future has folded in on itself." But it sparked her interest in pursuing the meaning of her new life, and to find a philosophical footing within it. Therefore, if an illness is viewed as an opportunity to philosophize, it "can be seen as dramatically changing the ways of being that are available to a person and thus prompting, provoking, or inviting them to modify their being."

Such an endeavor of reflective coping recalls the ancient Greek notion that philosophy is about learning how to die. Here it is not a physical death of the body itself, but at least a death of some vital part of the living self. Suspending a previous life requires learning how to bear illness well—living alongside a disability, reckoning with the pain, and processing the shock and sadness. She recalls the Stoic thinker Epictetus, who wrote, "What is it to bear a fever well? Not to blame God or man; not to be afflicted at that which happens, to expect death well and nobly, to do what must be done."

And modifying one's own being can mean harnessing the illness as an opportunity for post-traumatic growth, taking the perspective away from long-term goals in the future, and focusing in on the present moment, dwelling in the current experience. We can cope with illness by keeping stock of what is still possible.

In that respect, she finds sustenance in the words of Friedrich Nietzsche, whose own struggle with neurological disease reoriented his philosophical outlook:

"It was as if I discovered life anew, myself included; I tasted all the good things, even the small ones, as no other could easily taste them—I turned my will to health, to life, into my philosophy...the years when my vitality was at its lowest were when I stopped being a pessimist."

FORGING A REALISTIC HOPE

One frame of mind that has guided me through some of my worst relapses has been what business consultant Jim Collins has called the "Stockdale Paradox." It's the idea that in times of greatest hardship, you "must maintain unwavering faith that you can and will prevail in the end, regardless of the difficulties, and at the same time, have the discipline to confront the most brutal facts of your current reality, whatever they might be." Collins coined the term in his 2001 book *Good to Great* after interviewing Admiral James Stockdale, who had been the senior ranking U.S. military officer held at the infamous "Hanoi Hilton" prison in Vietnam. Collins asked Stockdale who among the captives was most likely to die, and the admiral—who became a Stoic philosopher after the war—said, "Oh, that's easy. The optimists." Prisoners who naively clung to a falsely positive belief of being released and home by Christmas were the ones most likely to succumb to hopelessness and despair. When the arbitrary deadline they'd held in their minds came and went, a physical and emotional collapse ensued.

The survivors had a different mindset, one which could combine acknowledgment of their circumstances' stark reality with an unwavering faith that things can and would get better. Holding those two ideas together simultaneously is also a way of navigating the uncertainty and unrelenting hell of a disease you don't deserve.

The concept of "unwavering faith" aligns closely with that of hope. And while religious practices have preached the benefits and rewards of faith and hope for millennia, science and the field of positive psychology are beginning to unravel its utility as well. In his book *The Anatomy of Hope*, Dr. Jeremy Groopman distinguishes between two types of hope: true hope and false hope. Groopman, a physician-scientist at Harvard Medical School, was once a patient navigating the complexities of chronic pain. Initially, as both a patient and a practitioner, Groopman struggled with the idealized versions of hope reflected in pop culture and its ties to uncorroborated follies like wishful thinking. However, after experiencing his own success with hope, Groopman decided to take his subjective experience and explore the idea of hope objectively through science. Groopman's book reflects his decades of research on the effect true hope has on people facing serious and terminal illnesses. According to Groopman, two key elements of hope—belief and expectation—can be cardinal components of the placebo response. When patients hope for or expect a treatment, the placebo effect can trigger a cascade of pain-relieving endorphins in the brain.

In alignment with hope, researchers have been exploring mindset as a way to elicit progress across many disciplines. Originally investigated in the classroom by psychologist Carol Dwerk, a concept known as *growth mindset* explores how believing in one's potential and growth helps us see a future where options exist, allowing us to set expectations and goals. That, in turn, changes our behavior. According to researchers in the field, growth mindset is in juxtaposition to a fixed mindset where goal-oriented effort is blunted by an inescapable view of oneself and the world. Fixed mindset might include giving up easily and having low expectations for oneself. A growth mindset includes developing flexible beliefs about one's potential, seeing challenges as learning experiences and opportunities, and having resilience to setbacks. But could growth mindset be applied to our wellness as well? Could hope change our brains? Could our mindset change our actions? Some wellness programs seem to think so. Other medical practitioners believe positive psychology around health is akin to the placebo effect. And while there is a small, but growing body of research to affirm that mindset can affect physiological outcomes and symptom severity, science has not shown us that mindset can alter serious disease processes such as cancer outcomes. However, if a growth mindset can promote goal-setting and includes being open to trying a new potential treatment, the outcome may change. Mix that with a dose of endorphin release, and you might have the ingredients for progress.

While mindset, hope, and optimism may have their place as supportive therapies for people experiencing chronic conditions, it's also important to acknowledge how harmful these seemingly positive tools can be if used incorrectly or taken to the extreme. When medical practitioners, friends, or family offer these tools in a package that claims to cure disease, they unwittingly minimize the complexity and seriousness of devastating physical disease. When doctors suggest a change in mindset without properly acknowledging or medically addressing the depth of their patient's physical pain and suffering, patients can be left feeling the opposite of hope.

These facts are particularly challenging in the face of contested or invisible diseases such as Long Covid. There may be great potential to keeping hope and seeing your future abilities as flexible. But I've always found these truths must be balanced with pacing, respecting one's boundaries, and an acceptance of reality. A true hope.

And perhaps the truest hope I know is a faith in the resilience of regular people with lived experience of a problem to gather together, of strangers unified through no other connection than their own shared suffering. I believe in the power of connective technologies that provide a forum for shared communities to flourish, propping each other up with mutual support when whole systems seem to have failed. I believe in the power of regular people to help write or reform policy, and to endeavor in a collective effort ceaselessly to try and change the world. And whether we actually change it or not, I believe in that collective striving, in the sparks that fly out from the friction of striking against a rocky adversary. I believe in that tension of idealism and cynicism, which is our constant, universal act of becoming in this world.

Acknowledgments

First and foremost, I'm thankful to the dozens who generously gave their time for long interviews, especially in the midst of a strange disease. I hope this book helps you feel validated in your experience and contributes to a more just world.

I am grateful to my parents, Mary and Tom Prior. None of this is possible without your love, commitment, and unfailing belief. I'm so fortunate to have won the lottery with such deeply supportive and caring parents. They hosted me and cooked for me during several months of this project, enabling me to focus solely on writing. And both reviewed multiple drafts with me line by line along the way, improving anything from minor punctuation errors to major structural changes.

Elizabeth Weaver, my researcher, was like a divine gift. She serves on the neuroscience faculty at Georgia State as an adjunct working on interdisciplinary policy and administration, lives with ME/CFS, and moonlights with her firm, Brain Wheel, providing research and design for non-fiction books. I couldn't have dreamt up a better partner and friend to soldier through brainstorming, early drafts, and the formidable process of endnotes with me. She stepped in to help write a few sections as well, including on shame, infection theory, gaslighting, sexism, and hope. I will cherish our masked-up, socially distanced outdoor selfies as cicadas chirped in the Georgia summer and the air sparked with ideas and fireflies.

I thank my high school teachers Scott Daniel, the man who taught me to love to write, and Pam Stanescu, whose love of learning thrilled all of us and whose love toward me ensured I wouldn't fail in my moments of greatest need.

I am grateful to the institutions which have anchored my life, and built me into the writer, advocate, and man I am today.

At CNN, I was blessed with thousands of colleagues engaged in the collective endeavor to tell the story of our times with rigor, thoughtfulness, and high professionalism. From all of you, I have learned the craft of journalism, singing in many keys across quick news hits, lengthy reported features, and producing for television. You've all pushed me to be both dreamily ambitious and meticulously careful. Colleen Covino and Cristina Hernandez fought to give me the writing opportunities that could fill my soul. A dedicated editor, Brandon Griggs, helped my feature stories shine with cinematic pace and flair. Ben Tinker, David Allan, Katia Hetter, Justin Lear, Saeed Ahmed, Calvin Houts, Linda Rathke, and Damon Peebles all cultivated my creativity and curiosity. Thank you to CNN for giving me several months off to start this manuscript.

The Stanford Medicine X community, founded by the visionary Dr. Larry Chu, inspired me to believe that patient voices matter. The values of the collective ensured I didn't ever feel alone or abnormal in living with a chronic illness. My fellow ePatients affirmed that experiences of suffering can be a profound gift to others, making us *more than* and not *less than*. Medicine X has been a catalyst to write about patients from the spectrum of diseases who were unwilling to accept the status quo and took it upon themselves to innovate, advocate, and instigate a more inclusive healthcare future in which patients take their rightful place at the center. Their examples, including Doug Lindsay, Andrea Downing, Grace Anne Dorney Koppel, and dozens of others, are a light.

The #MEAction Network, founded by Jennifer Brea and Beth Mazur, has provided a global structure pushing for health equity for those with ME. It's one of the great honors of my life to work with so many talented, altruistic people on a mission far larger than myself.

Thank you to my agent Jennifer Weis, for believing in this project with such enthusiasm, and injecting confidence into me from our very first meeting. I thank Pam Weintraub for introducing me to Jennifer after ScienceWriters 2020.

At Post Hill Press, thank you to Debra Englander for spotting the potential for this book when it was in its early proposal stages and offering me the opportunity to publish it. Thank you to managing editor Heather King for ably managing each stage of the process, and to Devan Murphy for her superb and thoughtful copyedits, strengthening the manuscript. And thank you to Devon Brown for being sharp in running publicity.

I felt deeply supported by my fact checker, Maya Dusenbery, herself the author of *Doing Harm*, a book about contested illnesses and sexism in medicine. She brought extraordinary subject matter expertise as we tightened the scientific facts in the text. Any remaining errors are, of course, my own.

My friends Doug Lindsay, David Tuller, Brian Vastag, Beth Mazur, Imraan Sumar, Travis Preston, and Cecily McMillan all walked with me in this journey, joyfully supporting long workshop sessions and pushing to make the book everything it could be. Though she didn't live to see the pandemic or this book, I felt the presence of the late Cindy Shepler, who for years had breathed hope into me and preached the interconnectedness of all autoimmune diseases. At Hutchins State Jail in Texas, James McMillan reviewed and discussed the progress of the book with me weekly.

Bibliography

Chapter 1: A Future in Jeopardy

"It's important to remember,"...Alex Azar, "Remarks by President Trump, Vice President Pence, and Members of the Coronavirus Task Force in Press Conference," transcript of speech delivered at the James S. Brady Press Briefing Room, February 29, 2020, https://trumpwhitehouse.archives.gov/briefings-statements/remarks-president-trump-vice-president-pence-members-coronavirus-task-force-press-conference-2/.

*But like seven million others in the U.S....*Rafael Harpaz, MD, MPH, "Prevalence of Immunosuppression Among US Adults, 2013," JAMA Network, December 20, 2016, https://jamanetwork.com/journals/jama/fullarticle/2572798.

"To keep new cases from entering our shores,"...Donald Trump, "Read President Trump's Speech on Coronavirus Pandemic: Full Transcript," *The New York Times*, March 11, 2020, https://www.nytimes.com/2020/03/11/us/politics/trump-coronavirus-speech.html.

*I have told the stories...*Ryan Prior, "I Can't Shake Covid-19: Warnings from Young Survivors Still Suffering," CNN, July 19, 2020, https://www.cnn.com/2020/07/18/health/long-term-effects-young-people-covid-wellness/index.html; "Redefining Covid-19: Months after Infection, Patients Report Breathing Difficulty, Excessive Fatigue," CNN, September 13, 2020, https://www.cnn.com/2020/09/13/health/long-haul-covid-fatigue-breathing-wellness/index.html; "Covid-19's Effects Include Seizures and Movement Disorders—Even in Some

Moderate Cases, Study Finds," CNN, December 10, 2020, https://www.cnn.com/2020/12/10/health/effects-on-the-brain-covid-19-wellness/index.html; "A Third of Covid-19 Survivors Suffer 'Brain Disease,' Study Shows," CNN, April 6, 2021, https://www.cnn.com/2021/04/06/health/covid-neurological-psychological-lancet-wellness/index.html.

*A 2009 study of 369 SARS survivors...*Marco Ho-Bun Lam, Yun-Kwok Wing, Mandy Wai-Man Yu, Chi-Ming Leung, Ronald C. W. Ma, Alice P. S. Kong, W.Y. So, Samson Yat-Yuk Fong, and Siu-Ping Lam, "Mental Morbidities and Chronic Fatigue in Severe Acute Respiratory Syndrome Survivors: Long-Term Follow-Up," *Archives of Internal Medicine* 169, no. 22 (2009): 2142-47. doi:10.1001/archinternmed.2009.384.

irreversible paralysis in about 1 in 200 patients..."Poliomyelitis," World Health Organization, July 22, 2019, https://www.who.int/news-room/fact-sheets/detail/poliomyelitis.

the virus also caused post-polio syndrome..."Post-Polio Syndrome," Centers for Disease Control and Prevention, Last modified September 23, 2021, https://www.cdc.gov/polio/what-is-polio/pps.html.

Ebola killed more than a third..."2014-2016 Ebola Outbreak in West Africa," Centers for Disease Control and Prevention, Last modified March 8, 2019, https://www.cdc.gov/vhf/ebola/history/2014-2016-outbreak/index.html.

*more than 70 percent of survivors...*Nell G Bond, Donald S Grant, Sarah T Himmelfarb, Emily J Engel, Foday Al-Hasan, Michael Gbakie, Fatima Kamara, Lansana Kanneh, Ibrahim Mustapha, Adaora Okoli, William Fischer, David Wohl, Robert F Garry, Robert Samuels, Jeffrey G Shaffer, John S Schieffelin, "Post-Ebola Syndrome Presents With Multiple Overlapping Symptom Clusters: Evidence From an Ongoing Cohort Study in Eastern Sierra Leone," Oxford Academic, September 15, 2021, https://academic.oup.com/cid/article/73/6/1046/6209860.

*the CDC released a study of 292 Covid-19 patients...*Mark W. Tenforde, Sara S. Kim, Christopher J. Lindsell, Erica Billig Rose, Nathan I.

Shapiro, D. Clark Files, Kevin W. Gibbs, Heidi L. Erickson, Jay S. Steingrub, Howard A. Smithline, et al., IVY Network Investigators, CDC COVID-19 Response Team, "Symptom Duration and Risk Factors for Delayed Return to Usual Health among Outpatients with Covid-19 in a Multistate Health Care Systems Network—United States, March–June 2020," *Morbidity and Mortality Weekly Report* 69, no. 30 (June 2020): 993-98. https://doi.org/10.15585/mmwr.mm6930e1.

one in ten people were sick for at least three weeks..."How Long Does Covid-19 Last?" ZOE Covid Study, June 6, 2020, https://covid.joinzoe. com/post/covid-long-term...

I wrote a story for USA Today...Ryan Prior, "Viewpoint: The Real Story of Chronic Fatigue Syndrome," *USA Today*, October 02, 2012, https://www.usatoday.com/story/college/2012/10/02/viewpoint-the-real-story-of-chronic-fatigue-syndrome/37397751/.

*I wrote about Stanford's Ron Davis...*Ryan Prior, "He Pioneered Technology That Fueled the Human Genome Project. Now His Greatest Challenge Is Curing His Own Son," CNN, May 12, 2019, https://www.cnn.com/2019/05/12/health/stanford-geneticist-chron-ic-fatigue-syndrome-trnd/index.html.

*I profiled Doug Lindsay...*Ryan Prior, "This College Dropout Was Bedridden for 11 Years. Then He Invented a Surgery and Cured Himself," CNN, July 27, 2019, https://www.cnn.com/2019/07/27/ health/doug-lindsay-invented-surgery-trnd/index.html.

*a series of features on Dr. David Fajgenbaum...*Ryan Prior, "This Med Student Was Given Last Rites Before Finding a Treatment That Saved His Life. His Method Could Help Millions," CNN, September 14, 2019, https://www.cnn.com/2019/09/14/health/castleman-fajgen-baum-chasing-my-cure-wellness-trnd/index.html; "After Saving His Own Life With a Repurposed Drug, a Professor Reviews Every Drug Being Tried Against Covid-19. Here's What He's Found," CNN, July

27, 2020, https://www.cnn.com/2020/06/27/health/coronavirus-treatment-fajgenbaum-drug-review-scn-wellness/index.html.

up to 100 million long haulers worldwide...Chen Chen, Spencer R. Haupert, Lauren Zimmermann, Xu Shi, Lars G. Fritsche, and Bhramar Mukherjee, "Global Prevalence of Post-Acute Sequelae of COVID-19 (PASC) or Long COVID: A Meta-Analysis and Systematic Review," *MedRXiv*, November 16, 2021, https://www.medrxiv.org/content/10.1101/2021.11.15.21266377v1.

More than 150 million Americans...Christine Buttorff, Teague Ruder, and Melissa Bauman, "Multiple Chronic Conditions in the United States," RAND, May 31, 2017, https://www.rand.org/pubs/tools/TL221.html.

Chapter 2: A Surprising Problem

A growing body of research shows that...*"Introduction to COVID-19 Racial and Ethnic Health Disparities," Center for Disease Control and Prevention, last modified December 10, 2020, https://www.cdc.gov/coronavirus/2019-ncov/community/health-equity/racial-ethnic-disparities/index.html; Wyatt Koma, Samantha Artiga, Tricia Neuman, Gary Claxton, Matthew Rae, Jennifer Kates, and Josh Michaud, "Low-Income and Communities of Color at Higher Risk of Serious Illness if Infected with Coronavirus," KFF, May 2020, https://www.kff.org/coronavirus-covid-19/issue-brief/low-income-and-communities-of-color-at-higher-risk-of-serious-illness-if-infected-with-coronavirus/; Neal Marquez, MPH1; Julie A. Ward, MN, RN2; Kalind Parish, MA3; et al, "COVID-19 Incidence and Mortality in Federal and State Prisons Compared With the US Population, April 5, 2020, to April 3, 2021," JAMA Network, October 6, 2021, https://jamanetwork.com/journals/jama/fullarticle/2784944; Irene Gibson, Marc R. Rosenblum, Bryan Baker, and Alexander Eastman, "COVID-19 Vulnerability by Immigration Status," US Department of Homeland Security, May 2021, https://www.dhs.gov/sites/default/files/publications/immigration-statistics/research_reports/research_paper_covid-19_vulnerability_by_immigration_status_may_2021.pdf; Lindsey Dawson, Ashley Kirzinger, and Jennifer Kates, "The Impact of the Covid-19 Pandemic on LGBT People," KFF, March, 11, 2021. https://www.kff.org/coronavirus-covid-19/poll-finding/the-impact-of-the-covid-19-pandemic-on-lgbt-people/.

experts worry they will be further alienated...Elizabeth Cooney, "Researchers Fear People of Color May Be Disproportionately Affected by Long Covid," STAT, May 10, 2021, https://www.statnews.com/2021/05/10/with-long-covid-history-may-be-repeating-itself-among-people-of-color/.

more severe outcomes occurred in communities of color..."Risk for COVID-19 Infection, Hospitalization, and Death By Race/Ethnicity," Center for Disease Control and Prevention, last modified March 25, 2022, https://www.cdc.gov/coronavirus/2019-ncov/covid-data/investigations-discovery/hospitalization-death-by-race-ethnicity.html.

Amy Carrillo, a forty-three-year-old from Kansas...Amy Carrillo, Interview by Ryan Prior, August 23, 2021.

Michael Sieverts was another...Michael Sieverts, Interview by Ryan Prior, 2021.

Clare Daly, thirty-eight, the chief product officer...Clare Daly, Interview by Ryan Prior, August 23, 2021.

Yvette Walker, a fifty-one-year-old writer...Yvette Walker, Interview by Ryan Prior, August 26, 2021.

Kimberly Shay's taste buds...Kimberly Shay, Interview by Ryan Prior, August 23, 2021.

Courtney Garvin, a singer and guitarist...Courtney Garvin, Interview by Ryan Prior, August 23, 2021.

*And for Molly Adams...*Molly Adams, Interview by Ryan Prior, August 23, 2021.

*Bahtiyar Bozkurt, a thirty-seven-year-old engineer...*Bahtiyar Bozkurt, Interview by Ryan Prior, August 24, 2021.

*Cali Wilson was similarly...*Cali Wilson, Interview by Ryan Prior, August 23, 2021.

*Marie, a twenty-six-year-old hacker...*Marie, Interview by Ryan Prior, August 26, 2021.

*Rabia Jaffer, a teacher from Toronto...*Rabia Jaffer, Interview by Ryan Prior, August 23, 2021.

*Marjorie Roberts, a life coach from Georgia...*Marjorie Roberts, Interview by Ryan Prior, August 23, 2021.

*Dani Mortell had summited...*Dani Mortel, Interview by Ryan Prior, August 23, 2021.

*Kimberley Grant, a social worker...*Kimberley Grant, Interview by Ryan Prior, August 23, 2021.

*For Alexis Misko, an occupational therapist...*Alexis Misko, Interview by Ryan Prior, August 23, 2021.

*Esther La Russa, a cashier from Illinois...*Esther La Russa, Interview by Ryan Prior, August 23, 2021.

*Felipe Andrés Araya Casanova, a thirty-two-year-old...*Felipe Andrés Araya Casanova, Interview by Ryan Prior, August 23, 2021.

*Eva Amat, a fifty-one-year-old secretary...*Eva Amat, Interview by Ryan Prior, August 27, 2021.

*Joni Savolainen, a thirty-five-year-old...*Joni Savolainen, Interview by Ryan Prior, August 21, 2021.

Jenna, a young woman working...Jenna, Interview by Ryan Prior, August 27, 2021.

Enya Vermeyen, a mathematics teacher...Enya Vermeyen, Interview by Ryan Prior, August 24, 2021.

Deborah Lee, a twenty-six-year-old...Deborah Lee, Interview by Ryan Prior, August 23, 2021.

James McMillan, incarcerated...James McMillan, Interview by Ryan Prior, August 26, 2021.

Amanda Finley experienced...Amanda Finley, Interview by Ryan Prior, October 21, 2021.

Álvaro Rial, thirty...Álvaro Rial, Interview by Ryan Prior, August 24, 2021.

MIS-C had appeared in about 7,880 U.S. pediatric Covid cases..."Health Department-Reported Cases of Multisystem Inflammatory Syndrome in Children (MIS-C) in the United States," Centers for Disease Control and Prevention, Last modified (May 2022), https://covid.cdc.gov/covid-data-tracker/#mis-national-surveillance.

have less access to post-acute hospital care...Moses J.E. Flash et al, "Disparities in Post-Intensive Care Syndrome During the Covid-19 Pandemic: Challenges and Solutions." NEJM, 2020, https://doi.org/10.1056/CAT.20.0568.

in an estimated 10 percent to 30 percent of those infected..."Prevalence of Ongoing Symptoms Following Coronavirus (COVID-19) Infection in the UK: 1 April 2021," Office for National Statistics, April, 1, 2021, https://www.ons.gov.uk/peoplepopulationandcommunity/healthandsocialcare/conditionsanddiseases/bulletins/prevalenceofongoingsymptomsfollowingcoronaviruscovid19infectionintheuk/1april2021; Jennifer K. Logue, BS1; Nicholas M. Franko, BS1; Denise J. McCulloch, MD, MPH1; et al, "Sequelae in Adults at 6 Months After COVID-19 Infection," JAMA Network, February 19, 2021, https://

jamanetwork.com/journals/jamanetworkopen/fullarticle/2776560; Chen Chen, Spencer R. Haupert, Lauren Zimmermann, Xu Shi, Lars G. Fritsche, Bhramar Mukherjee, "Global Prevalence of Post-Acute Sequelae of COVID-19 (PASC) or Long COVID: A Meta-Analysis and Systematic Review," PubMed, April 2022, https://pubmed.ncbi.nlm.nih.gov/35429399/.

The Covid death rate in most developed countries…"Mortality Analyses," Johns Hopkins University & Medicine, last modified April 26, 2022, https://coronavirus.jhu.edu/data/mortality.

the World Health Organization's report in February 2020…"Report of the WHO-China Joint Mission on the Coronavirus Disease 2019 (COVID-19)," World Health Organization, February 2020, https://www.who.int/docs/default-source/coronaviruse/who-china-joint-mission-on-covid-19-final-report.pdf.

*One of those citizen scientists was…*Ben Zimmer, "Long hauler: When Covid-19's Symptoms Last and Last," *Wall Street Journal,* January 1, 2021, https://www.wsj.com/articles/long-hauler-when-covid-19s-symptoms-last-and-last-11609524809.

Chapter 3: A Groundswell of Patient Activism

*Fiona Lowenstein, a twenty-six-year-old freelance writer…*Fiona Lowenstein, Interview by Ryan Prior, 2021.

*The op-ed recounted how the coronavirus…*Fiona Lowenstein, "I'm 26. Coronavirus Sent Me to the Hospital." *New York Times,* March 23, 2020, https://www.nytimes.com/2020/03/23/opinion/coronavirus-young-people.html.

*This second piece, published on April 13, 2020…*Fiona Lowenstein, "We Need to Talk About What Coronavirus Recoveries Look Like," *The New York Times,* April 13, 2020, https://www.nytimes.com/2020/04/13/opinion/coronavirus-recovery.html.

Alison Sbrana had fallen ill...Alison Sbrana, Interview by Ryan Prior, 2021.

10 percent with mono develop long-term symptoms...D S Buchwald, et al. "Acute Infectious Mononucleosis: Characteristics of Patients Who Report Failure to Recover," *The American Journal of Medicine* 109,7 (2000): 531-7, doi:10.1016/s0002-9343(00)00560-x https://pubmed.ncbi.nlm.nih.gov/11063953/.

women more than twice as likely as men...Lawrence B. Afrin, Joseph H. Butterfield, Martin Raithel, and Gerhard J. Molderings, "Often Seen, Rarely Recognized: Mast Cell Activation Disease – a Guide to Diagnosis and Therapeutic Options," *Annals of Medicine* 48, no. 3: 190-201. https://doi.org/10.3109/07853890.2016.1161231; I.J. Bakken et al, "Two Age Peaks in the Incidence of Chronic Fatigue Syndrome/Myalgic Encephalomyelitis: A Population-Based Registry Study from Norway," *BMC Med* 12, 167 (October 2014), https://doi.org/10.1186/s12916-014-0167-5; B. H. Shaw, L. E. Stiles, K. Bourne, E. A. Green, et al, "The Face of Postural Tachycardia Syndrome – Insights From a Large Cross-Sectional Online Community-Based Survey," *Journal of Internal Medicine* 286, no 4 (October 2019): 438-448. https://doi.org/10.1111/joim.12895.

Hannah Davis, who was a thirty-two-year-old...Hannah Davis, Interview by Ryan Prior, 2021.

Gina Assaf, a design strategist...Gina Assaf, Interview by Ryan Prior, 2021.

Lisa McCorkell, twenty-eight...Lisa McCorkell, Interview by Ryan Prior, 2021.

Hannah Wei, a Canadian product consultant...Hannah Wei, Interview by Ryan Prior, 2021.

Athena Akrami, a neuroscientist...Athena Akrami, Interview by Ryan Prior, 2021.

The survey generated 640 responses...Gina Assaf, Hannah Davis, Lisa McCorkell, Hannah Wei, O'Neil Brooke, Athena Akrami, Ryan Low et al, "What Does Covid-19 Recovery Actually Look Like?" Patient-Led Research Collaborative, May 11, 2020, https://patientresearchcovid19.com/research/report-1/.

a June 4, 2020 piece in The Atlantic...Ed Yong, "Covid-19 Can Last for Several Months," *The Atlantic*, June 4, 2020, https://www.theatlantic.com/health/archive/2020/06/covid-19-coronavirus-longterm-symp-toms-months/612679/.

an archeologist named Elisa Perego...Elisa Perego, Email to Ryan Prior, August 16, 2021.

Claire Hastie, a corporate consultant...Claire Hastie, Interview by Ryan Prior, 2021.

Long Covid is just as likely to stem from a mild case...Jennifer Logue et al, "Sequelae in Adults at 6 Months After COVID-19 Infection," *JAMA Network* 4, (February 2021), https://jamanetwork.com/journals/jamanetworkopen/fullarticle/2776560.

"Message in a Bottle" YouTube video...LongCovidSOS Team, "Message in a Bottle Long Covid SOS," United Kingdom, 2020, https://www.you-tube.com/watch?v=IIeOoS_A4c8.

published a British Medical Journal *opinion piece*...Amali Lokugamage, Sharon Taylor, and Clare Rayner, "Patients' Experiences of 'Longcovid' Are Missing from the NHS Narrative," B*MJ Opinion*, July 10, 2020. https://blogs.bmj.com/bmj/2020/07/10/patients-experiences-of-long-covid-are-missing-from-the-nhs-narrative/.

a virtual press conference about Covid-19...Adeeba Kamarulzaman, Anthony Fauci, Claudio Fenizia, Andrew Hill, Kristen Marks, and Carina Marquez, "Official Press Conference: COVID-19 Conference Highlights (Thursday, 9 July)," International AIDS Conference,

July 9, 2020, conference recording https://www.youtube.com/watch?v=UMmT48IC0us.

*Terri Wilder, a social worker...*Terri Wilder, Interview by Ryan Prior, 2021.

*organized a virtual meeting...*Brianna Sacks, "COVID Is Making Younger, Healthy People Debilitatingly Sick For Months. Now They're Fighting For Recognition," Buzzfeed, Last modified August 25, 2020, https://www.buzzfeednews.com/article/briannasacks/covid-long-haulers-who-coronavirus.

*They documented more than 200 symptoms...*Hannah E. Davis, Gina S. Assaf, Lisa McCorkell, Hannah Wei, Ryan J. Low, Yochai Re'em, Signe Redfield, Jared P. Austin, and Athena Akrami, "Characterizing Long Covid in an International Cohort: 7 Months of Symptoms and Their Impact," MedRxiv, (2020), 2020.12.24.20248802.

*published in the peer reviewed journal...*Hannah E. Davis et al, "Characterizing Long COVID in an International Cohort: 7 months of Symptoms and Their Impact," *The Lancet* 38, (August 2021), https://www.thelancet.com/journals/eclinm/article/PIIS2589-5370(21)00299-6/fulltext.

*Perego published an article...*Felicity Callard and Elisa Perego, "How and Why Patients Made Long Covid," Short Communication, *Social Science & Medicine* 268, (2020), doi:10.1016/j.socscimed.2020.113426

The WHO reported 1.65 million social media mentions..."Update on Clinical Long-Term Effects of Covid-19," World Health Organization, Last Modified March 26, 2021, https://www.who.int/docs/default-source/coronaviruse/risk-comms-updates/update54_clinical_long_term_effects.pdf?sfvrsn=3e63eee5_8.

Chapter 4: Patients Become the Experts

Our word patient *comes to us from the Latin "patiens"*...J Neuberger, "Do We Need a New Word for Patients? Let's Do Away with 'Patients.'" [In eng]. *BMJ (Clinical research ed.)* 318, no. 7200 (1999): 1756-57. https://doi.org/10.1136/bmj.318.7200.1756. https://pubmed.ncbi.nlm. nih.gov/10381717.

Fiona Lowenstein, Body Politic's founder...Fiona Lowenstein, Interview by Ryan Prior, 2021.

series of one-pagers..."Post-COVID Conditions: Information for Healthcare Providers," Centers for Disease Control and Prevention," Last modified July 9, 2021, https://www.cdc.gov/coronavirus/2019-ncov/hcp/clinical-care/post-covid-conditions.html.

NIH Director Francis Collins highlighted...Francis Collins, "Trying to Make Sense of Long Covid Syndrome," NIH ed., (2021), https://directors blog.nih.gov/2021/01/19/trying-to-make-sense-of-long-covid-syndrome/.

penned a Wall Street Journal *opinion piece*...Jeremy Devine, "The Dubious Origins of Long Covid," *Wall Street Journal*, March 22, 2021. https://www.wsj.com/articles/the-dubious-origins-of-long-covid-11616452583.

"Mickey Mouse science at best"...Mike Mariani, "The Great Gaslighting: How COVID Longhaulers are Still Fighting for Recognition," *The Guardian*, February 3, 2022, https://www.theguardian.com/society/2022/feb/03/long-covid-fight-recognition-gaslighting-pandemic.

"It's possible that I would not be studying...Ziyad Al-Aly, Interview by Ryan Prior, 2021.

His team's study was published...Ziyad Al-Aly, Yan Xie, and Benjamin Bowe, "High-Dimensional Characterization of Post-Acute Sequelae of Covid-19," *Nature* 594, no. 7862 (2021): 259-64, https://doi.org/10.1038/s41586-021-03553-9.

Kramer, an Oscar-nominated screenwriter...Randy Shilts, *And the Band Played On: Politics, People, and the Aids Epidemic.* New York, New York: St Martin's Press, 2007.

the 2012 documentary How to Survive a Plague...David France, "How to Survive a Plague," 2012. https://surviveaplague.com.

Davis resonated with a different type...Hannah Davis, Interview Ryan Prior, 2021.

Claire Hastie, the founder...Clarie Hastie, Interview by Ryan Prior, 2021.

a global conference on Long Covid..."Long COVID Forum: 9-10 December 2020," International Severe Acute Respiratory and emerging Infection Consortium, last modified December 9, 2020, https://isaric.org/event/long-covid-joint-research-forum-virtual-events-9-10-december-2020/.

an agenda identifying research priorities...G. Carson and Long Covid Group, "Research Priorities for Long Covid: Refined Through an International Multi-Stakeholder Forum," *BMC Med* 19, no 84 (2021), https://bmcmedicine.biomedcentral.com/articles/10.1186/s12916-021-01947-0.

"I have these weird neurological symptoms...Chelsea Cirruzzo, "'It's Personal and It's Policy': Sen. Tim Kaine Details His Bout with Long Covid," U.S. News & World Report, March 24, 2021. https://www.usnews.com/news/health-news/articles/2021-03-24/tim-kaine-on-bout-with-long-covid-its-personal-and-its-policy.

testify in front of the House Energy and Commerce Committee..."The Long Haul: Forging a Path through the Lingering Effects of COVID-19," The Subcommittee on Health of the Committee on Energy and Commerce, April 28, 2021, recorded hearing, https://energycommerce.house.gov/committee-activity/hearings/hearing-on-the-long-haul-forging-a-path-through-the-lingering-effects-of.

For her testimony, Lisa McCorkell...Lisa McCorkell, Interview by Ryan Prior, 2021.

interim guidelines for treating post-Covid conditions..."Evaluating and Caring for Patients with Post-Covid Conditions: Interim Guidance," Centers for Disease Control and Prevention, Last Modified June 14, 2021, https://www.cdc.gov/coronavirus/2019-ncov/hcp/clinical-care/post-covid-index.html.

And Alison Sbrana, seven years after...Alison Sbrana, Interview by Ryan Prior, 2021.

"It is beautiful to see this..."A Brief but Spectacular Take on Chronic Illness," PBS, https://www.pbs.org/video/brief-but-spectacular-1619123266/.

$1.15 billion check for research...Francis S. Collins, "NIH launches new initiative to study 'Long COVID,'" National Institutes of Health, February 23, 2021, https://www.nih.gov/about-nih/who-we-are/nih-director/statements/nih-launches-new-initiative-study-long-covid.

introduce the Covid-19 Long Haulers Act..."Nearly $100m in Long Covid Funding Introduced in Congress," PRNewswire Press Release, May 27, 2021. https://www.prnewswire.com/news-releases/nearly-100m-in-long-covid-funding-introduced-in-congress-301301363.html.

champion was Emily Taylor...Emily Taylor, Interview by Ryan Prior, 2021.

Only about a fifth..."Beyond Myalgic Encephalomyelitis/Chronic Fatigue Syndrome: Redefining an Illness," National Academy of Medicine, 2015, https://nap.nationalacademies.org/catalog/19012/beyond-myalgic-encephalomyelitischronic-fatigue-syndrome-redefining-an-illness.

allocating $15 million annually..."Estimates of Funding for Various Research, Condition, and Disease Categories (RCDC)," National Institute of Health, June 25, 2021, https://report.nih.gov/funding/categorical-spending#/.

the Covid-19 and Pandemic Response Centers of Excellence Act... "As Omicron Cases Are Detected In New York, Gillibrand Pushes For Creation Of Covid-19 And Pandemic Response Centers Of Excellence To Prepare For Future Variants And Help Prevent Public Health Emergencies," Kirsten Gillibrand U.S. Senator for New York, December 5, 2021, https://www.gillibrand.senate.gov/news/press/release/as-omicron-cases-are-detected-in-new-york-gillibrand-pushes-for-creation-of-covid-19-and-pandemic-response-centers-of-excellence-to-prepare-for-future-variants-and-help-prevent-public-health-emergencies.

The White House Covid-19 Health Equity Task Force... "Presidential COVID-19 Health Equity Task Force," U.S. Department of Health and Human Services Office of Minority Health, October 2021, https://www.minorityhealth.hhs.gov/assets/pdf/HETF_Report_508_102821_9am_508Team%20WIP11-compressed.pdf.

recommendations presented by Davis and McCorkell... Hannah Davis and Lisa McCorkell, "White House Covid-19 Equity Task Force Presentation", Patient-Led Research Collaborative, 2021, https://docs.google.com/presentation/d/1QoXnLSwV-tB7Le9R9SiF6Xouf9q0t-TOuQKF3KYZIf1Q/mobilepresent?slide=id.gdd634b6900_0_101.

More than eighty Long Covid clinics... Erika Edwards, "Inside 'Post-Covid' Clinics: How Specialized Centers are Trying to Treat Long-Haulers," *NBC News*, March 1, 2021, https://www.nbcnews.com/health/health-news/inside-post-covid-clinics-how-specialized-centers-are-trying-treat-n1258879.

Dr. David Putrino, the Director of Rehabilitation Innovation... David Putrino, Interview with Ryan Prior, 2022.

Chapter 5: A Lifelong Mission

In a press conference to launch…"CDC Launches 'Get Informed. Get Diagnosed. Get Help.' Campaign," CDC Newsroom Press Release, November 3, 2006, https://www.cdc.gov/media/pressrel/r061103.htm.

an important study by Dr. Ian Lipkin…Harvey J. Alter et al, "A Multicenter Blinded Analysis Indicates No Association between Chronic Fatigue Syndrome/Myalgic Encephalomyelitis and either Xenotropic Murine Leukemia Virus-Related Virus or Polytropic Murine Leukemia Virus," *ASM Journals* 3, no 5 (September 2012), https://journals.asm.org/doi/full/10.1128/mBio.00266-12.

a more personal USA Today *column*…Ryan Prior, "Viewpoint: The Real Story of Chronic Fatigue Syndrome," *USA Today*, October 02, 2012, https://www.usatoday.com/story/college/2012/10/02/viewpoint-the-real-story-of-chronic-fatigue-syndrome/37397751/.

The Atlantic *published a story*…Nicole Allan, "Who Will Tomorrow's Historians Consider Today's Greatest Inventors?" *The Atlantic*, November 2013, https://www.theatlantic.com/magazine/archive/2013/11/the-inventors/309534/.

the most serious journalistic investigation into ME/CFS…Hillary Johnson, *Osler's Web: Inside the Labyrinth of the Chronic Fatigue Syndrome Epidemic*, (United States: Penguin US, 1996).

patients had a host of abnormalities…Klimas NG, Salvato FR, Morgan R, Fletcher MA. "Immunologic Abnormalities in Chronic Fatigue Syndrome," *J Clin Microbiol* 28, (June 1990:1403-10), doi: 10.1128/jcm.28.6.1403-1410.1990. PMID: 2166084; PMCID: PMC267940.

published a paper in the journal Annals of Internal Medicine…D. Buchwald, P. R. Cheney, D. L. Peterson, B. Henry, S. B. Wormsley, A. Geiger, D. V. Ablashi, et al, "A Chronic Illness Characterized by Fatigue, Neurologic and Immunologic Disorders, and Active Human

Herpesvirus Type 6 Infection," [In eng]. *Ann Intern Med* 116, no. 2 (January 1992): 103-13, https://doi.org/10.7326/0003-4819-116-2-103.

just 43 percent of the $23 million...June Gibbs Brown, "Audit of Costs Charged to the Chronic Fatigue Syndrome Program at the Centers for Disease Control and Prevention (CIN: A-04-98-04226)," Office of Inspector General, May 10, 1999, https://oig.hhs.gov/oas/reports/region4/49804226.pdf.

Davis sought two NIH grants...Olga Khazan, "The Tragic Neglect of Chronic Fatigue Syndrome," *The Atlantic*, October 8, 2015, https://www.theatlantic.com/health/archive/2015/10/chronic-fatigue-patients-push-for-an-elusive-cure/409534/.

30 percent of medical school curricula...Mark Peterson, Thomas W. Peterson, Sarah Emerson, Eric Regalbuto, Meredyth Evans, and Leonard Jason, "Coverage of CFS within U.S. Medical Schools," *Universal Journal of Public Health* 1, no. 4 (2013). https://doi.org/10.13189/ujph.2013.010404.

Discover *magazine called Lipkin*...Grant Delin, "Discover Interview: The World's Most Celebrated Virus Hunter, Ian Lipkin," *Discover Magazine*, 2012, https://www.discovermagazine.com/health/discover-interview-the-worlds-most-celebrated-virus-hunter-ian-lipkin.

a $766,000 grant to complement...Olga Khazan, "The Tragic Neglect of Chronic Fatigue Syndrome."

her own documentary about the disease...*Unrest*, Directed by Jennifer Bea, Shella Films, 2017.

Newt Gingrich had penned a 2015 op-ed...Newt Gingrich, "Newt Gingrich: Double the N.I.H. Budget," *The New York Times*, April 22, 2015, https://www.nytimes.com/2015/04/22/opinion/double-the-nih-budget.html.

an estimated $17 to $24 billion...Leonard A. Jason, Mary C. Benton, Lisa Valentine, Abra Johnson, and Susan Torres-Harding, "The Economic Impact of ME/CFS: Individual and Societal Costs," [In eng], *Dynamic medicine*, 7 (2008): 6-6. https://doi.org/10.1186/1476-5918-7-6.

a similar disease, multiple sclerosis, had only about one-third...Ashley R. Valdez, Elizabeth E. Hancock, Seyi Adebayo, David J. Kiernicki, Daniel Proskauer, John R. Attewell, Lucinda Bateman, et al, "Estimating Prevalence, Demographics, and Costs of ME/CFS Using Large Scale Medical Claims Data and Machine Learning," [In English]. *Frontiers in Pediatrics* 6, (2019), https://doi.org/10.3389/fped.2018.00412.

ought to have been $203 million annually...Arthur Mirin, Mary Dimmock, and Leonard Jason, "Research Update: The Relation between ME/CFS Disease Burden and Research Funding in the USA," Work 66, no. 2 (2019): 277–82. https://doi.org/10.3233/WOR-203173.

slot at the Stanford Medicine X conference...Ryan Prior, "Epatient Ignite! Ryan Prior," In Stanford Medicine X, 8:56, 2017. https://www.youtube.com/watch?v=wajdSXwRaJA.

in Man's Search for Meaning...Viktor Frankl, *Man's Search for Meaning* (Boston: Beacon Press, 1959).

Rilke's semi-autobiographical novel...Rainer Maria Rilke, "For the Sake of a Single Poem," *In the Notebooks of Malte Laurids Brigge* (Austria-Hungary, 1910).

six times greater risk of suicide...Dr. Emmert Roberts et al, "Mortality of people with chronic fatigue syndrome: a retrospective cohort study in England and Wales from the South London and Maudsley NHS Foundation Trust Biomedical Research Centre (SLaM BRC) Clinical Record Interactive Search (CRIS) Register," *The Lancet* 387, no 10028 (April 2016): 1638-1643, https://www.thelancet.com/journals/lancet/article/PIIS0140-6736(15)01223-4/fulltext.

Buddhist nun Pema Chödrön...Pema Chödrön, *When Things Fall Apart: Heart Advice for Difficult Times* (Boston: Shambhala: 2000).

Chapter 6: We Predicted This

Leonard Jason, a professor of psychology...Leonard Jason, Interview with Ryan Prior, 2021.

a four-year study of mononucleosis...Leonard A Jason, Joseph Cotler, Mohammed F Islam, Madison Sunnquist, and Ben Z Katz, "Risks for Developing Myalgic Encephalomyelitis/Chronic Fatigue Syndrome in College Students Following Infectious Mononucleosis: A Prospective Cohort Study," *Clinical Infectious Diseases*, (2020), https://doi.org/10.1093/cid/ciaa1886.

"If you look at all the pandemics...Leonard Jason, Interview by Ryan Prior, 2021.

a century of post-infectious syndromes...Mohammed Islam, Joseph Cotler, and Leonard Jason, "Post-Viral Fatigue and Covid-19: Lessons from Past Epidemics," Review. *Fatigue: Biomedicine, Health & Behavior* 8, no. 20 (2020): 61-69, https://www.tandfonline.com/doi/epub/10.1080/21641846.2020.1778227.

a 2006 study conducted in Australia...I. Hickie, T. Davenport, D. Wakefield, U. Vollmer-Conna, B. Cameron, S. D. Vernon, W. C. Reeves, and A. Lloyd, "Post-Infective and Chronic Fatigue Syndromes Precipitated by Viral and Non-Viral Pathogens: Prospective Cohort Study," [In eng]. *BMJ* 333, no. 7568 (Sep 16, 2006): 575, https://doi.org/10.1136/bmj.38933.585764.AE.

A study in Houston, Texas...Kristy O. Murray et al, "Survival Analysis, Long-Term Outcomes, and Percentage of Recovery Up to 8 Years Post-Infection Among the Houston West Nile Virus Cohort," *PloS One* 9, no 7 (July 2014), https://www.ncbi.nlm.nih.gov/pmc/articles/PMC4108377/.

28 percent of those recovering from Ebola...Himiede W Wilson et al, "Post-Ebola Syndrome Among Ebola Virus Disease Survivors in Montserrado County, Liberia 2016," *BioMed Research International*, (June 2018), https://www.ncbi.nlm.nih.gov/pmc/articles/PMC6046154/.

It showed that 40 percent of patients reported chronic fatigue...Marco Ho-Bun Lam, Yun-Kwok Wing, Mandy Wai-Man Yu, Chi-Ming Leung, Ronald C. W. Ma, Alice P. S. Kong, W.Y. So, Samson Yat-Yuk Fong, and Siu-Ping Lam, "Mental Morbidities and Chronic Fatigue in Severe Acute Respiratory Syndrome Survivors: Long-Term Follow-Up," *Archives of Internal Medicine* 169, no. 22 (2009): 2142-47, doi:10.1001/archinternmed.2009.384.

there's likely some kind of a wrench in the machinery...Gerwyn Morris and Michae Maes, "Mitochondrial Dysfunctions in Myalgic Encephalomyelitis / Chronic Fatigue Syndrome Explained by Activated Immuno-Inflammatory, Oxidative and Nitrosative Stress Pathways," *Metab Brain Dis* 29, (March 2014): 19-36, https://link.springer.com/article/10.1007/s11011-013-9435-x.

Dr. David Putrino was in a unique position...David Putrino, Interview by Ryan Prior, 2022.

redesign the Precision Recovery app...L. Tabacof, C. Kellner, E. Breyman, S. Dewil, S. Braren, L. Nasr, J. Tosto, M. Cortes, and D. Putrino, "Remote Patient Monitoring for Home Management of Coronavirus Disease 2019 in New York: A Cross-Sectional Observational Study," [In eng]. *Telemed J E Health* 27, no. 6 (Jun 2021): 641-48, https://doi.org/10.1089/tmj.2020.0339.

people with Long Covid have hypocapnia...Jamie Wood et al, "Levels of end-tidal carbon dioxide are low despite normal respiratory rate in individuals with long COVID," *Journal of Breath Research* 16, no 1 (December 2021), https://iopscience.iop.org/article/10.1088/1752-7163/ac3c18/pdf.

Chapter 7: Covid for Christmas

my most personal story for CNN...Ryan Prior, "My Friend Chose an Assisted Death in Switzerland. Her Dying Wish was to Tell You Why,"

CNN, June 7, 2020, https://www.cnn.com/2020/06/07/health/cindy-shepler-assisted-death-wellness-trnd/index.html.

a book by Franciscan priest Richard Rohr...Richard Rohr, *The Universal Christ* (New York: Convergent Books, 2019).

Social Security Disability Insurance and Supplemental Security Income... "Chart Book: Social Security Disability Insurance," Center on Budget and Policy Priorities, Last Modified February 12, 2021, https://www. cbpp.org/research/social-security/social-security-disability-insurance-0.

40 percent of workers...Martin J. Walsh and William W. Beach, "National Compensation Survey: Employee Benefits in the United States," U.S. Bureau of Labor Statistics, March 2021, https://www.bls. gov/ncs/ebs/benefits/2021/employee-benefits-in-the-united-states-march-2021.pdf.

words of the Greek playwright Aeschylus...Edith Hamilton, *The Greek Way* (New York: W.W. Norton & Company, 2010), https://books.google.com/books/about/The_Greek_Way.html?id=D3QwvF3GWOkC.

In his classic book Man's Search for Meaning...Viktor Frankl, *Man's Search for Meaning* (Boston: Beacon Press, 1959).

Susan Sontag's famous collection of essays...Susan Sontag, *Illness as Metaphor* (New York: Knopf Doubleday Publishing Group, 1978).

Chapter 8: Unraveling the Mystery

Athena Akrami was unique...Athena Akrami, Interview by Ryan Prior, 2021.

a preprint paper offering a set of hypotheses...Russell N. Low et al, "A Cytokine-based Model for the Pathophysiology of Long COVID Symptoms," *OSF Preprints*, (November 2020), https://doi.org/10.31219/osf.io/7gcnv.

Dr. Noah Greenspan, a pulmonary rehab therapist...Noah Greenspan, Interview by Ryan Prior, 2021.

produce a documentary film...*Long Haul*, directed by Noah Greenspan (A Pulmonary Wellness Foundation Film, 2021), 38:36, https://www. longhaul.movie/.

Michael VanElzakker is a neuroscientist...Michael VanElzakker, Interview by Ryan Prior & Elizabeth Weaver, 2021.

he published his vagus nerve infection hypothesis...Michael B.VanElzakker, "Chronic Fatigue Syndrome from Vagus Nerve Infection: A Psychoneuroimmunological Hypothesis," *Medical Hypothesis* 81, no 3 (September 2013): 414-423, https://www.science-direct.com/science/article/abs/pii/S0306987713002752?via%3Dihub.

he and microbiologist Amy Proal authored...Amy D. Proal and Michael B. VanElzakker, "Long Covid or Post-Acute Sequelae of Covid-19 (PascPASC): An Overview of Biological Factors That May Contribute to Persistent Symptoms," [In English], *Frontiers in Microbiology* 12, (June 2021), https://doi.org/10.3389/fmicb.2021.698169.

intrigued by one German study...Jakob Matschke, Marc Lütgehetmann, Christian Hagel, Jan P. Sperhake, Ann Sophie Schröder, Carolin Edler, Herbert Mushumba et al, "Neuropathology of Patients with Covid-19 in Germany: A Post-Mortem Case Series," *The Lancet Neurology* 19, no. 11 (2020): 919-29, https://doi.org/10.1016/S1474-4422(20)30308-2.

Geralyn Lucas, an author...Geralyn Lucas, Interview by Ryan Prior, 2021.

long haulers reported feeling partially or totally recovered...Ryan Prior, "Some Covid-19 Long Haulers Say Vaccines May Be Relieving Their Symptoms. Researchers Are Looking into It," CNN, March 4, 2021, https://www.cnn.com/2021/04/03/health/long-haulers-vaccine-well-ness/index.html.

Several informal patient surveys…"The Impact of COVID Vaccination on Symptoms of Long Covid. An international survey of 900 people with Lived Experience," LongCovidSOS, Last accessed April 9, 2022, https://3ca26cd7-266e-4609-b25f-6f3d1497c4cf.filesusr.com/ugd/8bd4fe_a338597f76bf4279a851a7a4cb0e0a74.pdf; RUN-DMC / Gez Medinger, "First Vaccine Reaction Data For Long Covid | Pfizer, AstraZeneca and Moderna Analyzed," YouTube, February 23, 2021, https://www.youtube.com/watch?v=Lio2ByLW4WE; Francis Stead Sellers, "Could Long Covid Unlock Clues to Chronic Fatigue and Other Poorly Understood Conditions?" *Washington Post*, November 7, 2021, https://www.washingtonpost.com/health/2021/11/07/long-covid-fatigue-research/.

16.6 percent of long haulers…Viet-Thi Tran, Elodie Perrodeau, Julia Saldanha, Isabelle Pane, and Philippe Ravaud, "Efficacy of Covid-19 Vaccination on the Symptoms of Patients with Long Covid: A Target Trial Emulation Using Data from the Compare E-Cohort in France," *The Lancet*, Preprint, (September 2021), https://papers.ssrn.com/sol3/papers.cfm?abstract_id=3932953.

Akiko Iwasaki, a professor…Akiko Iwasaki, Interview by Ryan Prior, 2021.

the most notable patient survey…"The Impact of COVID Vaccination on Symptoms of Long Covid. An International Survey of 900 People with Lived Experience," LongCovidSOS, Last Accessed April 9, 2022, https://3ca26cd7-266e-4609-b25f-6f3d1497c4cf.filesusr.com/ugd/8bd4fe_a338597f76bf4279a851a7a4cb0e0a74.pdf.

recruited participants into the study…Caroline Leiber, "In Search of Answers About Long Covid-19, Scientists Turn to Social Media," *Yale School of Medicine*, January 26, 2022. https://medicine.yale.edu/news-article/in-search-of-answers-about-long-covid-19-scientists-turn-to-social-media/.

Chapter 9: The NIH Goes Big

Dr. Avindra Nath, the clinical director...Avindra Nath, Interview by Ryan Prior, 2021.

About 10 percent of its funding..."Budget," National Institute of Health. Last modified June 29, 2020, https://www.nih.gov/about-nih/what-we-do/budget.

supporting basic *research*..."Basic Research—Digital Media Kit," National Institutes of Health, last modified March 12, 2021, https://www.nih.gov/news-events/basic-research-digital-media-kit.

led to the gene editing tool CRISPR...Loureiro, Alexandre, and Gabriela Jorge da Silva, "CRISPR-Cas: Converting A Bacterial Defence Mechanism into A State-of-the-Art Genetic Manipulation Tool," *Antibiotics* 8, no.1 (January 2019):18, https://doi.org/10.3390/antibiotics8010018.

Nath began giving presentations...Anonymous source at the NIH. Personal communication to Ryan Prior, October 13, 2020.

Researching Covid to Enhance Recovery, or RECOVER Initiative... "Recover: Researching Covid to Enhance Recovery," Recover, Last accessed April 26, 2022, https://recovercovid.org.

problems that had plagued early research...Ryan Prior, "Here's How to Design Drug Trials to Defeat the Next Pandemic," CNN, July 4, 2021, https://www.cnn.com/2021/07/04/health/drug-trials-covid-pandemic/index.html.

Some 92 percent of the trials...Kushal T. Kadakia et al, "Leveraging Open Science to Accelerate Research," *The New England Journal of Medicine*, (April 2021), https://www.nejm.org/doi/full/10.1056/NEJMp2034518.

a large UK trial showing...Dylan Scott, "How the UK Found the First Effective Covid-19 Treatment — and Saved a Million Lives," *Vox*,

April 26, 2021, https://www.vox.com/22397833/dexamethasone-coronavirus-uk-recovery-trial.

NIH director Francis Collins said..."The Long Haul: Forging a Path through the Lingering Effects of Covid-19," United States Congress House Energy and Commerce Committee, April, 2021.

*said Dr. Walter Koroshetz...*Walter Koroshetz, Interview by Ryan Prior & Elizabeth Weaver, 2021.

*Karyn Bishof, the founder...*Karyn Bishof, Interview by Ryan Prior, October 26, 2021.

*Harvard's Michael VanElzakker...*Michael VanElzakker, Interview by Ryan Prior & Elizabeth Weaver, 2021.

*Mt. Sinai's David Putrino...*David Putrino, Interview by Ryan Prior, 2022.

*a study on high-intensity interval training...*TK https://anesthesiology.duke.edu/?p=857965

a panel discussion on Long Covid..."Understanding Long COVID: The Unseen Public Health Crisis," Harvard T.H. Chan School of Public Health, educational video, November 19, 2021, https://www.hsph.harvard.edu/event/understanding-long-covid-the-unseen-public-health-crisis/.

*the PLRC published an open letter...*The Patient-Led Research Collaborative, "Open Letter Regarding the RECOVER Initiative to Study Long COVID," Patient-Led Research Collaborative, November 29, 2021, https://patientresearchcovid19.com/open-letter-regarding-the-recover-initiative-to-study-long-covid/.

*the Body Politic had urged the NIH...*Fiona Lowenstien and Angela Vázquez, "Open Letter to the NIH," Body Politic, April 22, 2021, https://www.wearebodypolitic.com/bodytype/2021/4/22/open-letter-to-nih.

half of long haulers met the diagnostic criteria...C Kedor et al, "Chronic COVID-19 Syndrome and Chronic Fatigue Syndrome (ME/CFS) Following the First Pandemic Wave in Germany—A First Analysis of a Prospective Observational Study," MedRXiv, (February 2021), https://www.medrxiv.org/content/10.1101/2021.02.06.21249256v1.

Chapter 10: Gaslighting, Disbelief, and the Search for Answers

Oxford University Press named it..."Word of the Year 2018: Shortlist," Oxford Languages, 2018, https://languages.oup.com/word-of-the-year/2018-shortlist/.

women's unexplained physical symptoms are often "all in their heads"... Diane E. Hoffmann and Anita J. Tarzian, "The Girl Who Cried Pain: A Bias against Women in the Treatment of Pain," *SSRN*, (2001), https://doi.org/http://dx.doi.org/10.2139/ssrn.383803.

as journalist Maya Dusenbery...Maya Dusenbery, *Doing Harm: The Truth About How Bad Medicine and Lazy Science Leave Women Dismissed, Misdiagnosed and Sick* (San Francisco, California: HarperOne, 2018).

83 percent of women with chronic pain..."Women in Pain Survey," The National Pain Report and For Grace, September 12, 2014, https://www.surveymonkey.com/results/SM-P5J5P29L/.

wait longer for pain treatment...Esther H Chen et al, "Gender Disparity in Analgesic Treatment of Emergency Department Patients with Acute Abdominal Pain," *Academic Emergency Medicine: Official Journal of the Society for Academic Emergency Medicine* 15, no 5 (2008): 414-8, https://pubmed.ncbi.nlm.nih.gov/18439195/.

women have historically been underrepresented...Carolyn M Mazure and Daniel P Jones, "Twenty Years and Still Counting: Including Women as Participants and Studying Sex and Gender in Biomedical

Research," *BMC Women's Health* 15, no 94 (October 2015), https://pubmed.ncbi.nlm.nih.gov/26503700/.

for those with poorly understood conditions...Anne Werner and Kirsti Malterud, "It is Hard Work Behaving as a Credible Patient: Encounters Between Women with Chronic Pain and Their Doctors," *Social Science & Medicine* 57, no 8 (2003): 1409-1419, https://pubmed.ncbi.nlm.nih.gov/12927471/.

Researchers from the University of Virginia showed...Kelly M. Hoffman, Sophie Trawalter, Jordan R. Axt, and M. Norman Oliver, "Racial Bias in Pain Assessment and Treatment Recommendations, and False Beliefs About Biological Differences between Blacks and Whites," *Proceedings of the National Academy of Sciences of the United States of America* 113, no. 16 (2016): 4296-301. https://www.pnas.org/doi/full/10.1073/pnas.1516047113.

A 2013 review published in the American Medical Association's Journal of Ethics...Ronald Wyatt, "Pain and Ethnicity," *Virtual Mentor* 15, no 5 (May 2013): 449-454, https://journalofethics.ama-assn.org/article/pain-and-ethnicity/2013-05.

In her paper "The Sociology of Gaslighting"...Paige L. Sweet, "The Sociology of Gaslighting," *American Sociological Review* 84, no. 5 (2019): 851-75, https://doi.org/10.1177/0003122419874843.

The UK-based Long Covid Support organization ran a survey..."Long Covid Assessment Services Patient Feedback," Long Covid, May 2021, https://drive.google.com/file/d/1UFEUgw1LEOz4Jx_wGwknrtbGHt0TkZk9/view.

Guardian *columnist George Monbiot found*...George Monbiot, "We're About to See a Wave of Long Covid. When Will Ministers Take It Seriously?" *The Guardian*, January 21, 2021, https://www.theguardian.com/commentisfree/2021/jan/21/were-about-to-see-a-wave-of-long-covid-when-will-ministers-take-it-seriously.

*presentation that an Oxford psychiatrist gave...*Michael Sharpe, "Post COVID-19 Syndrome (long Covid),"Swiss Re, February 2021, https://www.swissre.com/dam/jcr:788aa287-7026-430a-8c14-f656421b6e71/swiss-re-institute-event-secondary-covid19-impacts-presentation-michael-sharpe.pdf.

*wrote a follow-up column...*George Monbiot, "Apparently Just by Talking About It, I'm Super-Spreading Long Covid," *The Guardian*, April 14, 2021, https://www.theguardian.com/commentisfree/2021/apr/14/super-spreading-long-covid-professor-press-coverage.

*Showing that this occurs...*Staci Stevens et al, "Cardiopulmonary Exercise Test Methodology for Assessing Exertion Intolerance in Myalgic Encephalomyelitis/Chronic Fatigue Syndrome," *Frontiers in Pediatrics* 6, (September 2018), https://www.ncbi.nlm.nih.gov/pmc/articles/PMC6131594/

*publication of the PACE Trial...*P. D. White, K. A. Goldsmith, A. L. Johnson, L. Potts, R. Walwyn, J. C. DeCesare, H. L. Baber, et al, "Comparison of Adaptive Pacing Therapy, Cognitive Behaviour Therapy, Graded Exercise Therapy, and Specialist Medical Care for Chronic Fatigue Syndrome (Pace): A Randomised Trial," *The Lancet* 377, no. 9768 (2011): 823-36, https://doi.org/10.1016/S0140-6736(11)60096-2.

*The study became mired in controversy...*Julie Rehmeyer, "Bad Science Misled Millions with Chronic Fatigue Syndrome. Here's How We Fought Back," *STAT*, September 21, 2016, https://www.statnews.com/2016/09/21/chronic-fatigue-syndrome-pace-trial/.

A report by the UK-based ME Association..."ME/CFS Illness Management Survey Results 'No Decisions About Me without Me,'" ME Association, May 2015, https://meassociation.org.uk/wp-content/uploads/2015-ME-Association-Illness-Management-Report-No-decisions-about-me-without-me-30.05.15.pdf.

*a 15,000-word analysis disputing the study's methods...*David Tuller, "Trial by Error: The Troubling Case of the Pace Chronic Fatigue Syndrome Study," Vincent Racaniello ed. *Virology Blog: About Viruses and Viral Disease*, October 21, 2015, https://www.virology.ws/2015/10/21/trial-by-error-i/.

*"When I wrote it, I made sure to say...*David Tuller, Interview by Ryan Prior, 2021.

sign an open letter to The Lancet...Ronald W. Davis et al, "An Open Letter to The Lancet, again," Virology, February 10, 2016, https://www.virology.ws/2016/02/10/open-letter-lancet-again/.

*Patients and independent scientists who analyzed the data...*Carolyn E. Wilshire, Kindlon, et al., "Rethinking the Treatment of Chronic Fatigue Syndrome—A Reanalysis and Evaluation of Findings from a Recent Major Trial of Graded Exercise and CBT," *BMC Psychol* 6, no 6 (March 2018), https://bmcpsychology.biomedcentral.com/articles/10.1186/s40359-018-0218-3.

A 2015 report by the U.S. Institute of Medicine..."Beyond Myalgic Encephalomyelitis/Chronic Fatigue Syndrome: Redefining an Illness," National Academy of Medicine, (2015), https://nap.nationalacademies.org/catalog/19012/beyond-myalgic-encephalomyelitischronic-fatigue-syndrome-redefining-an-illness.

*the CDC dropped its recommendation...*David Tuller, "Trial by Error: The CDC Drops CBT/GET," Vincent Racaniello ed. *Virology Blog: About Viruses and Viral Disease*, July 10, 2017, https://www.virology.ws/2017/07/10/trial-by-error-the-cdc-drops-cbtget/.

*The U.S. federal Agency for Healthcare Research and Quality said...*Beth Smith et al, "Diagnosis and Treatment of Myalgic Encephalomyelitis/Chronic Fatigue Syndrome," Rockville (MD): Agency for Healthcare Research and Quality, no 219 ((July 2016), https://www.ncbi.nlm.nih.gov/books/NBK379582/.

A similar evidence review…"NICE ME/CFS Guideline Outlines Steps for Better Diagnosis and Management," National Institute for Health and Care Excellence, October 28, 2021, https://www.nice.org.uk/news/article/nice-me-cfs-guideline-outlines-steps-for-better-diagnosis-and-management.

*"I don't know if I can concretely say…*David Lee, Interview by Ryan Prior, 2021.

A 2019 article in the journal BMC Medical Education…David R. Chen and Kelsey C. Priest, "Pimping: A Tradition of Gendered Disempowerment," *BMC Medical Education* 19, no. 345 (October 2019), https://doi.org/10.1186/s12909-019-1761-1.

*instills a fear of making a mistake…*Abraar Karan, "Medical Students Need to be Quizzed, but 'Pimping' Isn't Effective," Statnews, February 3, 2017, https://www.statnews.com/2017/02/03/medical-students-pimping-testing-knowledge/.

*Cynthia Adinig, a thirty-four-year-old graphic designer…*Cynthia Adinig, Interview by Ryan Prior, 2021.

*Albert Camus wrote in 1942…*Albert Camus, *The Myth of Sisyphus* (France: Editions Gallimard, 1942).

Chapter 11: Chronicles of Uncertain Recoveries

*Maneesh Juneja is a consultant…*Maneesh Juneja, Interview by Ryan Prior, 2021.

One doctor wrote him…"Long Covid: How Becoming a Patient Shaped My Thinking as a Futurist," Academy Health, 2021. https://academyhealth.org/professional-resources/training/prof-dev/long-covid-how-becoming-patient-shaped-my-thinking-futurist.

CDC released their guidelines for post-Covid conditions…"Evaluating and Caring for Patients with Post-COVID Conditions: Interim

Guidance," Centers for Disease Control and Prevention, June 14, 2021, https://www.cdc.gov/coronavirus/2019-ncov/hcp/clinical-care/post-covid-index.html

Gay's journey began in March 2020...Mara Gay, Interview by Ryan Prior, 2021.

Desmond Tutu's The Book of Forgiving...D. Tutu and M. Tutu, *The Book of Forgiving: The Fourfold Path for Healing Ourselves and Our World*, (New York: HarperCollins, 2014), https://books.google.com/books?id=RfhNAgAAQBAJ.

Chapter 12: Precursors: ME/CFS and Lyme

Dr. Nancy Klimas treated many...Nancy Klimas, Interview by Ryan Prior, 2022.

It made her recall...Dr. Nancy Klimas, "Long Covid & Post-Viral ME/CFS: Modeling Complex Illnesses," Webinar from Long Covid Alliance, 2021. https://longcovidalliance.org/body-politic-x-dr-nancy-klimas-long-covid-post-viral-me-cfs-modeling-complex-illnesses/.

may miss more than half of cases...Raphael B. Stricker and Lorraine Johnson, "Lyme Disease: Call for a 'Manhattan Project' to Combat the Epidemic," *PLOS Pathogens* 10, no. 1 (2014), https://doi.org/10.1371/journal.ppat.1003796.

the agency estimates..."How Many People Get Lyme Disease?" Centers for Disease Control and Prevention, Last modified January 13, 2021, https://www.cdc.gov/lyme/stats/humancases.html.

10 to 20 percent of those infected remaining ill...John Aucott et al, "Risk of post-treatment Lyme disease in patients with ideally-treated early Lyme disease: A prospective cohort study," *International Journal of Infectious Disease* 116, (March 2022): 230-237, https://www.sciencedirect.com/science/article/pii/S1201971222000352.

Lyme has been the subject of decades of heated debate...Pamela Weintraub, *Cure Unknown: Inside the Lyme Epidemic*, (New York: St. Martin's Press, 2009).

said Dr. John Aucott...John Aucott, Interview by Ryan Prior, 2021.

The team had found elevated levels...John Aucott et al, "CCL19 as a Chemokine Risk Factor for Posttreatment Lyme Disease Syndrome: a Prospective Clinical Cohort Study," *Clinical and Vaccine Immunology* 23, no 9 (September 2016):757-766, https://www.ncbi.nlm.nih.gov/pmc/articles/PMC5014924/.

They also found that gene regulation patterns...Daniel J.B. Clarke et al, "Predicting Lyme Disease From Patients' Peripheral Blood Mononuclear Cells Profiled With RNA-Sequencing," *Frontiers in Immunology* 12, (March 2021), https://www.frontiersin.org/articles/10.3389/fimmu.2021.636289/full.

other Lyme studies of the metabolome...Bryna L Fitzgerald et al, "Metabolic Response in Patients With Post-treatment Lyme Disease Symptoms/Syndrome," *Clinical Infectious Diseases: an official publication of the Infectious Diseases Society of America* 73, no 7 (2021): 2342-2349, https://pubmed.ncbi.nlm.nih.gov/32975577/.

Early autopsy studies by the NIH...Myoung-Hwa Lee et al, "Microvascular Injury in the Brains of Patients with Covid-19," *The New England Journal of Medicine* 384, no 5 (2021): 481-483, https://www.ncbi.nlm.nih.gov/pmc/articles/PMC7787217/.

a German study of patients...Jakob Matschke et al, "Neuropathology of Patients with COVID-19 in Germany: A Post-Mortem Case Series," *The Lancet* 19, no 11 (November 2020): 919-929, https://www.thelancet.com/journals/laneur/article/PIIS1474-4422(20)30308-2/fulltext.

a more robust autopsy study...Daniel Chertow et al, "SARS-CoV-2 infection and persistence throughout the human body and brain,"

Biological Sciences, (December 2021), https://www.researchsquare. com/article/rs-1139035/v1.

In a 2018 neuroimaging study...Jennifer M. Coughlin, Ting Yang, Alison W. Rebman, Kathleen T. Bechtold, Yong Du, William B. Mathews, Wojciech G. Lesniak, et al, "Imaging Glial Activation in Patients with Post-Treatment Lyme Disease Symptoms: A Pilot Study Using [11c]Dpa-713 Pet," *Journal of Neuroinflammation* 15, no. 1 (2018): 346, https://doi.org/10.1186/s12974-018-1381-4.

launched a two-year "Crash Course" study..."Crash Course," Stanford Medicine, Last accessed May 2, 2022, https://snyderlabs.stanford.edu/ crashcourse/.

Chapter 13: Theory of Everything

said Dr. Lucinda Bateman...Lucinda Bateman, Interview by Ryan Prior, 2021.

Ron Davis, professor of genetics...Ron Davis, Interview by Ryan Prior & Elizabeth Weaver, 2022.

It published the 2015 report..."Beyond Myalgic Encephalomyelitis/ Chronic Fatigue Syndrome: Redefining an Illness." National Academy of Medicine. https://nap.nationalacademies.org/catalog/19012/beyond-myalgic-encephalomyelitischronic-fatigue-syndrome-redefining-an-illness

The OMF funded a study of severe ME/CFS...Chia-Jung Chang et al, "A Comprehensive Examination of Severely Ill ME/CFS Patients," *Healthcare* 9, no. 10 (September 2021): 1290, https://www.mdpi. com/2227-9032/9/10/1290?fbclid=IwAR3OVmfTMmj3RvNdN-ZL3-juIRbPHClmWvUqfi5y8VO7Beass6wWcKoM1lhk.

they published initial findings...R. Esfandyarpour, A. Kashi, M. Nemat-Gorgani, J. Wilhelmy, and R. W. Davis, "A Nanoelectronics-

Blood-Based Diagnostic Biomarker for Myalgic Encephalomyelitis/ Chronic Fatigue Syndrome (ME/CFS)," *Proceedings of the National Academy of Sciences* 116, no. 21 (2019): 10250, https://doi.org/10.1073/ pnas.1901274116.

*They enrolled Covid-19 patients in a new study...*Ronald Tompkins, "Long Covid to ME/CFS A Potential Second Pandemic," Open Medicine Foundation, March 11, 2021, https://www.omf.ngo/ post-covid-syndrome-to-me-cfs/.

*She highlighted their ongoing lines of research...*Hannah Davis, Hannah Davis. "Long COVID: Current Research & Research Needs," Power-Point Presentation to NIH Recover Initiative, June 2021, https://docs. google.com/presentation/d/1_meYPsbEGS0QHa17Lk2-023zaPxqih-qMMAkP6-QY_RE/edit#slide=id.gd7355e9495_0_173.

*complicated two-step...*Tracie White, *The Puzzle Solver* (New York: Hachette, 2021).

*a new compound called BC 007...*Bettina Hohberger et al, "Case Report: Neutralization of Autoantibodies Targeting G-Protein-Coupled Receptors Improves Capillary Impairment and Fatigue Symptoms After COVID-19 Infection," *Front. Med.* 8, (November 2021), https:// www.frontiersin.org/articles/10.3389/fmed.2021.754667/full.

*Proal worked with her colleague...*Amy Proal, Interview by Ryan Prior & Elizabeth Weaver, 2022.

*a preprint in December 2021...*Daniel Chertow et al, "SARS-CoV-2 Infection and Persistence Throughout the Human Body and Brain," Research Square, December 20, 2021, https://www.researchsquare. com/article/rs-1139035/v1.

*during a Senate health committee hearing...*U.S. Senate Committee on Health, Education, Labor & Pensions, Hearing, "Addressing New Variants: A Federal Perspective on the COVID-19 Response," recorded at G50 Dirksen Senate Office Building, January 11, 2022, https://www.

help.senate.gov/hearings/addressing-new-variants-a-federal-perspec-
tive-on-the-covid-19-response.

*two-thirds showed Epstein-Barr virus reactivation...*Jeffrey E. Gold,
Ramazan A. Okyay, Warren E. Licht, and David J. Hurley, "Investigation
of Long COVID Prevalence and Its Relationship to Epstein-Barr Virus
Reactivation," *Pathogens* 10, no. 6 (June 2021): 763, https://www.mdpi.
com/2076-0817/10/6/763.

*The clots could be a major contributor...*Modjtaba Emadi-Baygi et al,
"Corona Virus Disease 2019 (COVID-19) as a System-Level Infectious
Disease with Distinct Sex Disparities," Frontiers in Immunology12,
778913 (November 2021), https://www.ncbi.nlm.nih.gov/pmc/
articles/PMC8667725/.

*Dr. David Systrom used a process...*Inderjit Singh, MD et al, "Persistent
Exertional Intolerance After COVID-19 Insights From Invasive
Cardiopulmonary Exercise Testing," *Chest Infections: Original Research*
161, no 1 (January 2022): 54-63, https://www.ncbi.nlm.nih.gov/pmc/
articles/PMC8354807

*implicated in a number of post-pathogen disease states...*D. J. Harrington,
"Bacterial Collagenases and Collagen-Degrading Enzymes and Their
Potential Role in Human Disease," *Infection and immunity* 64, no. 6
(1996): 1885-1891, https://doi.org/10.1128/iai.64.6.1885-1891.1996.
https://pubmed.ncbi.nlm.nih.gov/8675283.

*a plethora of structural instabilities...*Fraser Henderson, Claudio
Austin, Edward Benzel, Paolo Bolognese, Richard Ellenbogen,
Clair Francomano, Candace Ireton et al, "Neurological and Spinal
Manifestations of the Ehlers–Danlos Syndromes," *American Journal
of Medical Genetics*, (2017), https://onlinelibrary.wiley.com/doi/
epdf/10.1002/ajmg.c.31549; Fraser Henderson, "Cranio-Cervical
Instability in Patients with Hypermobility Connective Disorders."
Journal of Spine 5, no 2 (2016), DOI:10.4172/2165-7939.1000299.

Proal ran through a few different scenarios... "The Global Interdependence Center – Solve Long Covid Initiative Program Series: Medical Research," Global Interdependence Center, January 7, 2022, https://www.interdependence.org/resources/the-global-interdependence-center-solve-long-covid-initiative-program-series-medical-research/#.YmscnvXMKL8.

a paper in Immunologic Research...Amy D Proal et al, "Immunostimulation in the Treatment for Chronic Fatigue Syndrome/Myalgic Encephalomyelitis," *Immunologic Research* 56, no 2 (2013): 398-412, https://pubmed.ncbi.nlm.nih.gov/23576059/.

Pretorius and her team found the microclots... E. Pretorius, M. Vlok, C. Venter et al, "Persistent Clotting Protein Pathology in Long COVID/Post-Acute Sequelae of COVID-19 (PASC) is Accompanied By Increased Levels of Antiplasmin," *Cardiovasc Diabetol* 20, no 172 (2021), https://cardiab.biomedcentral.com/articles/10.1186/s12933-021-01359-7.

The South African researchers found a strong signal... Etheresia Pretorius et al, "Combined Triple Treatment of Fibrin Amyloid Microclots and Platelet Pathology in Individuals with Long COVID/Post-Acute Sequelae of COVID-19 (PASC) Can Resolve Their Persistent Symptoms," PREPRINT (Version 1) available at Research Square, (December 2021), https://www.researchsquare.com/article/rs-1205453/v1.

scientist Leslie Norins offered $1 million... "$1 Million Prize for Alzheimer's Disease Germ Announced by Dr. Leslie Norins on Alzgerm.Org," *PRNewswire* Press Release, January 16, 2018. https://www.prnewswire.com/news-releases/1-million-prize-for-alzheimers-disease-germ-announced-by-dr-leslie-norins-on-alzgermorg-300582042.html.

Epstein-Barr virus was a precursor for multiple sclerosis... Kjetil Bjornevik, Marianna Cortese, Brian C. Healy, Jens Kuhle, Michael J.

Mina, Yumei Leng, Stephen J. Elledge, et al, "Longitudinal Analysis Reveals High Prevalence of Epstein-Barr Virus Associated with Multiple Sclerosis," *Science* 375, no. 6578 (2022): 296-301, https://doi.org/doi:10.1126/science.abj8222.

One group of experiments led by Ruth Itzhaki...G A Jamieson et al, "Latent Herpes Simplex Virus Type 1 in Normal and Alzheimer's Disease Brains," *Journal of Medical Virology* 33, no 4 (1991): 224-247, https://pubmed.ncbi.nlm.nih.gov/1649907/; Professor Ruth F Itzhaki PhD et al, "Herpes Simplex Virus Type 1 in Brain and Risk of Alzheimer's Disease," *The Lancet* 349, no 9047 (January 1997): 241-244, https://www.sciencedirect.com/science/article/abs/pii/S014067369 6101495.

this finding has been replicated...Matthew A. Wozniak and Ruth F. Itzhaki, "Antiviral Agents in Alzheimer's Disease: Hope for the Future?" *Therapeutic Advances in Neurological Disorders* 3, no. 3 (2010): 141-52, https://doi.org/10.1177/1756285610370069, https://pubmed.ncbi.nlm.nih.gov/21179606.

Although no single lab won..."Nobody finds the Alzheimer's Germ in $1 Million Challenge, but eight researchers split $200K, says Dr. Leslie Norins of Alzheimer's Germ Quest," *PRNewswire*, February 23, 2021, https://www.prnewswire.com/news-releases/nobody-finds-the-alzheimers-germ-in-1-million-challenge-but-eight-researchers-split-200k-says-dr-leslie-norins-of-alzheimers-germ-quest-3012 32177.html.

a large study in 2018 showed that treatment...Nian-Sheng Tzeng, Chi-Hsiang Chung, Fu-Huang Lin, Chien-Ping Chiang, Chin-Bin Yeh, San-Yuan Huang, Ru-Band Lu, et al, "Anti-Herpetic Medications and Reduced Risk of Dementia in Patients with Herpes Simplex Virus Infections—a Nationwide, Population-Based Cohort Study in Taiwan," *Neurotherapeutics* 15, no. 2 (2018): 417-29, https://doi.org/10.1007/s13311-018-0611-x.

a herpes zoster infection...Vincent Chin-Hung Chen, MD, PhD, "Herpes Zoster and Dementia: A Nationwide Population-Based Cohort Study," *Journal of Clinical Psychiatry* 79, no 1 (2018): 16, https://www.psychiatrist.com/jcp/neurologic/dementia/herpes-zoster-and-dementia/.

bacterium associated with gum disease...Stephen S. Dominy, Casey Lynch, Florian Ermini, Malgorzata Benedyk, Agata Marczyk, Andrei Konradi, Mai Nguyen, et al, "*Porphyromonas Gingivalis* in Alzheimer's Disease Brains: Evidence for Disease Causation and Treatment with Small-Molecule Inhibitors," *Science Advances* 5, no. 1 (2019), https://doi.org/doi:10.1126/sciadv.aau3333.

the Alzheimer's Association and representatives..."International Brain Study: Sars-Cov-2 Impact on Behavior and Cognition," Alzheimer's Association Press Release, Last accessed April 7, 2022. https://www.alz.org/research/for_researchers/partnerships/sars-cov2-global-brain-study.

show markedly slowed metabolism...Robert K. Naviaux et al, "Metabolic features of chronic fatigue syndrome," *Biological Sciences* 113, no 37 (August 2016): 5472-5480, https://www.pnas.org/doi/abs/10.1073/pnas.1607571113.

Chapter 14: A New Epidemic of Disability

an annual $17 to 24 billion impact...Jason, "The Economic Impact of ME/CFS: Individual and Societal Costs," *Dynamic Medicine*, https://doi.org/10.1186/1476-5918-7-6.

co-wrote a New York Times *opinion piece*...Fiona Lowenstein and Hannah Davis, "Long Covid Is Not Rare. It's a Health Crisis," *The New York Times*, March 17, 2021, https://www.nytimes.com/2021/03/17/opinion/long-covid.html.

polio was disabling about 35,000 people..."Polio Elimination in the United States," Centers for Disease Control and Prevention, Last modified September 28, 2021, https://www.cdc.gov/polio/what-is-polio/polio-us.html.

according to a study by the nation's Office of National Statistics... "Prevalence of Ongoing Symptoms Following Coronavirus (COVID-19) Infection in the UK: 1 April 2021," https://www.ons.gov.uk/peoplepopulationandcommunity/healthandsocialcare/condition-sanddiseases/bulletins/prevalenceofongoingsymptomsfollowingcoro-naviruscovid19infectionintheuk/1april2021

*Davis and McCorkell presented the PLRC findings...*Davis, "White House Covid-19 Equity Task Force Presentation," https://docs.google.com/presentation/d/1QoXnLSwV-tB7Le9R9SiF6Xouf9q0tTOuQK-F3KYZIf1Q/mobilepresent?slide=id.gdd634b6900_0_101.

*President Joe Biden said in a Rose Garden speech...*President Biden, "Remarks by President Biden Celebrating the 31st Anniversary of the Americans with Disabilities Act," transcript of speech delivered at the Rose Garden, July 26, 2021, https://www.whitehouse.gov/briefing-room/speeches-remarks/2021/07/26/remarks-by-pres-ident-biden-celebrating-the-31st-anniversary-of-the-ameri-cans-with-disabilities-act/.

*a statement from Body Politic praising the move...*Fiona Lowenstein, "Body Politic and PLRC Statement on Federal Long Covid Disability Rights Guidance," We Are Body Politic, July 27, 2021, https://www.wearebodypolitic.com/bodytype/2021/7/27/body-politic-and-pa-tient-led-research-collaborative-applaud-federal-long-covid-dis-ability-rights-guidance-on-anniversary-of-americans-with-disabi-lities-act.

*the codes can get a bit absurd...*Katie Bo Williams, "The 16 Most Absurd Icd-10 Codes," Healthcare Dive, August 15, 2015, https://www.healthcaredive.com/news/the-16-most-absurd-icd-10-codes/285737/.

the ICD-10 code U09.9 went live..."New ICD-10-CM code for Post-COVID Conditions, following the 2019 Novel Coronavirus (COVID-

19)," Centers for Disease Control and Prevention, October 1, 2021, https://www.cdc.gov/nchs/data/icd/announcement-new-icd-code-for-post-covid-condition-april-2022-final.pdf.

the World Health Organization published its case definition…"A Clinical Case Definition of Post COVID-19 Condition by a Delphi Consensus, 6 October 2021," World Health Organization, October 6, 2021, https://www.who.int/publications/i/item/WHO-2019-nCoV-Post_COVID-19_condition-Clinical_case_definition-2021.1

*Karyn Bishof, a co-founder of the Long Covid Alliance…*Bishof, Karyn. Interview by Ryan Prior, 2021.

*"Originally, before Covid…*Jayani Delgado, Interview by Ryan Prior, 2021.

just 34 percent of applicants ultimately win benefits…"Chart Book: Social Security Disability Insurance," Center on Budget and Policy Priorities, Last Modified February 12, 2021, https://www.cbpp.org/research/social-security/social-security-disability-insurance-0.

*according to a 2014 analysis…*David A. Weaver, "Social Security Disability Benefits: Characteristics of the Approved and Denied Populations," *Sage Journals* 32, no 1 (June 2020): 51-62, https://journals.sagepub.com/doi/abs/10.1177/1044207320933538.

*according to Rebecca Vallas…*Rebecca Vallas, Interview by Ryan Prior, 2021.

*the SSA's 1,200 field offices were closed…*Jonathan Stein and David A. Weaver, "Half a Million Poor and Disabled Americans Left Behind by Social Security," The Hill, November 15, 2021, https://thehill.com/opinion/finance/581522-half-a-million-poor-and-disabled-americans-left-behind-by-social-security/?rl=1.

*1.6 million jobs in the U.S.…*Katie Bach, "Is 'Long Covid' Worsening the Labor Shortage?" *Brookings*, January 11, 2022. https://www.brookings.edu/research/is-long-covid-worsening-the-labor-shortage/.

Chapter 15: The ePatient Revolution and Crowdsourcing Research

*Susannah Fox was one of the people...*Susannah Fox, Interview by Ryan Prior, 2021.

*she wrote in a blog post...*Susannah Fox, "Crazy. Crazy. Long Covid. Obvious," Susannah Fox (blog), January 25, 2021, https://susannahfox. com/2021/01/25/crazy-crazy-longcovid-obvious/.

*digital health version of the Cajun Navy...*Susannah Fox "We Need a Digital Health Cajun Navy," Susannah Fox (blog), June 10, 2019, https:// susannahfox.com/2019/06/10/we-need-a-digital-health-cajun-navy/.

the launch of the site PatientsLikeMe..."Patients Like Me," Patients Like Me, Last Accessed April 7, 2022. https://www.patientslikeme. com/about.

*self-reported data from 348 users on the site...*Paul Wicks, Timothy E. Vaughan, Michael P. Massagli, and James Heywood, "Accelerated Clinical Discovery Using Self-Reported Patient Data Collected Online and a Patient-Matching Algorithm," *Nature Biotechnology* 29, no. 5 (May 2011): 411-414, https://doi.org/10.1038/nbt.1837.

*a story deBronkart tells in his 2011 TEDx talk...*Dave deBronkart, "Meet E-Patient Dave," TED Talk, 2011, https://www.ted.com/talks/ dave_debronkart_meet_e_patient_dave?language=en#t-616926.

*DeBronkart's story ended up on the front page...*Lisa Wangness, "Electronic Health Records Raise Doubt," *The Boston Globe*, April 13, 2009, https://archive.boston.com/news/nation/washington/ articles/2009/04/13/electronic_health_records_raise_doubt/.

*"Gimme my damn data...*Dave deBronkart, "A Movement Is Born: 'Gimme My Damn Data,'" Tincture, June 6, 2019, https://tincture. io/a-movement-is-born-gimme-my-damn-data-a8eee0f520c0.

a concept from Wired *magazine co-founder*...Kevin Kelly, "The Natural History of a New Idea." The Technium, Last accessed May 1, 2022, https://kk.org/thetechnium/natural-history/.

"Crazy. Crazy. Long Covid. Obvious."...Fox, "Crazy. Crazy. Long Covid. Obvious."

Distilled into ten design principles..."Our Stanford Medicine X Design Principles," Everyone Included, Last accessed May 1, 2022, https://everyoneincluded.org/#design.

The process begins by empathizing...Ramunus Balcaitis, "Design Thinking Models. Stanford d.School," *EMPATHIZE@IT EMPATHIZE. DESIGN. BUILD.* June, 2019. https://empathizeit.com/design-thinking-models-stanford-d-school/.

has now raised..."The Power of 10" Drive-in Gala Celebrates Historic Milestone For Emily's Entourage," Emily's Entourage, December 23, 2021, https://www.emilysentourage.org/the-power-of-10-drive-in-gala-celebrates-historic-milestone-for-emilys-entourage/?fbclid=IwAR2jsD7DM5evYY5jqZ1pJAknC6OZqPcKDTPltRvyn-4BVfQ7zIvWlmFuyFQc.

received a quarter-million dollar grant..."The Promise of Patient-Led Research Integration into Clinical Registries and Research," Patient Centered Outcomes Research Institute, Last accessed April 7, 2022, https://www.pcori.org/research-results/2021/promise-patient-led-research-integration-clinical-registries-and-research.

They won a $3 million grant..."Patient-Led Research Collaborative Receives $3M in Funding for Long COVID Research from Balvi, a New Fund for High-Impact COVID Projects from Ethereum Co-Found Vitalik Buterin," Patient-Led Research Collaborative, April 22, 2022, https://patientresearchcovid19.com/press-releases/.

Chapter 16: Expectant Hope

in late December 2021...Austin Landis and Reuben Jones, "Long Covid Still a Risk with Omicrons Despite Milder Illness," NY1, December 29, 2021, https://www.ny1.com/nyc/all-boroughs/news/2021/12/29/fauci-interview-long-covid-still-a-risk-with-milder-omicron-cases.

Long Covid is more likely in individuals...C. Cervia et al, "Immunoglobulin Signature Predicts Risk of Post-Acute COVID-19 Syndrome," *Nature Communications* 13, 446 (January 2022), https://www.nature.com/articles/s41467-021-27797-1; Yapeng Su et al, "Multiple Early Factors Anticipate Post-Acute COVID-19 Sequelae," *Cell* 185, no 5 (March 2022): 881-895, https://www.sciencedirect.com/science/article/pii/S0092867422000721.

the chemokine CCL11 being strongly associated...Anthony Fernández-Castañeda et al, "Mild Respiratory SARS-CoV-2 Infection Can Cause Multi-Lineage Cellular Dysregulation and Myelin Loss in the Brain," *BioRxiv* 20, (January 2022), Preprint, https://www.ncbi.nlm.nih.gov/pmc/articles/PMC8764721/.

Karyn Bishof assembled a list...Karyn Bishof n.d., "A Comprehensive Guide for Covid-19 Longhaulers and Physicians: The PASC Master Document," Last accessed April 8, 2022, https://docs.google.com/document/d/1VfENjAiOBKryT-dIOFyU8CyEAAKVR5xk-9WyvlZF-u4M/edit.

Long hauler Sandhya Kamphampati advised...Sandhya Kamphampati, "Being a Covid Long Hauler Taught Me to be Fearless, Push Back, and Take Lots of Notes," *LA Times*, August 5, 202, https://www.latimes.com/science/story/2021-08-05/heres-how-to-effectively-communicate-with-healthcare-professionals.

the Job Accommodation Network...Job Accommodation Network, Last accessed April 7, 2022, https://askjan.org.

famous theory of the five stages of grief...Elisabeth Kübler-Ross, *On Death and Dying* (New York: Macmillan, 1969).

In her book The Phenomenology of Illness...Carel Havi, *Phenomenology of Illness*, 1st ed. (Oxford: OUP Oxford, 2016).

Jim Collins has called the "Stockdale Paradox."...Jim Collins, *Good to Great*, (New York: Harper Business, 2001).

Dr. Jeremy Groopman distinguishes between...Jeremy E. Groopman, *The Anatomy of Hope: How People Prevail in the Face of Illness*. (New York: Random House, 2005).

a concept known as growth mindset...Carol S. Dwerk, *Mindset: The New Psychology of Success*, (New York: Ballantine Books, 2007).

a small, but growing body of research...Alia J Crum et al, "Mind Over Milkshakes: Mindsets, Not Just Nutrients, Determine Ghrelin Response," *Health Psychology: Official Journal of the Division of Health Psychology, American Psychological Association* 30, no 4 (2011): 424-9, https://pubmed.ncbi.nlm.nih.gov/21574706/; Abiola Keller et al, "Does the Perception that Stress Affects Health Matter? The Association with Health and Mortality," *Health Psychology: Official Journal of the Division of Health Psychology, American Psychological Association* 31, no 5 (2012): 677-84, https://pubmed.ncbi.nlm.nih.gov/22201278/; Alia J Crum and Ellen J Langer, "Mind-Set Matters: Exercise and the Placebo Effect," *Psychological Science* 18, no 2 (2007): 165-171, https://dash.harvard.edu/bitstream/handle/1/3196007/Langer_ExcersisePlaceboEffect.pdf?sequence=1%3FviewType=Print&viewClass=Print

science has not shown us that mindset...J. C. Coyne, M. Stefanek, and S. C. Palmer, "Psychotherapy and Survival in Cancer: The Conflict Between Hope and Evidence," *Psychological Bulletin* 133, no 3 (2007): 367-394, https://doi.apa.org/doiLanding?doi=10.1037%2F0033-2909.133.3.367.